OTHER A TO Z GUIDES FROM
THE SCARECROW PRESS, INC.

The A to Z of
Early North America

Cameron B. Wesson

The A to Z Guide Series, No. 40

The Scarecrow Press, Inc.
Lanham • Toronto • Plymouth, UK
2009

Published by Scarecrow Press, Inc.
A wholly owned subsidiary of
The Rowman & Littlefield Publishing Group, Inc.
4501 Forbes Boulevard, Suite 200, Lanham, Maryland 20706
http://www.scarecrowpress.com

Estover Road, Plymouth PL6 7PY, United Kingdom

British Library Cataloguing in Publication Information Available

Library of Congress Cataloging-in-Publication Data

The hardback version of this book was cataloged by the Library of Congress as
follows:

Wesson, Cameron B., 1968–
    Historical dictionary of early North America / Cameron B. Wesson.
        p. cm. — (Historical dictionaries of ancient civilizations and historical eras ;
    no. 15)
    Includes bibliographical references.
    1. North America—History—Dictionaries. 2. Indians of North America—
History—Dictionaries. I. Title. II. Series.
    E35.W475 2005
    970.01'03—dc22   2004010700

ISBN 978-0-8108-6823-6 (pbk. : alk. paper)
ISBN 978-0-8108-6339-2 (ebook)

Dedicated to the indigenous peoples of North America and those who have devoted themselves to their study.

Contents

Editor's Foreword

Among the world's major civilizations, ancient North America is one we hear relatively little about. There are some "good" reasons, if that expression can be used, in that there are no giant monuments or overgrown palaces and temples, and it is much more widely dispersed, hardly the sort of thing to put on the tourist circuit. There are probably also some "bad" reasons, and that expression can probably be used fairly. For the modern United States and Canada were built on the ruins of the civilizations that went before and, to justify this occupation of foreign lands, were denigrated to the point that it was questioned just how civilized they were. But, as this book will show, the indigenous populations of North America created impressive societies, erected some reasonably sized cities, left huge mounds, engaged in trade, and had a varied economic, social, and religious life but were just not strong enough to resist foreign intrusion.

This makes it much harder to write a reference work like this, for it is necessary to describe numerous different ethnic groups and societies over a truly extensive period and covering a vast continent. Moreover, it is necessary to track down the details through countless excavations and digs in often-inaccessible places and, worse, sometimes already covered over by modernity. In this case, since history was not written and recorded by most peoples, it is often a matter of conjecture as to how they lived, and it is simply impossible to trace their history far back in time. On the other hand, the results of this research are precious. Thus, no matter how bare, the chronology does make it possible to locate different cultures in time; the introduction to see how they related to the different epochs and regions, and to one another as well as to the colonialists; and the bibliography to gain access to further information. Obviously, the core is the dictionary, which provides a wealth of details on all relevant aspects, including the intriguing one of how the archaeologists, anthropologists, ethnologists, and others managed to amass so much information out of such limited remains.

This volume was written by Cameron B. Wesson, a specialist on the political economy of the Native Americans of the Eastern Woodlands. He has written extensively on the archaeology of southeastern North America. More important, he is an active archaeologist, excavating various sites in the Southeast and Midwest. But, to write this book, he also had to take a very careful look at many other aspects and many other peoples in many other regions. That he managed to cover so much ground is noteworthy, as is his ability to explain the techniques and tools of those engaged in recovering the past. This makes *The A to Z of Early North America* a good place to start one's investigation into an impressive, if less heralded, center of civilization.

Jon Woronoff
Series Editor

Acknowledgments

This dictionary would not have been possible without the patient support of the series editor, Jon Woronoff. I would like to acknowledge his direction and encouragement throughout the production of this volume. I also wish to thank Shannon Freeman for his editorial assistance. In addition, the Department of Anthropology and the College of Liberal Arts and Sciences of the University of Illinois at Chicago provided support for my efforts. I hope that this work provides students and professionals alike with a better understanding of the field.

Cameron B. Wesson

Reader's Note

All dates used in dictionary entries are presented as B.P. (years before present) in accordance with standard North American archaeological practice. This dating system was devised to normalize worldwide archaeological dating conventions. However, the term *B.P.* does not refer to dates before the immediate present, but to the year 1950 (when the use of radiocarbon dating became the accepted standard for absolute dating in archaeology). To aid readers unfamiliar with the use of the B.P. dating convention, I have also included B.C. and A.D. dates in parentheses. In addition, boldfaced type is used throughout the text to indicate that a term has its own entry elsewhere in the dictionary.

Acronyms and Abbreviations

AAA	American Anthropological Association
AMS	Accelerator mass spectrometry dating
CLIMAP	Climate and environment monitoring with GPS atmospheric profiling
CRM	Cultural resource management
FCR	Fire-cracked rock
NAGPRA	Native American Grave Protection and Repatriation Act
SAA	Society for American Archaeology
TL	Thermoluminescence dating
TVA	Tennessee Valley Authority

Maps

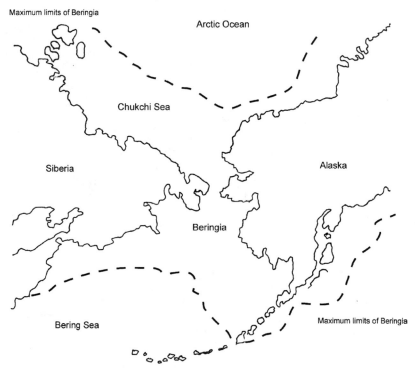

Geographical Extent of Beringia, circa 15,000 B.P. (13,000 B.C.)

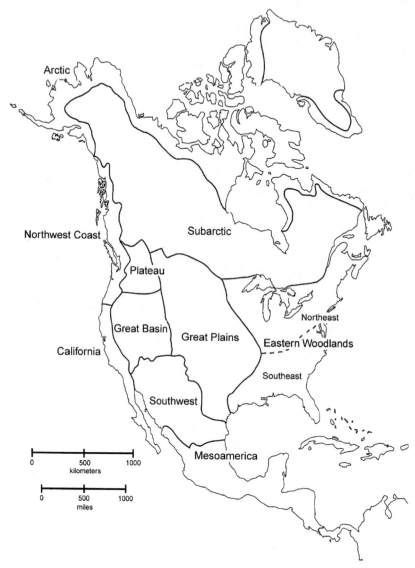

Arctic

Northwest Coast

Subarctic

Plateau

Great Basin

Great Plains

Northeast

Eastern Woodlands

California

Southeast

Southwest

0   500   1000
kilometers

0   500   1000
miles

Mesoamerica

Culture Areas of North America

Chronology

13,000+ B.P. (11,000 B.C.) Most widely accepted date for the initial arrival of Paleoindians from Asia via the Bering Land Bridge; Clovis and other early big-game hunting cultures.

10,000 B.P. (8000 B.C.) Extinction of most species of megafauna in North America.

9000 B.P. (7000 B.C.) Archaic period begins; regional diversification of subsistence practices with an increased reliance upon plant collection.

5000 B.P. (3000 B.C.) Arrival of groups ancestral to modern Eskimo and Inuit from northeastern Asia; the first permanent occupation of the Arctic region and more extensive occupation of the Subarctic.

4000 B.P. (2000 B.C.) Poverty Point culture develops in the Southeast.

3000 B.P. (1000 B.C.) Woodland period in Eastern Woodlands; increased sedentism; villages; ceramic production; horticulture and mixed foraging; complex earthen architecture.

2800 B.P. (800 B.C.) Adena Tradition develops along the Ohio River and its tributaries; greater subsistence reliance upon plants; evidence of extensive long-distance trade networks across the midcontinent; complex mortuary customs with increasing importance of burial goods and social status.

2000 B.P. (A.D. 1) Hopewell Tradition develops along the Ohio River and its tributaries; complex earthen architecture; domestication of local plant species; greater sedentism; Hopewell Interaction Sphere; increased social ranking and status differentiation between members of society.

1750 B.P. (A.D. 300) Development of Anasazi, Hohokam, and Mogollon cultures in the Southwest; increased social complexity;

greater population nucleation; domesticated plants become increasingly important to local subsistence practices.

950 B.P. (A.D. 1000) Exploration of the northeastern Atlantic Coast of North America by Leif Ericsson; occupation of L'Anse aux Meadows by the Norse; first definitive archaeological evidence of contacts between Europeans and Native Americans; Mississippian period in Southeast and Midwest.

750 B.P. (A.D. 1200) Extended drought conditions in the Southwest result in the demise of most large settlements and a reversion back to smaller villages.

458 B.P. (A.D. 1492) Landing of Christopher Columbus in the Caribbean and the beginning of the first prolonged contacts between Europeans and Native Americans.

453 B.P. (A.D. 1497) Exploration of the northeastern Atlantic Coast of North America by John Cabot.

437 B.P. (A.D. 1513) Claiming of Florida by Spanish expedition of Juan Ponce de León.

429 B.P. (A.D. 1521) Failed effort to colonize Florida by a Spanish party under the command of Juan Ponce de León.

426 B.P. (A.D. 1524) Exploration of the Atlantic Coast of North America by Giovanni da Verrazano in search of a westward passage to Asia.

422 B.P. (A.D. 1528) Exploration of Florida by Panfilo de Narváez's party; resulting capture of Alva Nuñez Cabeza de Vaca and other members of the expedition.

416 B.P. (A.D. 1534) First voyage of Jacques Cartier to North America in search of the Northwest Passage to Asia.

411 B.P. (A.D. 1539) Exploration of the Southeast by Hernando de Soto's party begins.

410 B.P. (A.D. 1540) Exploration of the Southwest by Francisco Coronado's party.

374 B.P. (A.D. 1576) First of three voyages to North America by Martin Frobisher in search of the Northwest Passage to Asia.

365 B.P. (A.D. 1585) Establishment of English colony on Roanoke Island by Sir Walter Raleigh.

349 B.P. (A.D. 1601) Exploration of the Southwest and southern Great Plains by Juan de Oñate's party.

147 B.P. (A.D. 1803) Lewis and Clark expedition embarks on a journey to survey the lands and people brought under the control of the United States with the Louisiana Purchase.

100 B.P. (A.D. 1850) Detailed survey of Native American earthworks in the Ohio River valley by Ephraim Squire and Edwin Davis.

Introduction

Those unfamiliar with the prehistory of North America have a general perception of the cultures of the continent that includes Native Americans living in tipis, wearing feathered headdresses and buckskin clothing, and following migratory bison herds on the Great Plains. Although these practices were part of some Native American societies, they do not represent adequately the diversity of cultural practices by the overwhelming majority of Native American peoples. Media misrepresentations shaped by television and movies along with a focus on select regions and periods in the history of the United States have produced an extremely distorted view of the indigenous inhabitants of the continent and their cultures.

North America has a long and complex history of human occupation. The diverse environmental zones of the continent, from the frozen tundra of the Arctic to the scorching deserts of the Southwest, encouraged considerable regional variation in cultural development. Archaeologists and ethnologists have relied upon these regional distinctions in the analysis of indigenous North American cultures, resulting in the division of the continent into distinct culture areas: Arctic, California, Eastern Woodlands (frequently subdivided into the Northeast and Southeast), Great Basin, Great Plains, Northwest Coast, Plateau, Southwest, and Subarctic. Additionally, although geographically part of the North American continent, the Mesoamerican culture area (stretching from central Mexico into northern Central America) was home to a series of cultural traditions that are commonly seen as unique among those of the continent. Given the previous treatment of Mesoamerican cultures in this series (Palka, 2000), the cultures of this region have not been addressed in the present historical dictionary.

Over the past century, archaeological and ethnological research throughout all regions of North America has revealed much about the indigenous peoples of the continent. These efforts have helped to refine our understanding of the regional variation in Native American cultures while simultaneously revealing many social and cultural similarities among these groups. In addition, such research has dispelled many of the early ethnocentric notions proposed for the prehistory of the continent. Early European settlers argued that Native Americans were themselves relatively recent arrivals to the continent and thus could be displaced from their territories with little second thought. The massive earthworks of the Eastern Woodlands also were conveniently seen as evidence of previous occupations by the Lost Tribes of Israel, Phoenicians, Egyptians, or other nonindigenous peoples, thus limiting Native American claims to the land. Archaeological research has shown these contentions to be unfounded, revealing instead a long, complex history of indigenous occupation of North America.

THE FIRST NORTH AMERICANS: PALEOINDIAN PERIOD CULTURES

The indigenous peoples of North America are thought to have developed out of the early hunting and gathering peoples who first migrated into the Americas more than 13,000 years ago. The first humans in North America were big-game hunters who immigrated into the continent during the last glacial period across the now-submerged Bering Land Bridge. During the Pleistocene epoch, a time period when the earth's temperatures were considerably lower than those at present, glaciers covered much of the North American continent. Environmental reconstructions indicate that these glaciers contained so much water that mean sea levels were lowered by almost 100 meters (325 feet) below their present levels. This reduction in sea levels revealed a narrow strip of land, called Beringia, linking Asia to North America. This landmass facilitated the migration of caribou and other migratory animals between the continents, with human hunters following these animals into North America. With the advent of the Holocene epoch (circa 10,000 B.P. [8000 B.C.]) and more modern temperatures, the glaciers melted, releasing massive amounts of water back into the oceans and raising sea levels to near their present levels. This rise in sea levels resulted in the covering of Beringia by the Bering Sea and the geographic isolation of North America from Asia.

Those peoples who were in North America during this interglacial period would have been unable to move back into Asia and thus became the first permanent residents of North America. Known simply as Paleoindians, these first North American peoples were experienced big-game (megafauna) hunters who adapted their subsistence practices to target the mammoth, mastodon, bison, and other large animals indigenous to North America. These early hunters, referred to as the Clovis culture, quickly spread throughout all regions of North America, adapting their hunting techniques to take advantage of the megafauna in each regional environment and thus leading to a gradual regional diversification in subsistence practices, tool types, and other cultural materials.

Although the overland migration of hunting peoples from Asia has been the preferred explanation for the initial peopling of the Americas for almost a century, alternate hypotheses have also been proposed. One of the most intriguing is the possibility that a much earlier movement of Asian peoples into the Americas may have taken place more than 30,000 years ago. Advocates of this view, termed the *pre-Clovis hypothesis*, suggest that the first human residents of North America were foraging peoples. Recent archaeological research in South America does suggest an earlier date for the earliest human occupation of the Americas, with Tom Dillehay's research at Monte Verde, Chile, indicating that significant numbers of humans were present in South America as early as 12,000 B.P. (10,000 B.C.; Dillehay, 2000). Advocates of the Pre-Clovis Hypothesis surmise that for people to be present in South America by this time, they must have arrived much earlier in North America.

Although some archaeological sites in North America (most notably Meadowcroft Rockshelter) seem to support an earlier presence of humans in the Americas, the ephemeral nature of most proposed pre-Clovis sites and the lack of definitive, human-made tools at these sites make this idea an intriguing, but as yet unsubstantiated, proposition for most North American archaeologists. Current archaeological research in the Arctic and Subarctic regions as well as core testing in the Bering Sea will hopefully resolve these issues within the next few decades. Regardless of the definitive date for their entry into the Americas, archaeological, linguistic, and genetic data all indicate that Native American populations are closely related to the indigenous peoples of northeast Asia.

By 12,000 B.P. (10,000 B.C.), ample evidence exists of a human presence in almost all corners of North America. The extinction of most species of North American megafauna around 10,000 B.P. (8000 B.C.) forced Native Americans to alter their subsistence practices. Although the direct human contribution to the extinction of megafauna is hotly contested, there is evidence that a combination of environmental change and human hunting dramatically reduced populations of these animals. The eventual extinction of North American megafauna resulted in local Paleoindian groups shifting their hunting strategies toward smaller game animals and supplementing their diets increasingly with the gathering of wild plant resources. Because the plants and animals of each region were highly varied, the cultures that developed in each environmental zone became increasingly specialized on local resources, and thus the archaeological record indicates growing differences between Native American cultures in each region of the continent.

ARCHAIC PERIOD CULTURES

By 9000 B.P. (7000 B.C.), the changing ways of life for Native American peoples ushered in what archaeologists refer to as the Archaic period. Although the manifestations of this period vary by culture area, they generally consist of increased territoriality, as groups begin to confine their seasonal migrations to a geographically circumscribed home territory (base camps). There is also a continued diversification of tools and a general broadening of the subsistence practices to include a wider range of animal species and a greater emphasis on plant foods. Although Archaic period diets varied according to locally available resources, people came to rely increasingly on native plant species. Archaic peoples also developed new technologies like the grooved axe, net sinkers, and atlatls. Later, Archaic peoples began to carve vessels from steatite, a soft, easily manipulated local stone, suggesting changes in the processing, preparation, and storage of foodstuffs. Additionally, there is evidence of increasing sedentism during the Archaic period, with some groups residing in one location for extended periods of time. Although the Archaic period ends in some regions by about 3000 B.P. (1000 B.C.), in many areas of North America indigenous peoples continued to practice Archaic lifestyles even after contacts with Europeans in the 18th and 19th centuries.

During both the Paleoindian and Archaic periods, societies tended to consist of small groups of closely related peoples usually numbering 50 or less. These groups, called *band societies* by archaeologists and ethnologists, are generally egalitarian in nature with reciprocal exchanges being the norm. There were no permanent positions of authority, and little formal social ranking in these societies. In band societies, political and judicial decisions are made by the group as a whole in accordance with preexisting customs. Given their highly mobile lifestyles, there is also limited accumulation of material goods and a lack of long-term food storage technologies.

The largest and most intriguing North American society of the Archaic period is that of the Poverty Point culture. Developing in the present-day region of northeastern Louisiana at approximately 4000 B.P. (2000 B.C), Poverty Point culture demonstrates the presence of long-distance trade networks that brought raw materials (chert, galena, hematite, magnetite, slate, and steatite) and finished goods (adzes, hoes, drills, perforators, celts, plummets, gorgets, beads, pendants, and figurines) to the region from throughout the Great Plains and Eastern Woodlands. Poverty Point peoples practiced broad-spectrum foraging, but the biotic diversity of thelower Mississippi Valley was rich enough to permit them to become one of the earliest semisedentary foraging societies of North America. Poverty Point peoples also constructed some of the earliest and largest earthworks in North America, with these constructions thought to contain astronomical alignments as well as larger social meanings. The best examples of these structures are found at the Poverty Point site, the largest and most important center of Poverty Point cultural development.

Although it was unique for its time, the size, architectural complexity, and degree of sedentism present at Poverty Point indicate a markedly different social, political, and economic environment from that of the Paleoindians and contemporary Archaic societies. Archaeological research at Poverty Point suggests a degree of hierarchical social organization and a reduction in egalitarianism. Although the material manifestations of this process are yet to be examined fully, most scholars interpret Poverty Point as evidence of a Big Personage society (originally referred to as Big Man societies). In these societies, individuals

with the personal characteristics favored by society are given a dispro-
portionate ability to make decisions affecting society as a whole. However, the power and prestige of Big Persons are directly proportionate to
their current social standing, meaning that inherited social position is
absent. This flexibility ensures that social power is not concentrated
permanently in the hands of a few select individuals, but is always
placed in check by the will of the society as a whole.

WOODLAND PERIOD CULTURES

By about 3000 B.P. (1000 B.C.), continuing cultural trends begun in the
Archaic period, many societies in eastern North America became increasingly sedentary and more reliant upon the cultivation of local plant
species. During what is commonly referred to as the Woodland period,
these people not only began to live in permanent and semipermanent
villages, but they also engaged in the widespread production of ceramic
vessels for food preparation and storage. Although ceramics were produced in small numbers by Archaic peoples as early as 4000 B.P. (2000
B.C.), they become increasingly important as these societies developed
from foragers to food producers. Not coincidentally, the increase in ceramic production takes place at the same time that indigenous peoples
domesticated a series of formerly wild plant species. Plant domestication and small-scale horticultural food production would ultimately
change not only subsistence practices, but social relationships as well.

Societies of the Woodland period demonstrate marked increases in
local populations as well as contacts with nonlocal peoples. It is during
this period that eastern North America witnessed the development of
two major cultural traditions: the Adena Complex and Hopewell culture. The Adena complex, based along the Ohio River Valley and its
tributaries, indicates elaborations in the interment of the dead, the erec-
tion of public structures, and the development of long-distance trade
networks. Slightly later in time, the Hopewell culture builds upon these
developments and extends their influence throughout the Eastern
Woodlands of North America. The Hopewell are noted for their highly
elaborate material culture, consisting of exotic raw materials and finely
produced finished goods, as well as the construction of extensive geometric earthworks. Although there are considerable regional variations

in the Hopewell style through the Eastern Woodlands, the most elaborate Hopewell sites are found in the Scioto River valley of Ohio.

Both the Adena and Hopewell are thought to have influenced the cultural development of societies throughout the Eastern Woodlands, with their influence also thought to have extended onto the eastern Great Plains as well. They are presently interpreted as representing an expansion of Big Personage societies throughout eastern North America, with social power and prestige becoming increasingly concentrated within a select group of individuals. In fact, some archaeologists suggest that these social distinctions may have become more regularized within Hopewell society, and may possibly represent a transition to chiefdoms in the region. In neo-evolutionary terms, some scholars propose that both the Adena and Hopewell fall within the definition of tribal societies, where there are fewer positions of power than those who seek to hold power, but no permanent, stable political office in which all social decisions are based.

SOUTHWESTERN CULTURES: ANASAZI, MOGOLLON, AND HOHOKAM

At about 2000 B.P. (A.D. 1), the Southwest entered into a period of marked cultural development as well. The preceding Southwestern Archaic period was a time of culture change that included responses to warmer and drier environmental conditions in the region. Southwestern Archaic peoples were organized as small bands of mobile foragers with defined regional territories. These peoples primarily subsisted upon a wide variety of wild plants and animals, and were engaged in trade and exchange with other groups, resulting in broad similarities in culture. Toward the end of this period (circa 2200 [250 B.C.]), Southwestern Archaic peoples became more sedentary, with evidence of increased ceramic production and limited agriculture.

These trends culminated in the development of three distinct cultures in the Southwest: the Anasazi, Mogollon, and Hohokam at about 1750 B.P. (A.D. 300). These societies all consisted of village dwelling agriculturalists engaged in long-distance trade for exotic raw materials and finished goods. Each of these groups maintained their own distinct cultural practices, but all three became increasingly complex in terms of social and political life, with some scholars arguing for the development of both Big Personage societies and chiefdoms during this period. These cultural traditions exerted tremendous influence on cultural practices throughout the Southwest, with large, permanent river valley villages, such as those at Chaco Canyon, Mesa Verde, and Paquime, serving as ceremonial, political, social, and economic centers.

However, as with cultural development in all other regions of North America, even at the height of this regional population nucleation in river valleys and an increased dependence upon agriculture, other groups continued traditional nomadic foraging as their principal subsistence strategy. By around 750 B.P. (A.D. 1200), environmental conditions are thought to have become hotter and drier in the Southwest, with agricultural production compromised by an extended, regionwide drought. This prolonged drought is believed to have reduce the ability of Southwestern farmers to produce enough food to feed large settlements, with famine, warfare, and social collapse following closely on the heels of this environmental shift. Following this collapse in large-scale settlements in the region, many groups continued to practice village agriculture, becoming the historic Puebloan groups of the historic period, including the Hopi, Zuñi, Tewa, and others. During the period between 1150 and 950 B.P. (A.D. 800 to 1000), Athabaskan groups migrated into the Southwest from the north. These groups were nomadic foragers whose descendents include the historic Apache and Navajo.

MISSISSIPPIAN PERIOD CULTURES

By 1000 B.P. (A.D. 1000), a new cultural tradition develops in the Eastern Woodlands, only this time it is centered along the Mississippi River. Known as the *Mississippian period*, this era is marked by the development of large-scale maize agriculture, permanently sedentary villages and cities, widespread similarities in material culture and iconography, as well as the institution of permanent hereditary social inequality. Unlike bands or tribes, these societies are thought to be chiefdoms: societies in which there is a permanent position of power in which social power resides. In addition, based upon archaeological and historic evidence, the position of chief was hereditary, with the prestige and authority of the office of chief permanently vested in one social group.

Mississippian societies also yield evidence of large-scale warfare and conquest, with major Mississippian societies like those at Cahokia, Moundville, and Etowah thought to have conquered neighboring groups for the purpose of extorting tribute payments and other forms of sociopolitical dependence.

Archaeological investigation at Mississippian sites reveals marked distinctions between political elites and commoners. These distinctions include differential access to high status, exotic raw materials, and finished goods. In addition, at Cahokia and Moundville there appears to have been spatial segregation between these groups, with elites residing either within or in close proximity to prominent public structures. Analysis of artifacts from across the Eastern Woodlands indicates the presence of a similar iconographic program for the decoration of high-status goods during the Mississippian period. Termed the Southeastern Ceremonial Complex, this cultural complex includes similar decorative styles and the use of complex anthropomorphic and zoomorphic imagery in the decoration of ceramics, shell gorgets, and other items. This artistic complex is thought to have been related to the social and religious distinctions between elites and commoners, and served to mark elites as privileged in relation to the supernatural. Ethnohistoric documents also suggest that Mississippian elites held the power of life and death over their subjects, a social situation that is most definitely hierarchical. The degree of social and political integration and the sheer scale of Mississippian societies (with populations in the tens of thousands) have led most scholars to the conclusion that the Mississippian period was the pinnacle of indigenous cultural development in the Eastern Woodlands and possibly all of North America.

CULTURAL DEVELOPMENTS IN OTHER REGIONS

During these periods of dramatic increases in social and political complexity in the Eastern Woodlands and Southwest, Native American societies of other culture areas continued to change as well, just not as dramatically. Societies of the Great Plains diversified from east to west, with those of the eastern Plains adopting sedentary villages and agriculture from groups in the Eastern Woodlands. Meanwhile, groups of the western Plains continued to practice seasonally mobile foraging strategies. At the same time, groups of the Great Basin and Plateau continued to adapt to warmer and drier cultural conditions, developing their own unique forms of mobile foraging.

Native American groups of California continued their own unique cultural developments as well, with groups adapting to the diversity of environments of the Pacific Coast and interior mountain regions. Groups of the California culture area remained foragers; however, many groups were able to generate food surpluses given the tremendous biotic diversity of their local environments. The ease with which these food resources could be obtained led to expansive populations in the region, with the California culture area supporting one of the highest population densities of North America prior to European contacts. Groups in the California culture area vary from south to north, depending on their proximity to groups in other culture areas. Groups in the north were heavily impacted through trade with groups of the Northwest Coast culture area, adopting many of the cultural traits exhibited by these groups. At the same time, those of the southern portion of the region were engaged in trade and exchange with Southwestern groups along the Colorado River, with these peoples practicing small-scale horticulture and adopting many of the cultural practices of Southwestern peoples.

The Northwest Coast culture area was also a region with tremendous population density prior to European contacts. The complex foragers of the Northwest Coast developed subsistence strategies that took advantage of both terrestrial and aquatic food resources. These groups gathered a variety of plant resources and hunted deer, moose, elk, bear, mountain goat, sheep, fox, mink, and beaver, as well as whale, seal, sea lion, porpoise, sea otter, and numerous fish species. Given the tremendous biotic diversity of their natural environment, Northwest Coast societies were capable of supporting large social groups without the need for agriculture. These cultures are collectively considered to be the most sociopolitically complex foragers in the Americas and among the most complex in the world. Most groups were seasonally mobile, with the winter months spent in large coastal villages. With the abundant natural resources at their disposal, Northwest Coast groups developed hereditary social ranking, with an individual's social position related to that of their family and clan. Many scholars consider these societies to be representative of chiefdoms, although they are a distinct form of chiefdom from those found in the Eastern Woodlands and Southwest.

At the same time, the development of cultures in the Arctic and Subarctic show considerable geographic variations. These regions saw the least dense indigenous populations prior to European contact largely due to the presence of harsh climates and limited subsistence resources. Present evidence suggests that the first peoples to permanently settle the Arctic region arrived relatively late compared to other Native American groups (approximately 5000 B.P. [3000 B.C.]). Indigenous groups of both regions practice varied hunting and gathering subsistence regimes, with local groups adopting subsistence practices related to locally available food resources. Most Arctic groups share a reliance on maritime resources, but many also make use of caribou and other terrestrial resources when they are seasonally available. Groups of the Subarctic generally developed subsistence practices centered upon the hunting of caribou, deer, elk, and moose. Both groups demonstrate considerable seasonal mobility, with small social groups predominating. However, there are periodic larger gatherings of social groups during periods of maximum resource availability.

Throughout their history of occupation, each North American culture area saw immense cultural adaptations by indigenous peoples as they came to grips with changing environmental conditions and biotic communities. In addition, the archaeological record of North America is replete with evidence of innovations in technology and material culture related to the evolving lifeways of Native American peoples. Despite claims to the contrary in popular media accounts of Native American people, there are no unaltered cultures, and no "modern primitives." All existing cultures have their own unique periods of historical development, and although not all people have written records to recount the many changes that they have undergone with the passage of time, the archaeological record provides ample evidence that all groups change over time.

EUROPEAN CONTACTS

With the arrival of Europeans in North America during the late 15th and early 16th centuries, the direction and pace of Native American culture was irrevocably altered. Regardless of the culture area under consideration, contacts between Native Americans and Europeans resulted in extensive changes in indigenous cultures. Europeans introduced diseases for which Native American peoples had no natural immunities. These diseases quickly spread into pandemics (particularly smallpox), with most epidemiological estimates placing the rate of population loss from European diseases at almost 90 percent within the first century following initial contacts. This tremendous population loss, coupled with the continued expansion of European settlements and colonial endeavors, also had dramatic impacts on Native American peoples. The settlement of the Atlantic Coast forced many coastal groups to move inland, further disrupting indigenous societies of the interior of the continent. Additionally, the advent of commercial hunting with the deer skin trade further disrupted Native American cultures throughout the continent. Meanwhile, groups in portions of the Southwest, California, and Southeast were brought under the Spanish Mission system and forced to abandon almost all aspects of their precontact cultures. For Native Americans of the Eastern Woodlands and Great Plains, perhaps the greatest source of culture change was the annexation of their traditional territories and their removal to distant reservations or small allotments that were only fragments of their previous territories.

It is within this context of European contact that the common image of Native Americans was formed. The introduction of horses and guns to Native American peoples of the Great Plains produced some of the most efficient mobile hunting cultures ever documented. These Native American cultures quickly became the stereotypical image of the American Indian during the 19th century as the eastern United States was gradually depleted of Native Americans. Thus, the image of the nomadic cultures of the Great Plains became popularized in literature and art. However, these cultures underwent significant alterations as a result of European contacts and influence.

With the forced removal of most Native Americans from eastern North America by the late 19th century and the placement of nomadic Great Plains peoples on reservations, most scholars believed it to be only a matter of decades before the indigenous cultures of the continent disappeared. Franz Boas founded the field of American anthropology at the beginning of the 20th century with the imminent demise of Native American cultures in mind. The first generation of American anthropologists was charged with studying the physical, cultural, linguistic, and historical components of Native American peoples before they vanished. Luckily for all concerned, Native American cultures were more resilient than initially predicted.

Ethnologists and archaeologists continue to research Native American cultures, but are armed with a new set of anthropological questions. What they have learned is that the culture history of North America, whether prior to or following European contacts, is one of considerable social, cultural, economic, and technological change. Given this context of tremendous change during the 13,000 years or more of human occupation, it is important to realize the important place of archaeology in revealing the history of the human occupation of the Americas. Continued research holds the potential to extend not only our understanding of the temporal framework for the occupation of North America, but the developmental sequence of regional cultures as well.

The Dictionary

– A –

ABENAKI INDIANS. Algonquian-speaking Native American group who occupied northern New England and portions of the Canadian Maritimes when first recorded by Europeans. The Abenaki were village **agriculturalists** that cultivated **maize, beans**, and squash, and supplemented their diets by **hunting, fishing**, and collecting wild plants. They coalesced in large villages during the spring and summer months, with these encampments breaking into family groups during the late fall and winter. The Abenaki were dramatically impacted by contacts with Europeans, and the **Iroquois** played a major role in pressuring the Abenaki for territory in the **Northeast**. The Abenaki responded by forming their own confederacy with other small tribes in the region, but a series of smallpox epidemics in the 16th and 17th centuries had catastrophic results for the Abenaki, with their population dropping from an estimated 40,000 to 1,500 during this period. At present, there are approximately 15,000 Abenaki in the United States and Canada.

ABERDEEN SITE. Archaeological site located on the Thelon River, west of Hudson Bay in Canada. Evidence indicates that the Aberdeen site was occupied during the **Archaic** period, approximately 3000 B.P. (1000 B.C.). The inhabitants of this site were engaged in the seasonal **hunting** of **caribou**. The Aberdeen site is part of the **Shield Archaic**, and is important primarily because **tools** from the site evidence a mixture of **Great Plains** and Midwestern **lithic** (stone tool) **traditions**. This combination of traits from two distinct regions suggests that the occupants of the Aberdeen site migrated into the region from the Plains and Midwest following glacial retreat in the region.

ACCELERATOR MASS SPECTROMETRY DATING (AMS Dating). A particular type of **radiocarbon dating** in which the age of a sample is determined by counting radioactive carbon atoms directly with an accelerator mass spectrometer. Developed in 1979, AMS dating has an advantage over traditional radiocarbon dating methods because it can be used on extremely small carbon samples (as little as 100 micrograms [3.21×10^{-6} ounces]). Like other methods of radiocarbon dating, AMS dating can be used on almost all carbonaceous materials, and can yield accurate dates for materials as much as 50,000 B.P. in age. AMS dating has been particularly useful for North American archaeology in research directed at the role of **Paleoindians** in the **extinction** of North American **megafauna**.

ACCULTURATION. Process through which a **cultural** group adopts the material, social, and behavioral patterns of another society with which it has contact. **Anthropologists** have defined cases in which acculturation is symmetrical, with each society becoming increasingly like the other. However, in most cases the process of acculturation is decidedly asymmetrical, with one group's culture becoming increasingly like that of the culture with which it has contact. The term is often used in relation to the cultural changes experienced by Native American groups following their interaction with Europeans. The **Cherokee** are considered a particularly good example of the process of acculturation, having adopted European clothing, architecture, material culture, and a constitutional form of government following intense interaction with Europeans in the 18th and 19th centuries.

ACHIEVED STATUS. Social standing that reflects the ability of an individual to acquire a position in society as a result of his or her own accomplishments, abilities, and personal attributes. Achieved status varies throughout an individual's life, with one's social standing rising and falling due to recent successes or failures. Most Native American societies, like those of the **Woodland** period of the **Eastern Woodlands**, are thought to have practiced forms of social ranking in which personal achievements were the principal means of reckoning one's social status. Societies in which achieved status is the principal means of social ranking are often contrasted with those practicing **ascribed status**.

ACOMA INDIANS. A Native American society of the **Southwest**, the Acoma are thought to have developed out of earlier **Anasazi** peoples. The Acoma are mentioned in early historical accounts, and are noted for fighting several pitched battles with the Spanish during the 17th century. A large number of Acoma continue to reside in Acoma Pueblo, a village located atop a mesa in central New Mexico. Acoma Pueblo is argued to be the oldest continually inhabited settlement in the United States, with evidence of occupation as early as 800 B.P. (A.D. 1150). The Acoma are **agriculturalists**, cultivating **maize**, **beans, squash**, and **wheat**. At present, there are more than 3,000 Acoma living in New Mexico and Arizona.

ACORNS. A natural product of several species of oak tree, acorns were utilized as a food source by many Native American groups. However, before they are suitable for human consumption, acorns must be processed to remove poisonous tannic acids. The process of removing this poison frequently included pounding the acorns into meal, then using water to leach out the bitter acids. Acorns were utilized by early peoples in the **Eastern Woodlands**, where oak trees are abundant. They also became an important food for native peoples in western North America after the development of mortars and pestles at approximately 6000 B.P. (4000 B.C.).

ACOSTA, JOSÉ (1540–1600). Spanish **Jesuit** missionary to the Americas who wrote *Historia Natural y Moral de los Indias*. In this work, he described many of the **cultural** attributes of indigenous peoples and speculated that Native Americans were of Asian origin. He proposed that Native Americans originally migrated to the Americas over a now submerged landmass (presently referred to as **Beringia**) that linked North America to Asia. His ideas concerning the peopling of the Americas were not widely accepted at the time, but contemporary **archaeologists** generally accept an overland migration from Asia as the principal means by which native peoples made it into the Americas.

ADAIR, JAMES (1709–1783). Eighteenth-century Englishman who spent almost 40 years living among, and trading with, Native Americans in the **Southeast** (principally the **Chickasaw** and **Cherokee**).

His book, *The History of the American Indians*, provided descriptions of the locations, customs, histories, and activities of daily life of Southeastern **cultures**, and remains a valuable resource for contemporary **archaeologists** and **ethnohistorians**.

ADENA COMPLEX. Variously described as a **culture** and a ceremonial complex, Adena sites represent an Early **Woodland** cultural climax in portions of southern Ohio and Indiana, northern Kentucky, southwestern Pennsylvania, and northwestern West Virginia. The Adena Complex derives its name from the Adena mound group in Ross County, Ohio, originally excavated by W. C. Mills of the Ohio State Museum in 1901. The Adena Complex dates to the period from approximately 2500 to 1900 B.P. (500 B.C.–A.D. 100). Adena sites are characterized by the presence of large **burial mounds** and complex geometric **earthworks**. The largest Adena mound is the Grave Creek Mound in West Virginia (approximately 20 meters in height). Excavations in Adena mounds have revealed complex **burials** and elaborate mortuary practices, including the construction of central log tombs for those believed to have been the most powerful people in Adena society. Adena burials commonly contain stone and bone **tools**, **copper beads**, **mica**, seashells (see **shell midden** and **shell mound**, slate or **copper gorgets**, as well as distinctive tubular **pipes**. Some of the more elaborate Adena burials contain intricately carved stone tablets with **zoomorphic** designs and highly stylized copper ornaments. Many of these items are indicative of long-distance **trade** networks stretching across much of the **Eastern Woodlands** of North America.

ADOBE. Sun-dried bricks and the heavy clay from which these bricks are made. Adobe was a primary building material for many indigenous **cultures** of the American **Southwest** for thousands of years. Adobe is an excellent insulator, and is well suited to the temperature extremes of the region. In addition, when adobe bricks are heated (either intentionally or unintentionally) they undergo a chemical transformation similar to the firing of **ceramics**. This process causes adobe bricks to become more resistant to decay, making them an extremely durable building material. This heating process also allows archaeologists to use **thermoluminescence dating** (TL) to determine the age of adobe structures.

ADZE. An **axe**-like cutting tool used to shape wood. An adze consists of a thin arched **blade** (a thinned, convex head) set at a right angle and **hafted** to a wooden handle. Many Native American groups used adzes, but the elaborate woodworking **cultures** of the **Northwest Coast** provide perhaps the best examples of their use.

AGATE BASIN SITE. Archaeological site in eastern Wyoming related to a **Paleoindian bison** kill. The Agate Basin site possesses evidence of both the killing and postmortem **butchering** of bison by Paleoindians. The term *Agate Basin* has been extended to a series of archaeological sites in the northwestern **Great Plains** dating between 10,500 and 10,000 B.P. (circa 8500–8000 B.C.) with **artifact assemblages** primarily characterized by scrapers and bone needles. The name is also used to designate a specific type of **projectile point** used by Paleoindian **hunters**.

AGAVE. A family (*Agavaceae*) of succulent plants native to the hot, dry deserts of the American **Southwest** and **Great Basin**. Agave was important to Native Americans as a source of fibers used to produce clothing and other **artifacts** as well as a source of food and water. Agave leaves were harvested in the spring and baked in large communal earth ovens. Some **Mesoamerican** groups processed the sap of agave plants to produce *pulque*, a fermented, intoxicating beverage.

AGRICULTURE. The intentional **cultivation** of plants as a primary means of human **subsistence**. Native America agricultural practices consisted of planting individual seeding plants, followed by periods of tending and harvesting. Most plants grown by Native Americans were annuals or became annuals by **cultivation** and **domestication**. The dominant plants of Native American agriculture were **maize** (corn), **beans**, and **squash**. These three plants formed a symbiotic complex with corn stalks providing a climbing area that allowed bean plants to take advantage of light, while the roots of bean plants supported colonies of nitrogen-fixing bacteria. Squashes grow along the ground, covering the soil and helping to retain moisture.

Native Americans also cultivated a wide variety of indigenously domesticated plants, with many of these plants well adapted to specific local environmental conditions. Examples of regionally specific agricultural products include **chenopodium** and **sumpweed** in the **Eastern Woodlands**, as well as panic grass and jack beans in the **Southwest**. Following the establishment of European **colonies** in North America, the number of agricultural products increased dramatically to include European, Asian, and African domesticates. Much of our information about prehistoric agriculture is relatively recent and has been made possible through the practice of **flotation** and advances in the field of paleoethnobotany. *See also* CANAL SYSTEM.

ALEUT–ESKIMO LINGUISTIC GROUP. The single **language** family to which all **Eskimo** and **Aleutian** languages belong. This language family encompasses peoples from eastern Siberia and the Aleutian Islands, to Alaska, northern Canada, and Greenland. Aleut-Eskimo languages are closely related to Siberian language groups, with the strongest of these connections thought to be with the Chukchi and Ural–Altaic language groups. Eskimo languages are divided into two subgroups: Yupik (spoken on the Chukchi Peninsula of Siberia and in southwestern Alaska) and Inupiaq–Inuktitut (spoken across arctic Alaska and Canada to the coasts of Labrador and Greenland). Similarities between these languages provide definitive evidence of a northeast Asian origin for Native American peoples. In addition, strong similarities exist in the **cultural** traits of these groups, with scholars considering Aleut–Eskimo speakers to be the most Asian-like of all Native American groups. *See also* ALEUTIAN TRADITION.

ALEUTIAN TRADITION. A widespread set of **cultural** traits shared among Native American groups inhabiting the Aleutian Islands between 4500 and 200 B.P. (2500 B.C.–A.D. 1800). Although considerable stylistic variation exists in the **artifacts** of the Aleutian tradition, it is characterized by the presence of chipped-stone artifacts, an elaborate bone **tool** industry, and a **subsistence** strategy centered upon marine mammals and saltwater fish. The material culture of the Aleutian **tradition** differs markedly from that of other **Arctic** groups.

ALGONQUIAN LANGUAGE FAMILY. A Native American **language** family encompassing a number of distinct **cultural** groups across the **Eastern Woodlands** of North America. The Algonquian family is divided into Northern (**Cree**, **Kickapoo**, **Menomini**, **Miami**, **Ojibwa**, **Potawatomi**, **Sauk**, and Shawnee), Eastern (Abenake, **Delaware**, Massachusett, **Micmac**, and **Powhatan**), and Western (**Arapaho**, Atsina, **Blackfoot**, and **Cheyenne**) varieties. Some scholars contend that the majority of indigenous peoples in the **Eastern Woodlands** once spoke Algonquian languages, with these groups later displaced by peoples from other linguistic families and **culture** groups.

ALIBATES. A distinctive type of **lithic** material (agatized dolomite) used for making **projectile points** and other **tools**. A major source of North American alibates occurs in the Texas Panhandle along the Canadian River near the modern community of Fritch, Texas. Alibates was quarried by Native Americans for centuries, with the greatest intensity of this mining activity occurring during the **Antelope Creek focus** from 800 to 500 B.P. (circa A.D. 1150–1450). There is extensive **archaeological** evidence that alibates was used not only for tool production but also as a trade item that was highly prized by nonlocal groups.

ALTITHERMAL. A North American climatic episode characterized by drier and warmer environmental conditions than those at present. The altithermal began at approximately 8000 B.P. and lasted until about 4000 B.P. (circa 6000–2000 B.C.). Also referred to as the Holocene Climactic Optimum or the Hypsithermal, these changes in climate are believed to have spurred an expansion in North American prairies and the **fauna** that fed upon them (primarily **bison**). These climatic changes impacted humans by altering the carrying capacity of many environments and necessitating changes in human **subsistence** practices and settlement patterns. Some **archaeologists** have proposed that entire regions were abandoned during this period. The altithermal followed the **anathermal** climatic period.

ALVARADO, HERNANDO DE (1496–1542). Captain of artillery on the expedition of **Francisco Vasquez de Coronado** into the American **Southwest**. Alvarado split with the main party on August 29, 1540, and commanded a smaller expedition that explored the region to the east and the north for 80 days. Alvarado and his party ventured onto the southern **Great Plains**, becoming the first Europeans to directly encounter and describe the large herds of **bison** in the region.

AMERICAN ANTHROPOLOGICAL ASSOCIATION (AAA). Developing out of the **Anthropological** Society of Washington, the AAA (as it is commonly known) was officially founded in 1902. It is the largest professional anthropological organization in the world. The AAA publishes the *American Anthropologist*, the leading disciplinary journal in American anthropology.

AMERICAN BOTTOM. Name given to a section of the Mississippi River valley in west-central Illinois. This region is a relatively flat portion of the Mississippi River floodplain and was capable of supporting large Native American **agricultural** populations. The American Bottom has long been of interest to **archaeologists** and is considered the center of **Mississippian cultural** developments during the period from 1100 to 650 B.P. (A.D. 900–1350). The large Mississippian center of **Cahokia** and its allied communities are located within the American Bottom region.

ANANGULA SITE. Archaeological site located near Umnak Island in the Aleutian chain of Alaska. Evidence from this site indicates human presence as early as 8000 B.P. (6000 B.C). Archaeological materials at the site consist of various **blade** and microblade **tools** as well as several oval, semisubterranean houses. The site was occupied by a group of people who relied upon sea mammals and other marine resources for their primary **subsistence** needs.

ANASAZI CULTURE. Village **agricultural** peoples of the North American **Southwest** who occupied the Four Corners region of southeastern Utah, southwestern Colorado, northwestern New Mexico, and northeastern Arizona during the period from 1949 to 450 B.P. (A.D. 1–1500). The Anasazi were ancestors to many contemporary **Pueblo** Indians, including the **Acoma**, **Hopi**, and **Zuñi**. Depending on the translation, Anasazi is a **Navajo** word meaning "ancient ones," "early ancestors," or "old people." Major Anasazi settlements include **Chaco Canyon** and **Mesa Verde**, with the Anasazi **culture area** commonly divided into three regional variants, the Chacoan, Mesa Verde, and Kayenta.

The Anasazi cultural sequence was first defined by **A. V. Kidder**. Contemporary archaeologists recognize five general periods in Anasazi cultural development: **Basketmaker** (1850–1450 B.P. [A.D. 100–500]), defined by the appearance of **agriculture**; Modified Basketmaker (1450–1250 B.P. [A.D. 500–700]), defined by the appearance of **pottery**, **pit houses**, and the **bow and arrow**; Developmental Pueblo (1250–900 B.P. [A.D. 700–1050]), Classic Pueblo (900–650 B.P. [A.D. 1050–1300]), and Regressive Pueblo (650–400 B.P. [A.D. 1300–1550]), each characterized by an increasingly complex **subsistence** technology based on the intensive **cultivation** of **maize**, **beans** and **squash**, and the development of large, multiroom dwellings and sophisticated and regionally diverse **ceramics**.

ANATHERMAL. A North American climatic episode characterized by cooler and more moist environmental conditions than those at present. The anathermal began at approximately 11,000 B.P., lasting until 8000 B.P. (circa 9000–6000 B.C.). The anathermal immediately preceded the **altithermal**. The anathermal supported a different array of plant and animal communities than both previous and subsequent environmental periods, suggesting a unique set of human **subsistence** practices and settlement patterns during this time.

ANTELOPE. *See* PRONGHORN.

ANTELOPE CREEK FOCUS. A **cultural tradition** of the southern **Great Plains** primarily located in portions of western Oklahoma and the Texas panhandle. The Antelope Creek focus dates from 800 to 500 B.P. (circa A.D. 1200 to 1500) and is notable for evidence of long-distance **trade** relations with groups in both the **Southwest** and **Great Plains culture areas**. Much of this trade is thought to have involved the **exchange** of locally available **alibates** for items of seashell (see **shell midden** and **shell mound**), **pottery**, **obsidian**, and other exotic, nonlocal goods. Antelope Creek peoples are also notable for their construction of stone foundation houses and walls of **adobe** or masonry.

ANTHROPOLOGY. A social science discipline devoted to the holistic study of human beings. Established as an independent academic subject at the beginning of the 20th century, American anthropology has traditionally been divided into four subfields: physical anthropology, which assesses the biosocial nature of humans; **cultural** anthropology, which addresses the present cultural diversity of human cultures; linguistic anthropology, which examines human communication systems; and **archaeology**, which researches past human social development through material remains. Central to all of these subfields is the concept of culture. The interrelation of the four traditional subfields and the culture concept make American anthropology distinctive from that practiced in other world areas. *See also* AMERICAN ANTHROPOLOGICAL ASSOCIATION.

ANTHROPOMORPHIC. The use of human motifs to decorate an object. Native Americans used a variety of anthropomorphic representations, with human motifs appearing in **ceramics**, **earthworks**, **figurines**, **pipes**, **petroglyphs**, and other media.

ANTIQUITIES ACT OF 1906 (16 USC 431–433). The first legislation regulating the excavation and preservation of **archaeological** sites on federal lands in the United States. The Antiquities Act of 1906 protected archaeological sites on federal lands from the uncontrolled looting by **pot-hunters** that was common at the turn of the century. It also made provisions for the scientific collection of archaeological materials and their display in public museums.

ANVIL AND PADDLE TECHNIQUE. A technique for pottery manufacturing used by many Native American groups. This method is used to compress the walls of **ceramic** vessels before they are fired. An anvil is applied to one side of the vessel and a paddle to the other. The anvil normally consists of a piece of stone, wood, or ceramic that is flattened to provide a flat surface for the paddle to impact. The paddle is usually made of wood and may either be smooth or decorated with engraved designs. By compressing the walls of the vessel, air pockets that could potentially compromise the strength of the finished vessel are expelled prior to firing.

APACHE INDIANS. Native American group of the American **Southwest**, primarily located in Arizona and New Mexico. The Apache speak an **Athabaskan language** and are believed to have migrated into the **Southwest** from the **Great Plains** immediately prior to European contact. The name Apache is a **Zuñi** word for "enemy," and the Apache were in near constant conflict with the **Pima, Papago,** and other **Pueblo** peoples. The Apache are divided into Eastern (Mescalero, Jicarilla, Chiricahua, Lipan) and Western divisions. Present evidence indicates that the Apache did not practice **agriculture** before their arrival in the region, with this and many other traits borrowed from their Puebloan neighbors. The Apache resisted confinement on reservations, engaging in a 25-year armed struggle against the U.S. military (1861–1886). These hostilities ceased with the surrender of Geronimo. The Apache are composed of several distinct tribal groups, including the Mescaleros, Jicarillos, Faraones, Llaneros, Lipan, Chiracahua, Coyoteros, Aricaipa, and others. At present, there are more than 50,000 Apache living in the United States and Mexico.

APALACHEE INDIANS. A **Muskogean**-speaking Native American group originally located along the Apalachee River in northern Florida. They were one of the first Native American peoples to have direct contact with the expedition of **Hernando de Soto** (A.D. 1539–1542). Anhaica, the major Apalachee town, served as a winter camp for de Soto and his party. This is one of the few towns described in the accounts of the de Soto expedition that have been definitively identified **archaeologically**.

ARAPAHO INDIANS. An **Algonquian**-speaking group of Native Americans who lived along the Platte and Arkansas Rivers during the 19th century. The Arapaho were highly mobile **foragers**, with villages frequently moving to follow migratory **bison**. The Arapaho were trading partners with the **Arikara** and **Mandan**, but were frequently at war with the **Pawnee, Shoshone,** and **Ute**. At present, the Arapaho number approximately 1,000, with distinct populations in Wyoming and Oklahoma.

ARCHAEOASTRONOMY. The search for patterns in the **archaeological** record related to astronomical observations. Many archaeological sites in North America are thought to possess astronomical alignments (e.g., **Cahokia**, Mound City, and **Serpent Mound**). The presence of such patterns is thought to indicate a detailed knowledge of celestial events, the monitoring of changes in lunar and solar alignments, and an increased concern with observing the passage of time in ancient North American societies.

ARCHAEOLOGICAL CULTURE. A theoretical construct used by **archaeologists** to examine the temporal and spatial boundaries of past social groups. Archaeological **cultures** are considered to be the archaeological correlates of ethnographic cultures. This designation is based on consistent similarities in **artifact assemblages** thought to represent synonymous beliefs and behaviors in a particular region during a specific period of time.

ARCHAEOLOGY. A social science discipline devoted to the study of past human social development through material evidence of their **cultural** practices. Practiced in North America as a subfield of **anthropology**, in other world areas archaeology is considered either a component of history or an independent field of inquiry. The principal goal of archaeology is to reconstruct past human social and cultural life through the interpretation of material remains. Archaeological sites in North America provide essential information on the development of Native American **cultures** from the first period of human occupation.

Most scholars see the beginnings of a scientific archaeology in North America in the efforts of **Thomas Jefferson** on his Virginia property. However, the first generation of North American archaeologists was not professionally trained and was generally unsystematic in their investigative techniques. Pioneering efforts by avocational archaeologists such as Caleb Atwater, **Edwin Davis**, and **Ephraim Squire** in the Midwest; **Clarence B. Moore** and **Cyrus Thomas** in the **Southeast**; **William Henry Holmes** in the **Northeast**; and **Adolph Bandelier** and **John Wesley Powell** in the **Southwest** were important early steps in the development of the field, but their work would soon be superceded by that of professionally trained archaeologists. The first generation of professional North American archaeologists included some of the major figures in the development of the field, including **Joseph Caldwell, James Ford,**

James B. Griffin, A. V. Kidder, Paul S. Martin, Moreau Maxwell, William McKern, and **Gordon Willey.** These scholars influenced the development of **culture historical** perspectives among American archaeologists, while a later generation (heavily influenced by **Walter Taylor**), including **Lewis Binford,** Michael Schiffer, and **Patty Jo Watson,** would steer the field toward theoretical and methodological concerns of a more scientific and comparative nature, known as *processual archaeology. See also* ABERDEEN SITE; AGATE BASIN SITE; ANANGULA SITE; AVONLEA SITE; AZTALAN SITE; BAKER CAVE SITE; BAT CAVE SITE; BAUMER SITE; BLACK EARTH SITE; BLACK MESA SITE; BLACKWATER DRAW SITE; BONFIRE SHELTER SITE; BORAX LAKE SITE; BRAND SITE; BROKEN MAMMOTH SITE; CAHOKIA SITE; CASPER SITE; CHACO CANYON; CHALUKA SITE; CHETRO KETL; CLOVIS SITE; COLBY MAMMOTH SITE; COWBOY CAVE SITE; CROOKS SITE; DANGER CAVE SITE; DRAPER SITE; ETOWAH SITE; FOLSOM SITE; HARDAWAY SITE; ICEHOUSE BOTTOM SITE; JAKETOWN SITE; JESSE JENNINGS; JONES-MILLER SITE; KIMMSWICK SITE; KING SITE; MADELINE KNEBERG; KOLOMOKI SITE; KOSTER SITE; LACE SITE; LEHNER SITE; LINDENMEIER SITE; LITTLE EGYPT SITE; LITTLE SALT SPRINGS SITE; MCKEITHEN SITE; MEADOWCROFT ROCKSHELTER; MEAD SITE; MESA SITE; MESA VERDE; WARREN K. MOOREHEAD; MOUND CITY SITE; MOUNDVILLE SITE; MURRAY SPRINGS SITE; NACO SITE; NAMU SITE; NEWARK SITE; NODWELL SITE; ONION PORTAGE SITE; OZETTE SITE; PHILLIP PHILLIPS; POVERTY POINT SITE; QUEQERTASUSSUK SITE; ROGERS SHELTER SITE; RUSSELL CAVE SITE; SERPENT MOUND; SHOOP SITE; SLOAN SITE; SOCIETY FOR AMERICAN ARCHAEOLGY; ALBERT SPAULDING; SPIRO SITE; JOHN R. SWANTON; TATHAM MOUND SITE; TULAROSA CAVE SITE; VAIL SITE; ANTONIO J. WARING, JR.; WILLIAM S. WEBB; WALDO R. WEDEL; WILLIAMSON SITE; YOUNGER DRYAS.

ARCHAEOMAGNETIC DATING. Also referred to as paleomagnetic **dating,** archaeomagnetic dating consists of dating **archaeological**

materials by measuring the geomagnetic alignment of archaeological materials. Given periodic fluctuations in the earth's magnetic field, burned features and **artifacts** containing magnetic minerals can be used to measure the dominant magnetic field at the time they were heated. Measures of the direction and intensity of the earth's magnetic field contained in these materials are then used to date these objects. This technique is particularly useful in dating fire pits, **hearths**, kilns, and other clay-lined features.

ARCHAEOZOOLOGY. *See* ZOOARCHAEOLOGY.

ARCHAIC. General term applied to the **cultures** that developed out of the earlier **Paleoindian** groups of North America. The Archaic period is usually thought to have lasted from 9000 to 3000 B.P. (7000–1000 B.C.); however, in many regions of North America indigenous peoples continued to practice Archaic lifestyles until European contact. **Archaeological** data indicate that Archaic peoples exhibited increasingly diverse **subsistence** strategies and material cultures. Archaic peoples relied on an increased diversity of animal species, a greater emphasis on plant foods, and new tools for processing these new subsistence resources. Archaic peoples developed new technologies like the grooved **axe**, **net sinker**, and **atlatl**, with later Archaic peoples carving vessels from **steatite**.

ARCTIC CULTURE AREA. Geographic region consisting of the northernmost areas of North America and Siberia, from the Bering Sea to Greenland. The first peoples to settle this region arrived relatively late compared to other Native American peoples, with archaeologists dating their arrival to about 5000 B.P. (3000 B.C.). These groups are thought to have arrived in North America in skin and wooden boats or by riding ice floes. These groups were the ancestors of groups later known as the *Eskimos* and the *Aleuts*. Indigenous groups living in the Arctic **culture area** practice varied **hunting subsistence** regimes, with local groups adopting subsistence practices that favor locally available food resources. Most Arctic groups share a reliance on maritime resources, but many also make use of **caribou** and other terrestrial resources when they are seasonally available.

ARCTIC SMALL-TOOL TRADITION. A technological **tradition** of **artifact** manufacture found at **archaeological** sites in the **Arctic** region during the period from 4200 to 2100 B.P. (circa 2200–100 B.C.). **Tools** from this tradition are consistent with a **subsistence** economy based on **hunting** and **fishing** and are found throughout the Arctic region, from the Bering Straight to Greenland. **Assemblages** related to this tradition consist primarily of scrapers, burins, and microblade tools.

ARGILLITE. A compact metamorphic rock formed from siltstone, shale, or clay stone. Argillite is intermediate in structure between shale and slate, and was used by Native American groups of the **Northwest Coast** for the production of stone **tools** and **artifacts**, including ornate **pipes** and ceremonial **ceramic** vessels.

ARIKARA INDIANS. A Caddoan-speaking Native American group that occupied a number of villages along the middle Missouri River valley. The Arikara were village **agriculturalists** thought to have developed out of the Central **Plains** Tradition. Although they resided in **sedentary** villages, the Arikara also participated in a winter **bison** hunt that provided much of the meat that they consumed. The Arikara were dramatically impacted by European contact and trade, eventually ceding most of their lands to the United States in 1851. In the 1930s, the Arikara joined with the Mandan and Hidatsa to form the Three Affiliated Tribes. Today there are more than 11,000 members of the Three Affiliated Tribes living primarily in North Dakota.

ARROW. *See* BOW AND ARROW.

ARROWHEAD. *See* PROJECTILE POINT.

ARROYO HONDO PUEBLO. A major **Puebloan archaeological** site located near present-day Santa Fe, New Mexico. Arroyo Hondo was occupied from approximately 650 to 540 B.P. (A.D. 1300–1410), with several marked stages of population fluctuation during its occupation. The site's initial development is thought to represent the immigration of people from **Mesa Verde** and other areas of the **Southwest**. The site was almost completely abandoned by A.D. 1350, reoccupied again in the late 1380s, and finally destroyed by fire in A.D. 1410.

ARTIFACT. General term used by **archaeologists** to refer to any portable object that was made, modified, or used by humans at some time in the past. As such, the term is commonly used to denote both utilitarian and symbolic items. Artifact analyses provide archaeologists with a great deal of information about past **cultures**, and stylistic changes in artifacts over time provide archaeologists with a common way of dating their sites (**seriation**). *See also* TOOLS.

ARTIFICIAL CRANIAL DEFORMATION. The intentional distortion of a child's cranial bones during the earliest periods of growth. Many Native American **cultures**, including the **Choctaw** of the **Southeast**, practiced artificial cranial deformation as a way of altering an individual's appearance to meet **culturally** specific ideas of attractiveness and as an indicator of social status. The artificial shaping of a child's head was often accomplished through the use of a cradleboard or by tying constrictive bands of fabric around the head.

ASCRIBED STATUS. Social standing that is not directly representative of an individual's efforts or achievements, but is instead the result of inheritance or other hereditary factors. Ascribed social status is considered the antithesis of **achieved status**.

ASSEMBLAGE. The complete inventory of **artifacts** from a single, defined **archaeological** unit (stratum, site, or the like). Most commonly, assemblages are organized based on the diversity of artifact types recovered from discrete occupations at a site. Assemblage studies provide archaeologists with a measure of the diversity of artifacts used by a past society, permit evaluations of changes in material **culture** over time, and allow comparisons to be made between groups. *See also* SERIATION.

ASSINIBOINE INDIANS. An Apachean-speaking Native American group of the Canadian **Great Plains** descended from earlier Plains

hunting cultures. The Assiniboine had close **trade** relations with English traders at Hudson Bay during the **historic period**. They were skilled **bison** hunters who provided skins to the Europeans in exchange for European **trade** goods. Like other Native American groups, the Assiniboine were dramatically impacted by European introduced **diseases** and **trade**. They continued to have their lands encroached upon throughout the 18th and 19th centuries, and were eventually forced to settle on reservation lands in Montana. Today, there are more than 6,000 Assiniboine living in the United States and Canada.

ATHABASKAN LANGUAGE FAMILY. Family of Native American **languages** that includes more than 20 individual languages and **cultural** groups. Athabaskan speakers are found throughout the **Subarctic**, **Pacific Northwest**, and in the **southwestern** United States and Mexico. Thought to have originally inhabited portions of southwestern Canada, this group is considered ancestral to the **Apache** and **Navajo** of the American Southwest. The relationship between the Athabaskans and the indigenous **Puebloan** peoples is debated, but most scholars favor a date between 500 and 450 B.P. (A.D. 1450–1500) for the arrival of Athabaskan peoples in the Southwest. Linguist Edward Sapir grouped the Athabaskan language family with other language groups in a classification he named Na-Dene. However, this grouping remains controversial among linguists and **cultural anthropologists**.

ATLATL. A projectile technology consisting of a throwing stick used to extend the arm and propel a dart shaft through the air with greater force than is possible without its use. First recorded by Europeans among the Aztecs, *atlatl* is the Nahuatl word for "spearthrower." The atlatl works by extending the distance from the shoulder to the projectile and adding additional weight to the end of the shaft (**atlatl weight**), allowing darts to be thrown with increased accuracy and velocity, and over greater distances. The atlatl is generally associated with **Archaic cultures** and was the primary **hunting** weapon in western North America from around 8500 to 1700 B.P. (6500 B.C.–A.D. 300). The atlatl was eventually replaced by the greater efficiency of the **bow and arrow**.

ATLATL WEIGHT. Also referred to as **bannerstones**, these objects consist of ground and polished stones attached to the shaft of an **atlatl**. Such weights allow atlatl darts to be thrown with greater velocity than would otherwise be possible by increasing the force behind each throw and permitting improved balancing of the weapon while it is being thrown.

AVONLEA POINTS. Named for the **Avonlea site** in Saskatchewan, Canada, these side-notched **projectile points** are associated with groups of the Northeastern **Great Plains culture area**. Avonlea points commonly occur in association with **bison jumps** dating to approximately 2100 B.P. (100 B.C.). These broad, relatively small points allowed arrows to penetrate deeply into tough bison hide when shot at close range. Some scholars propose that these points were the first to be used with the **bow and arrow**. If this is the case, it is probable that these points mark the beginnings of complex and highly ritualized bison **hunting** on the Plains.

AVONLEA SITE. Archaeological site located in Saskatchewan, Canada, believed to possess the earliest evidence of the **bow and arrow** in the **Great Plains** area. This transition is reflected in the appearance of **Avonlea points** and other side-notched **projectile points**.

AWL. A sharply pointed **tool** made from bone, antler, metal, or wood used in sewing or hide working. The sharp point is used to make holes in leather for stitching thread, string, sinew, or fiber. Awls were also used in the production of coiled **basketry** by Native Americans in almost all regions of North America.

AXE. A stone implement with a sharp cutting edge, typically used for chopping or crushing. Axe heads were made of stone or **copper**, and are found throughout North America. Stone axes may be grooved or ungrooved, depending on their use and type of **hafting**. Ungrooved axe heads are typically referred to as celts. Axe heads were commonly manufactured from greenstone or other stones that could be shaped by chipping or grinding and were capable of withstanding high impact. **Microwear analysis** indicates that many axes were used for woodworking, while others appear to have been symbolic or ceremonial in nature. *See also* TOOLS.

AZTALAN SITE. A late prehistoric **mound** center located on the Crawfish River in southern Wisconsin. The Aztalan site has an earthen embankment and a **fortification** consisting of a wooden **palisade** with regularly spaced bastions that once encompassed an area of about nine hectares. Within the palisade are several earthen **mounds**, a large plaza, and domestic areas. Occupied between 900 and 700 B.P. (A.D. 1050–1250), Aztalan is unique because of strong **cultural** links to **Mississippian** sites to the south, particularly **Cahokia**. These connections to distant groups suggest that the occupants of the Aztalan site may have been either nonlocal peoples who migrated into the area or a local group who adopted the **cultural** practices of a distant society.

– B –

BAKER CAVE SITE. One of several cave sites in the lower Pecos Canyonland region of southwestern Texas. Baker cave is of particular importance to **archaeologists** because of its excellent preservation of both **artifacts** and ecofacts (environmental data). Excavations by Robert F. Heizer and Thomas R. Hester at Baker Cave were among the first to make use of **flotation** analysis in North America. The major occupation of the site occurred during the **Archaic** period, as early as 9000 B.P. (7000 B.C.), with evidence suggesting that the local environment was much wetter during this period than at present. Evidence from a subsequent occupation indicates that local environmental conditions became more like those at present during the period between 8000 and 5500 B.P (6000–3500 B.C.).

BALL COURT. Architectural feature common to many **archaeological** sites in the American **Southwest**. These structures normally consist of two parallel range **mounds** with an open space between for playing various forms of the ball game. Ball courts are a common feature of **Mesoamerican** archaeological sites, with their presence in the Southwest seen by some archaeologists as evidence of **culture**

contact between these regions. The occurrence of ball courts together with other items of Mesoamerican origin at **Hohokam** sites is thought to be particularly compelling evidence of contacts between Mexican groups and those in the Southwest. Regardless of its origin, the ball game was both a sporting event and a symbolic ritual event that brought communities together for social, political, and **religious** purposes. Because of these connections, ball courts are thought to have been important forms of public architecture.

BAND. Term used to describe the sociopolitical organization of small-scale societies. Bands are usually seasonally mobile **foraging** groups of less than 100 people. They are also characterized by increased egalitarianism and reciprocity, with little social differentiation between group members. **Paleoindian** societies are thought to have been band societies, with some groups in the **Arctic** and other remote regions of North America continuing to live in band societies.

BANDELIER, ADOLPH (1840–1914). Swiss-born amateur **anthropologist** who traveled the American **Southwest** in the 1880s investigating **archaeological** sites and recording oral histories. Highly influenced by **Lewis Henry Morgan**, Bandelier spent the majority of his life recording ethnographic and archaeological information from Native Americans in the Southwest, attempting to understand the historical connections between these groups and earlier **Puebloan cultures**. A group of Puebloan ruins on the Rio Grande River in north-central New Mexico bears his name.

BANNERSTONES. Polished stone **artifacts** used as **atlatl weights** by Native Americans during the **Archaic** period. Bannerstones were made in a variety of forms, including winged, boat, bird, or other **zoomorphic** shapes. Some are grooved or perforated, presumably for attachment to the **atlatl**. Although their primary function was as atlatl weights, given their highly ornate forms, some archaeologists believe that bannerstones were also used for symbolic and ceremonial purposes.

BARTRAM, WILLIAM (1739–1824). Son of famed American botanist John Bartram, William was a naturalist who traveled widely throughout the **Southeast** in the late 18th century. Bartram published an account of his travels through North and South Carolina, Florida, Georgia, Alabama, Mississippi, Louisiana, and Tennessee that contained excellent descriptions of the **flora**, **fauna**, and Native American **cultures** of the region. Although his work contains information on a number of Native American groups, his observations concerning the **Cherokee**, **Creek**, and Seminole remain his most important contribution to **archaeologists** and **ethnohistorians**.

BASKETMAKER CULTURE. A **cultural** period (circa 2200–1400 B.P. [200 B.C.–A.D. 500]) proposed for the American **Southwest** by **A. V. Kidder** after his work at **Pecos pueblo** in New Mexico. Evidence of Basketmaker culture is found in the presence of both **basketry** and highly distinctive black-on-white **ceramics**. Kidder believed the Basketmaker people to be the earliest **agriculturalists** and **ceramic** producers in the region. They are also notable for their construction of **pit houses** and use of the **bow and arrow**. Although the Basketmaker culture is still an important concept for Southwestern **archaeology**, Kidder's original chronological sequence has been modified by contemporary researchers.

BASKETRY. The weaving, coiling, or sewing of pliable plant materials to form containers. Materials used to produce baskets vary based on available resources and **cultural traditions**, but twigs, grasses, straw, cane, and other fibers were commonly used. Basketry was produced by indigenous peoples throughout North America, with the basketry of **Southwestern** and **Northwest Coast** groups providing perhaps the best Native American examples of this craft.

BAT CAVE SITE. Archaeological site in New Mexico that revealed the presence of **maize** in the American **Southwest** as early as 4000 B.P. (2000 B.C.). These findings encouraged other researchers, including **Richard S. McNeish**, to look for archaeobotanical remains in other cave contexts throughout **Mesoamerica** and the Southwest.

BAUMER SITE. An **archaeological** site in southern Illinois with indications of a cultural transition from the **Archaic** period to the **Woodland** period. The Baumer site lies along the Ohio River in the fertile

Black Bottom region and contains excellent evidence for the development of Woodland **cultural** practices out of earlier **Archaic** practices. There are indications that the people living at Baumer were increasingly reliant on stored plant foods and were more **sedentary** than their Archaic predecessors.

BAYTOWN CULTURE. A Late **Woodland cultural tradition** found in a large area of the lower Mississippi River valley (A.D. 300–700). Previously referred to as Deasonville, Baytown culture is thought to have developed out of the earlier Middle Woodland **Marksville** culture. Baytown culture is characterized by new **ceramic** forms, the presence of the **bow and arrow**, and an increased reliance on plant **cultivation**. Unlike other Late Woodland cultures, Baytown sites are not normally large centers with major **earthworks** but a series of smaller, dispersed settlements.

BEAD. Circular, tubular, or oblong ornament with a perforated center. Beads were frequently used as elements of jewelry and in other forms of adornment. Native American artisans produced beads from shell, stone, and bone. During the **historic period**, European glass beads become a common item of **trade** with Native Americans.

BEANS. Term referring to either the seeds or seedpods of a number of edible leguminous plants. Beans are protein rich and provide a good source of iron and B vitamins. Native American peoples cultivated several varieties of beans, with these foodstuffs serving as vital components of the "**Three Sisters**" of Native American **agriculture**.

BEAR. Large, short-legged mammal of the family Ursidae. Bears are omnivorous, with a large degree of variation in the degree of dietary preferences between species (e.g., some species are highly carnivorous). Bears are common throughout North America, but their range has been reduced due to **hunting** and loss of habitat. Native Americans used bears as sources of meat, hides, and oils, with these animals also figuring prominently in indigenous **religion** and lore.

BEAVER. Aquatic rodents of the family Castoridae. Beaver are notable for the construction of dams through the piling of sticks, stones, and mud. North American beavers were once found from the American **Southwest** to the **Arctic**, but both their number and geographical range have been limited by trapping during the **historic period**. European **traders** prized beaver pelts, and these items became important components of the Native American **fur trade**.

BELLA COOLA INDIANS. Native American group of the Pacific **Northwest Coast**. At the time of European contact, the Bella Coola were principally located along the northern banks of the Bella Coola River in present-day British Columbia, Canada. The Bella Coola are noted for their woodworking, particularly the production of highly ornate masks. Smallpox and other European-introduced **diseases** greatly reduced the Bella Coola during the 19th century. Today, there are more than 1,000 Bella Coola living in British Columbia.

BELLS, COPPER. Two groups of copper bells are identified by **archaeologists** in North America: those produced in **Mesoamerica** and those produced in Europe. Both were highly prized **trade** items, with those made in Mesoamerica traded primarily into Native American communities in the **Southwest**. European bells were made of **copper**, brass, and silver and were traded with native peoples of the **Eastern Woodlands** following their colonization of the region. Bells served as status markers, demonstrating that their owners possessed important **trade** connections with nonlocal societies.

BENEDICT, RUTH (1887–1948). Pioneering American **anthropologist** who received her Ph.D. from Columbia University in 1923. Benedict studied under **Franz Boas** and was later a faculty member at Columbia. While serving as Boas's assistant, Benedict became a major influence on young Margaret Mead. Her North American research was directed toward the **Kwakiutl** and **Zuñi**.

BEOTHUK INDIANS. An **Algonquian**-speaking group of Newfoundland and Labrador. The Beothuk primarily **subsisted** on maritime resources, including **seal** and smelt, but also took advantage of land mammals like **caribou** when they were available. The Beothuk were descendants of the **Maritime Archaic** people of the North Atlantic Coast, and were completely eradicated in the 19th century by a combination of European-introduced diseases and increased competition with the **Micmac** for limited food resources.

BERDACHE. A supernumerary gender recognized by many Native American groups of the **Great Plains** and **Southwest**. Berdache were normally biological males (but female cases are known) who adopted a gender role that blended both male and female roles. Berdache dressed as women and commonly served as village **shaman**.

BERINGIA. Landmass that linked Siberia and Alaska several times in the past, particularly during the **Pleistocene**, with the most recent linkage occurring at approximately 18,000 B.P. (16,000 B.C.). Beringia was exposed by the lower sea levels brought about by increased glaciation in the Northern Hemisphere. This glaciation reduced sea levels to more than 90 meters (300 feet) below their modern levels. Central Beringia was an exposed coastal plain believed to have provided the land route by which **Paleoindians** first reached the Americas. *See also* BERING LAND BRIDGE.

BERING LAND BRIDGE. Portion of **Beringia** connecting Siberia and Alaska at various intervals in the past due to increased glaciation in the Northern Hemisphere. The Bering Land Bridge was exposed most recently at approximately 18,000 B.P. (16,000 B.C.). This is the proposed route for the first peopling of the Americas by groups from northeastern Asia.

BIG-GAME HUNTING TRADITION. Cultural tradition characterized by the **hunting** of **megafauna** like **mammoth** and **bison**. This tradition was widespread in the **Paleoindian** period, but declined with the **extinction** of many species of megafauna. By the **Archaic** period, the big-game hunting tradition had been replaced in most regions by **subsistence** strategies focused on the increased **gathering** of plants and the hunting of smaller animal species. However, this tradition remained a dominant subsistence strategy for many groups on the **Plains** until European contact.

BIG MEN. Term first adopted by **anthropologists** to describe the principal members of Melanesian societies. This term distinguishes political leaders in societies lacking institutionalized sociopolitical hierarchies. In contrast to **chiefs**, big men possess no formally recognized or inherited power or sociopolitical position. Big men achieve and maintain their influence through personal qualities, the exchange of valuables, economic success, and the sponsorship of community feasts. Modern usage has seen this term modified to "big persons" or "big personage" in order to include societies in which women exhibit the same social and political abilities. *See also* ACHIEVED STATUS.

BINFORD, LEWIS R. (1930–). American **archaeologist** who is largely credited with promoting the development of **processual archaeology** (also referred to as *new archaeology*). Binford built upon the work of Leslie White, arguing that archaeologists could use the tenets of cultural materialism and an explicitly scientific methodology to interpret evidence of **culture** change in the archaeological record. Binford rejected the **culture historical** approach of American archaeology, emphasizing instead the interpretation of culture process through technological and ecological adaptations. Binford also advocated the use of **ethnoarchaeology** as a way of understanding the archaeological record.

BIRDSTONES. Polished stone implements with **zoomorphic** designs (carved in the form of birds) that are thought to have functioned as **atlatl weights.** Birdstones are closely related to **boatstones** and appeared in the **Eastern Woodlands** during the **Woodland** period. Birdstones and boatstones replace earlier **Archaic bannerstones**.

BIRNIRK STAGE. A variant of the **Old Bering Sea Stage** that developed along the Chukotkan coast of northwestern Alaska between 450 and 350 B.P. (A.D. 500–600). Birnirk people were primarily sea-mammal **hunters** who also engaged in a wide range of **fishing** and whaling activities. There is also evidence that they developed sleds presumably harnessed to teams of dogs.

BISON. Members of several species (genus *Bison*) of oxlike bovid with a shaggy mane, large forequarters, a convex forehead, short curved horns, and a pronounced shoulder hump. Several species of bison were common to North America prior to approximately 10,000 B.P. (8000 B.C.), with the only surviving North American species the comparatively smaller *Bison bison*. Mature males stand approximately two meters (six feet) in height, and weigh more than 900 kilograms (2,000 pounds). Bison are herd animals, and large herds numbering in the thousands were once common to the **Great Plains** of North America. The Native American peoples of the Plains relied upon bison as a food source, and developed a series of **cultural** adaptations (including seasonally mobile **hunting** practices) to make use of these animals. European hunting drove bison to near **extinction**, but modern management has stabilized North American bison populations.

BISON JUMP. Hunting strategy practiced by Native American groups of the **Great Plains** for obtaining large numbers of **bison** in a single hunting episode. Bison jumps were conducted at strategic locations such as cliffs, bluffs, sinkholes, and other locales that allowed large groups of bison to be stampeded over barriers and incapacitated by the fall. **Archaeological** examples of North American bison jumps are sites such as **Olsen-Chubbock** and **Head-Smashed-In**. Bison jumps are important archaeological sites because these hunting activities would have required a great deal of advanced planning and cooperation between a number of hunters. The presence of these sites on the Plains indicates the presence of such complex hunting activities as early as the **Paleoindian** period.

BLACK DRINK. Caffeinated beverage consumed by Native Americans of the **Southeast**. Black drink was produced from the leaves of the Yupon Holly (*Ilex vomitoria*), one of the few plants native to North America that contains caffeine. The black drink is a natural diuretic, and when consumed in large quantities it produces vomiting. These characteristics made the black drink a central component in purgative purification rituals for many Southeastern **cultures**. The black drink was primarily consumed by adult men, and played an important role in preparing for both **hunting** and **warfare**.

BLACK EARTH SITE. Archaic-period **archaeological** site in southeastern Illinois. Dated to approximately 6000 B.P. (4000

B.C.), the Black Earth site indicates a shift in **subsistence** strategies from upland to bottomland resources during the Middle Archaic period. Located on a swamp near Lake Saline, the Black Earth site has well-preserved evidence of the **flora** and **fauna** utilized by the site's residents. This site was apparently occupied on a multiseasonal basis, with local people taking advantage of the nearly year-round availability of aquatic plant and animal resources.

BLACKFOOT INDIANS. Group of three **Algonquian**-speaking Native American peoples of Alberta and Montana, composed of the Piegan, the Kainah (Blood), and the Siksika (Blackfoot proper). Given the name Blackfoot by Europeans based on the color of their black-dyed moccasins, these people were among the first Algonquians to migrate westward and among the first to acquire **horses** and **firearms**. Controlling a territory stretching from northern Saskatchewan to southwestern Montana, the Blackfoot were known as one of the strongest and most powerful groups on the northwestern **Great Plains**. They developed a highly mobile settlement system based largely on the seasonal migration of **bison** herds, but with the decline of these herds in the 19th century, the Blackfoot relied increasingly on the **trade** of **beaver** pelts to Europeans. Today there are more than 30,000 Blackfoot in the United States and Canada, with the majority residing on reservation lands in Montana.

BLACK HAWK (1767–1838). Sauk chief who resisted the confiscation of Native American lands east of the Mississippi River by the Treaty of St. Louis. He led a group of warriors across the Mississippi to recapture their lands, but his party was defeated in the Black Hawk War and he was captured by American forces in Wisconsin in 1832.

BLACK MESA SITE. Extensive plateau in northeastern Arizona with evidence of **Paleoindian** occupation as early as 9000 B.P. (7000 B.C.). Research by George Gumerman and Francis Smiley at Black Mesa also has revealed considerable **Basketmaker** and **Anasazi** occupations. **Archaeological** research at Black Mesa provides evidence on a range of **cultural** and environmental adaptations during the periods in which it was occupied.

BLACKWATER DRAW SITE. Archaeological site in New Mexico with evidence of a series of discrete occupations by **Clovis**, **Folsom**, and **Agate Basin** peoples. This site is the type site for the **Clovis culture**, and is one of the oldest presently known archaeological sites in North America (13,300 B.P. [11,300 B.C.]). Blackwater Draw is surrounded by a series of glacial lakes, and has yielded remains of many **extinct** forms of North American **megafauna**, including the camel, **horse**, **bison**, **mammoth**, llama, antelope, sloth, tapir, dire wolf, and smilodont (saber-toothed cat). Evidence from Blackwater Draw indicates the direct **association** of Clovis materials with the butchering of the mammoth, bison, and horse.

BLADE. Long, narrow **lithic** flake with parallel sides used as a cutting **tool**. Also called lamellar flakes, blades are usually struck from a prepared **core**. Blades are usually defined as being at least twice as long as they are wide. Blade tools are common on Native American **archaeological** sites and were used for a variety of cutting and scraping tasks. Recent advances in **microwear analysis** have allowed archaeologists to reconstruct the precise ways in which Native Americans used certain blade tools.

BLANK. Also called performs, blanks represent an advanced preliminary stage of **lithic tool** production. Blanks are commonly seen as representing the initial stages of "roughing-out" lithic materials prior to the production of formal tools. Archaeologists use these materials to reconstruct the stages and locations of lithic tool production. *See also* DEBITAGE.

BLITZKRIEG MODEL. Also referred to as the overkill model, this term is used to describe the impact of **Paleoindian** peoples on the **megafauna** of the North America. Based on research by **Vance C. Haynes** and **Paul S. Martin**, this model suggests that early humans spread throughout the Americas very rapidly (perhaps as quickly as 1,000 years). These early people are thought to have been highly skilled big-game **hunters**, with their hunting techniques contributing significantly to the **extinction** of megafauna in the Americas. Such views are based on the premise that there were no people in the Americas prior to the arrival of **Clovis** peoples. *See also* PRE-CLOVIS HYPOTHESIS.

BLUBBER. A thick layer of insulating fat common to marine mammals of the **Arctic** region. Blubber has been a major source of food and essential oils for Arctic peoples since at least the **Archaic** period.

BOAS, FRANZ (1858–1942). Pioneering **anthropologist** who founded the academic discipline of **anthropology** in the United States. Born in Germany, Franz Boas earned his Ph.D. from the University of Kiel in 1881. He conducted research on the **Eskimo** of Baffin Island and the **Kwakiutl** of British Columbia. Boaz was affiliated with the American Museum of Natural History from 1895 to 1905, and became the first professor of anthropology in the United States when he was hired by Columbia University in 1899. Boas helped to institute the four-field approach distinctive to American anthropology, and trained the first generation of U.S. anthropologists. Boas believed strongly in cultural relativism and historical particularism, views that were antagonistic to the prevailing evolutionist perspectives of **Louis Henry Morgan** and other social theorists of the era.

BOATS. A means of water conveyance powered by sail, paddle, or oar. Native Americans constructed a variety of boats, with the most common being the **dugout canoe**, **kayak**, and **umiak**.

BOATSTONES. A class of polished stone implements thought to have served as **atlatl weights**. Boatstones are closely related to **birdstones**, and appeared in the **Eastern Woodlands** during the **Woodland** period. Birdstones and boatstones are thought to have replaced earlier **Archaic bannerstones**.

BONFIRE SHELTER SITE. Rockshelter site in west-central Texas that is the southernmost site in North America with evidence of intensive **bison hunting**. This site contains a large number of bison bones associated with **Folsom** and **Plainview** points. In addition, a large number of bifaces and **flakes** were found at the site, indicating that the site may have functioned as a **butchering station**.

BONNEVILLE PERIOD. Cultural period lasting from 11,000 to 9500 B.P. (9000–7500 B.C.) in the eastern **Great Basin** region. Characterized by sites like **Danger Cave**, the Bonneville period is thought to be either contemporaneous with or immediately postdate **Paleoindian** occupation of the region. This was a period of considerable environmental change in the Great Basin, and the patterning of **archaeological** remains from this period are thought to indicate a transition from the **hunting** of **megafauna** to a diverse, broad-spectrum **subsistence** regimen represented by the **Desert Archaic tradition**.

BORAX LAKE SITE. Thought to be one of the earliest **Paleoindian** sites presently known in northern California, the Borax Lake site dates to approximately 12,000 B.P. (10,000 B.C.). This site is characterized by a scattering of **lithic** fragments, but the site **assemblage** does contain **Clovis** points.

BOREAL FOREST. The forested areas of the northern temperate zone. This forest is a dense mixture of coniferous trees, especially spruce, aspen, and birch. The boreal forest is the largest single vegetation zone in Canada, extending north to the edge of the **tundra**. The boreal forest provides one of the principal environmental zones occupied by the Native American peoples of the **Subarctic culture area**.

BOW AND ARROW. A projectile weapon consisting of two parts: a wooden bow with a tensed piece of cord stretched between its two ends, and a straight shafted wooden arrow with a sharp point at one end. The bow and arrow was a major technological advancement for Native Americans, allowing greater accuracy in the **hunting** of land mammals and waterfowl. The bow and arrow replaced the **atlatl** in many Native American groups, but the exact date of its introduction to (or development by) Native American peoples is presently unknown. Most **archaeologists** contend that the bow and arrow was introduced from Asia by people associated with the **Arctic small-tool tradition** at approximately 4000 B.P. (2000 B.C.). However, other scholars propose that a simple form of the bow and arrow was present as early as the **Archaic** period. In either case, the bow and arrow did not become well established until around 1200 B.P. (A.D. 700), when a more standardized arrow-tip technology came to be used, including small triangular and corner-notched **projectile points**.

BOYLSTON STREET FISH WEIR. The best-known prehistoric **fish weir** in the eastern United States. Designed to catch fish during periods of tidal action, the Boylston Street fish weir dates to the **Archaic** period. Located under the present-day streets of Boston, the weir covers almost two acres in area, and consists of approximately 65,000 wooden stakes interwoven with brush. Research by Dena Dincauze indicates that rather than one enormous fish weir, the Boylston Street weir actually represents a large number of smaller weirs constructed over many centuries. *See also* FISHING.

BRAND SITE. Archaeological site near the L'Anguille River in Arkansas. Excavated by Dan Morse, this site contains five distinct activity areas where **lithic artifacts** cluster in circular patterns. This distribution of cultural materials is thought to represent a series of **butchering** activities by **Dalton hunters** at approximately 10,500–9900 B.P. (8500–7900 B.C.). Other archaeological materials at the site suggest that various domestic activities were occurring at the site as well.

BROKEN MAMMOTH SITE. One of the oldest **Paleoindian archaeological** sites presently known in Alaska. Located in the Tanana Valley, between the Alaska Range and the Tanana-Yukon Upland, Broken Mammoth is one of three sites in the region dated between 11,000 and 12,000 B.P. (9000–10,000 B.C.), the others being **Mead** and Swan Point. At Broken Mammoth, ancient loess deposits helped to preserve the remains of wapiti, **bison**, and **mammoth** in good **stratigraphic** association with stone **tools**. Evidence from Broken Mammoth suggests that the site's inhabitants practiced a broad-based **hunting** and **foraging subsistence** regime.

BUFFALO. *See* BISON.

BUNDLES. Also referred to as "sacred bundles," these objects consisted of wrapped **bison** hides containing supernaturally powerful ritual objects. Bundles have powerful supernatural and **religious** associations. They were an important part of the spiritual life of many **Great Plains cultures**, and were closely associated with **agricultural** rituals related to planting and harvesting. *See also* SHAMANISM.

BUREAU OF AMERICAN ETHNOLOGY (BAE). Branch of the Smithsonian Institute charged with sponsoring and publishing **anthropological** and **archaeological** research on Native Americans. Functioning during the period from 1879 to 1965, the BAE supported numerous research projects and published hundreds of original reference materials on a variety of Native American issues.

BURIAL. Term referring to both the ritualistic manner in which human remains are interred and the location of their interment. Native Americans practiced a variety of death rituals and burial practices based on **cultural** and region **traditions**, including both primary and secondary burial practices. Primary burials are those where the deceased is placed in the ground in either a flexed or extended position and then permanently buried. Secondary burials are those where an individual is buried long enough for the flesh to decay, then disinterred for the purpose of disarticulation and reburial. Secondary burials often involve the wrapping of the bones within a textile bundle for reburial. The analysis of specific mortuary practices, **grave goods** placed with the deceased, as well as information on the nature of the remains themselves help **archaeologists** better understanding Native American cultural and **religious** practices and provide information on health, nutrition, and social status. *See also* BURIAL CHAMBERS; BURIAL MOUNDS; CAIRN; CREMATION; NATIVE AMERICAN GRAVE PROTECTION AND REPATRIATION ACT.

BURIAL CHAMBERS. Hollow vaults constructed for the **burial** of the dead. Central burial chambers were often constructed within **Adena** and **Hopewell mounds**. These chambers were commonly log-lined tombs over which earthen mounds were subsequently constructed.

BURIAL MOUNDS. Earthen **mounds** deliberately constructed as part of **burial** rituals. Interment within these structures is commonly interpreted by **archaeologists** as having been reserved for those of higher social status. In most cases, individuals were either interred on earthen platforms within log tombs or **cremated** and the remains placed in prepared basins within the mounds. Many burial mounds are accretional, with additional individuals buried within an existing mound and then covered over by the addition of new soils. Such mounds could hold the remains of several hundred individuals and be used for centuries.

BUTCHERING STATION. A site, or localized activity area within a site, dominated by evidence of the butchering of game animals. Evidence of butchering stations is usually found in the patterns of breakage and cut marks of butchering tools and on faunal remains. The **Casper** and **Olsen-Chubbock** sites are two North American examples of sites with well-defined butchering stations.

– C –

CABEZA DE VACA, ALVA NUÑEZ (1490–1557). Spanish explorer who journeyed to the Americas in 1528 as a member of the expedition of **Pánfilo de Narváez.** After being shipwrecked and taken captive by Native Americans, he spent eight years among the indigenous peoples of the Gulf Coast of present-day Texas. He and three companions escaped from their captors and journeyed on foot across Texas, New Mexico, and Arizona before arriving at the Spanish garrison in Culiacán, Mexico. The members of Cabeza de Vaca's party may have been the first Europeans to see **bison,** and their accounts of **Puebloan** groups inspired the legend of the Seven Cities of **Cibola.**

CABOT, JOHN (1461–1498). English explorer of Genoese birth who sailed from England to North America in 1497. Cabot landed at Newfoundland and sailed along the North Atlantic Coast, claiming this territory for England's King Henry VII. A second expedition in 1498 was considerably less successful, with Cabot and his party failing to return and presumably lost at sea. Cabot's explorations provided the basis for English territorial claims in North America.

CACTUS HILL SITE. Possible **pre-Clovis archaeological** site on the Nottaway River of Virginia. This site contains an **Archaic** period occupation that overlies an earlier **Paleoindian** occupation. **Radiocarbon dating** indicates that the earliest human occupation may have been as early as 17,000 B.P. (15,000 B.C.). Analysis of **lithics** from the site indicates that these materials are predecessors to **Clovis,** suggesting a possible **Southeastern** origin for Clovis culture. However, this interpretation of the Cactus Hill site remains controversial.

CADDO INDIANS. One of a number of Native American groups who speak a form of Hokan-Siouan known as *Caddoan*. Prior to European contact, these groups were organized into a loose confederacy of groups that occupied the Red River valley of Louisiana to the Brazos River valley in Texas, north into Kansas and Arkansas. This confederacy included the Caddo proper, as well as elements of the **Arikara**, **Pawnee**, and **Wichita**. They **traded** with **Mississippian** groups to the east, and were part of the **Southeastern Ceremonial Complex**. They were a semi**sedentary agricultural** people who lived in conical pole-and-thatch dwellings. During the 18th century, encroachments by Europeans and Americans reduced the Caddoan territory, and by 1835 they ceded their lands to the United States. Today, there are more than 1,000 Caddo living in Oklahoma and Texas.

CAHOKIA SITE. Major **Mississippian** period settlement located in the Black Bottom region of the Mississippi River floodplain near East St. Louis, Illinois. This site covers approximately 13 square kilometers, and is composed of plazas, residential areas, and over 80 earthen **mounds**. Cahokia is thought by many **archaeologists** to represent the center of the most sociopolitically complex Native American polity north of Mexico. It is estimated to have had a residential population of 10,000–20,000, with thousands more people living in surrounding satellite communities. Rising to prominence between 1050 and 600 B.P. (A.D. 900–1350), **archaeological** remains at Cahokia demonstrate that local elites controlled the production and exchange of exotic **trade** goods, and may have managed local **agricultural** surpluses. The principal architectural feature at Cahokia is **Monks Mound**, a large, flat-topped mound rising more than 30 meters (100 feet) above a rectangular plaza. Monks Mound is the largest Native American mound in the United States, taking its name from a 19th-century occupation of the site by Trappist monks.

CAIRN. A conical pile of stones constructed by humans. Native Americans of the **Great Basin** frequently constructed cairns as grave markers and as landmarks, although these structures are also common in other regions of North America as well. *See* BURIAL.

CALDWELL, JOSEPH R. (1916–1973). Archaeologist who worked primarily in the **Southeast** with the Smithsonian, National Park Service, Illinois State Museum, and University of Georgia. His most notable publication is *Trend and Tradition in the Prehistory of the Eastern United States*, in which he produced a systematic perspective on the prehistory of the Eastern Woodlands. Caldwell is also notable for his analysis of "**interaction spheres**" between the prehistoric peoples of eastern North America, particularly the **Hopewell** interaction sphere, and his concept of **primary forest efficiency**.

CALICO HILLS SITE. Archaeological site in the Mohave Desert, east of Barstow, California. Excavations at the site by Louis Leakey and Ruth Simpson are claimed to have produced **artifacts** as old as 100,000 B.P., suggesting a human presence in North America much earlier than previously estimated. However, most North American archaeologists do not accept materials from this purported occupation as legitimate human-produced artifacts, but as natural eoliths. There is a verified **Paleoindian** occupation at the site dated to around 10,000 B.P. (8000 B.C.), but this occupation is **stratigraphically** distinct from materials from the site claimed to be of exceptional antiquity.

CALIFORNIA CULTURE AREA. Corresponding roughly to the present-day boundaries of the state of California and the Mexican state of Baja California, this region was one of the most densely populated areas of North America prior to European contacts. Although there was a great deal of variation in the **cultural** practices of California groups, most were **foragers** who lived in small villages composed of related families. The largest Native American groups of the California culture area were the **Chumash**, Costano, Maisu, Miwok, Shasta, and Wintun. During the colonial period, many of these groups were relocated to Spanish missions and became known as the *Mission Indians*.

CALUMET. The French name given to the ceremonial **pipe** used by many Native American groups for smoking **tobacco**. These pipes, sometimes referred to as "peace pipes," consisted of a long, slender stem, frequently covered with feathers, with a pipe bowl at the end. Calumet pipes were ceremonial and symbolic **artifacts**, and were intimately related to powerful cosmological forces. They were commonly used during peace negotiations, adoption rituals, and other **religious** ceremonies. Calumet pipes also served as markers of elevated social rank for their owners.

CANAL SYSTEM. Artificial waterway constructed by humans to facilitate the movement of water to maximize **agricultural** productivity. The **Hohokam** of the **Southwest** constructed the most extensive irrigation canals in ancient North America. The canal systems of the Hohokam extend as much as 16 kilometers (10 miles) in length, bringing water to agricultural fields in naturally arid environments.

CANDLEFISH. Name given to a particular species of smelt (*eulachon*) found along the Pacific Coast from Oregon to Alaska. Possessing vast fat deposits, particularly during spawning, these fish can be dried and fitted with a wick, producing a rudimentary candle. Native peoples of the **Pacific Northwest** used these fish as both a source of food, oil, and as candles. *See also* FISHING.

CANNIBALISM. The consumption of human flesh by other humans. The term derives from a derogatory name given to the Carib people by the Spanish. Accusations by Europeans that nonwestern groups practiced cannibalism have been a common xenophobic ethnic slur since the era of first contacts. However, reliable, firsthand accounts of the practice are exceptionally rare, leading some historians to question whether cannibalism actually existed among the peoples of the Americas. Some scholars have suggested that rather than the ingestion of an entire corpse, most cannibalism takes the form of the ritual consumption of particular organs as a component in funeral rituals or as a means of sorcery. However, **archaeological** research into possible cannibalism among Native American peoples has intensified recently, with several **archaeological** studies suggesting that indigenous groups in the **Southwest** engaged in cannibalism during periods of excessive resource stress.

CANOES. A long, narrow watercraft propelled by the use of paddles. Native American peoples were highly skilled in the construction of canoes and other **boats**, with local rivers serving as the primary arteries for transportation and communication between societies. A common canoe among Native Americas was the **dugout**. These canoes were produced by hollowing out a large tree with the controlled use of fire, **adzes**, and other woodworking **tools**. Other canoes were produced through the use of bark (birch bark canoes) or **bison** hides (bullboats).

CAPE DENBIGH. Archaeological locality situated on the Seward Peninsula along the northern Bering Sea coast of Alaska. It serves as the type site for the Denbigh culture, and possesses evidence of human occupation from approximately 6000 to 3000 B.P. (4000–1000 B.C). The Denbigh culture is associated with the **Arctic small-tool tradition**, a **tool** complex consisting of small pressure flaked **blades** and bladelets. The occupants of Cape Denbigh were seasonally mobile, **subsisting** on coastal marine mammals during the summers and inland **caribou** during the winters.

CARBON-14 DATING. *See* RADIOCARBON DATING.

CARDIFF GIANT. An **archaeological** hoax perpetrated in Cardiff, New York, in 1869. Consisting of a supposed petrified man more than 3.3 meters (10 feet) in height, the Cardiff Giant attracted intense media and public attention, with thousands of people venturing to the site to view the giant. The local scientific community quickly recognized the Cardiff Giant as a hoax, revealing that it was nothing more than a carved block of gypsum. However, this hoax so captured the public imagination that Mark Twain used it as the subject of a short story. *See also* PSEUDOARCHAEOLOGY.

CARIBOU. Arctic deer (*Rangifer tarandus*) native to the **tundra**, **taiga**, and forests of North America. They are the only species of deer in which both sexes have antlers. North American caribou are divided into two groups: the woodland caribou of the forests and bogs from Newfoundland to British Columbia and the barren-ground caribou of the tundra from Alaska to northern Canada. Caribou stand approximately one meter tall (3 feet) at the shoulder and weigh up to 130 kilograms (300 lb.). Caribou were the focus of **subsistence hunting** practices for many Native American groups of the **Subarctic** and **Arctic**

regions. Caribou herds are also notable for their seasonal migrations between summer and winter ranges. Studies of the spatial distribution of **Paleoindian** hunting camps in the **Northeast** and Midwest are thought by some archaeologists to be related to Native American groups following caribou herds on their seasonal migrations.

CARTIER, JACQUES (1491–1557). French sailor who was commissioned to explore North America in the hopes of discovering a passage to Asia. Cartier landed in Newfoundland in 1534 and sailed completely around the Gulf of St. Lawrence. He returned in 1535, sailing as far inland as modern Quebec. He later returned to found a colony along the St. Lawrence River, but his efforts failed as the local **Huron** proved hostile to his settlement. Cartier's voyages formed the basis for French claims to the St. Lawrence Valley.

CASA GRANDE. Archaeological site in southern Arizona notable for a large coursed **adobe** structure ("Big House") four stories tall, crowned with a watchtower. Built by late Classic Period **Hohokam** peoples (circa 1350 A.D.), the Casa Grande ruins were the first archaeological preserve in the United States. Architectural features of Casa Grande suggest to some archaeologists the presence of **archaeoastronomical** alignments within the structure.

CASA RINCONADA. The largest great **kiva** within **Chaco Canyon**. This structure is more than 19 meters (63 feet) in diameter and has been suggested to contain **archaeoastronomical** alignments. Casa Rinconada is also unique among the kivas of Chaco Canyon because it is not directly associated with one of the large domestic room blocks in the canyon. **Archaeologists** have suggested a special role for this structure in the social, political, and **religious** rituals of **Chaco Canyon**'s **Anasazi** residents.

CASAS GRANDES. *See* PAQUIME.

CASPER SITE. Archaeological site near Casper, Wyoming, with evidence of **bison hunting** and processing at approximately 8000 B.P. (6000 B.C.). The Casper site is unique because it indicates that **Paleoindian** hunters used a large, parabolic sand dune to trap stampeding bison (a method referred to by some archaeologists as the cul-de-sac technique). Analysis of the bison remains at the site indicates a kill date during the early winter months, when large amounts of meat could be stored for later consumption.

CATAWBA INDIANS. Hokan-Souian–speaking Native American group of the **Southeast**. The Catawba were village **agriculturalists** who resided in portions of present-day South Carolina. The Catawba were heavily impacted by European contacts, and they struggled for control of the European **trade** with the **Cherokee** in a series of disastrous wars. The Catawbas were greatly reduced in number due to this warfare and the impact of smallpox and other European-introduced diseases. Today, more than 1,000 Catawbas continue to reside in South Carolina.

CATION-RATIO DATING. Dating method used to determine the age of rock carvings and engravings, with some studies indicating that it may also be used for other classes of **artifacts** with heavy patination caused by environmental exposure. This method relies on the solubility of cations of certain elements, with some materials leaching out of rock varnish more rapidly than others. Measuring the concentration of these cations on a surface reveals the age of the disturbance to the surface of the stone resulting from carving or engraving. This method has been of particular importance in the dating of rock carvings in the **Southwest** and **Great Basin** regions.

CATLIN, GEORGE (1796–1872). American painter, author, and lawyer, famous for his paintings of Native American life on the **Great Plains** in the 1830s. Catlin produced more than 500 paintings and sketches based on his travels among Native American peoples, with his artwork exhibited widely in the United States and Europe during his lifetime. He published several highly successful illustrated books on Native Americans, and his works form much of the Native American portrait art collections in the National Museum and the American Museum of Natural History. Catlin was the first non-Indian to observe the quarries that produced the material used in the construction of Native American **pipes**, with pipestone now commonly referred to as **catlinite**.

CATLINITE. A hard clay with a distinctive red or mottled pink and white color that was frequently used by Native Americans in the production of **tobacco pipes**. Also referred to as pipestone, catlinite naturally occurs in the Upper Missouri region of Minnesota, North Dakota, South Dakota, and Manitoba, Canada, but was traded throughout North America. Catlinite is named after the first non-Indian to observe the quarries that produced this material, **George Catlin**. *See also* CALUMET.

CAYUGA INDIANS. Native American society that occupied territory along Cayuga and Owasco Lakes in present-day New York. The Cayuga were one of the **Five Nations** of the **Iroquois** Confederacy. They were the least agricultural of the Iroquoian peoples, with seasonally mobile settlement practices and a **subsistence** economy that relied heavily upon **foraging** activities. The Cayuga, like most members of the Iroquois Confederacy, supported the English during the American Revolutionary War, and were subsequently forced from the state in the late 18th century.

CELT. Ungrooved, chisel-shaped **axe** used primarily for woodworking. Celt forms and materials varied over time, as did the method of **hafting**. These subtle stylistic changes allow archaeologists to date these tools, often without the aid of **stratigraphic** contexts.

CENTRAL PLAINS CULTURAL TRADITION. Generally found in areas of Kansas, Nebraska, Missouri, and Iowa, this cultural tradition is characterized by **agriculture** and the construction of **earthlodges**. Central **Plains** peoples are thought to have moved north in response to drought conditions during the 13th and 14th centuries. *See also* CROW CREEK SITE.

CENTRAL RIVERINE ARCHAIC TRADITION. The most elaborate Late **Archaic** tradition of the **Eastern Woodlands**. Developing among societies centered upon the major waterways of the Midwest and Southeast, including the Mississippi, Ohio, and Tennessee River valleys, the Central Riverine Archaic tradition is characterized by larger populations and increased social complexity. Because of the abundant **subsistence** resources made available in these river valleys during the Middle Holocene, people became more **sedentary** and utilized locally available resources more efficiently. *See also* GREEN RIVER CULTURE; KOSTER SITE; RIVERTON CULTURE.

CERAMICS. General term applied to fired-clay **artifacts**. Native American ceramics forms include a wide range of containers (pots, plates, bottles, and so on), figurines, and other types of artifacts. Ceramic were first produced in North America approximately 5000 B.P. (3000 B.C.), with this technique spreading rapidly across the continent. Most contemporary archaeologists view the development of ceramics as a Native American invention, with the earliest presently known ceramic-producing cultures located along the St. John's River in Florida. Other archaeologists contend that ceramic technology diffused into Florida from groups in the **Circum-Caribbean**. Regardless of their origin, ceramics were a dramatic technological improvement over the **basketry** and **steatite** containers that they largely replaced. Unlike these other container forms, ceramics resist water permeability and they can be used for direct cooking.

Ceramics are extremely useful to archaeologists studying Native American cultures because each group produced distinct ceramic forms. These distinctions have been used by archaeologists in the construction of **culture historical** frameworks and in the analysis of indigenous cultural contact and diffusion. Examples include the highly distinctive black on buff ceramics of the **Chaco Canyon Anasazi**, the highly detailed **zoomorphic** paintings found on **Mogollon** pottery, and the incised ceramics of the **Mississippians**. These stylistic variations are used to not only identify cultural groups, but are also useful in **dating archaeological** deposits. Through the use of **seriation** and other specific techniques, archaeologists are able to identify the changing stylistic preferences of a group of pottery producers and produce a temporal ordering for these remains.

Ceramics also reveal a great deal about the technological abilities of Native Americans, since they generally require a **tempering** agent to minimize the thermal expansion of the clay during firing. These tempering agents frequently include sand, grit, grog (crushed ceramics), limestone, bone, or plant fibers. Experimentation with different tempers allowed ceramic producers to vary the size, shape, and physical properties of ceramics to meet their desired needs. *See*

also ANVIL AND PADDLE TECHNIQUE; COILING; EARTHEN-
WARE; NEGATIVE PAINTING.

CHACO CANYON. Archaeological locality in northwestern New
Mexico with evidence of extensive human occupation during the
period from 1100 to 700 B.P. (A.D. 850–1250). Within the canyon
are 13 major archaeological sites, with nine large residential settlements within the canyon and on the surrounding hillsides, each
consisting of large multistory **pueblos**. These sites contain some of
the best examples of **Anasazi** stone masonry and are thought to
possess numerous **archaeoastronomical** alignments. Chaco
Canyon lies at the center of an extensive road network linking most
of the major Anasazi sites of the Four Corners region of the United
States. These roads are thought to have linked these people for the
purposes of **trade** and **religious** rituals, with Chaco Canyon serving as the dominant center for these activities. An extended drought
during the 13th century is thought to have brought about the collapse of Chacoan society and the eventual abandonment of the
canyon. *See also* ARCHAEOASTRONOMY; CHETRO KETL;
PUEBLO BONITO.

CHALCEDONY. Fine-grained, semitranslucent quartz with a crys-
talline structure so minute that it can only be seen with the use of a
microscope. Chalcedony is commonly pale blue, off-white, or light
gray in color, and was often heat-treated before being used to make
tools. Chalcedony was widely used for **lithic** tool production
throughout North America, with evidence that distinct forms of this
material were **traded** over large distances.

CHALUKA SITE. Archaeological site on Umnak Island, in the Aleutian chain of Alaska, occupied from approximately 4000 to 450 B.P.
(2000 B.C.–A.D. 1500). The Chaluka site contains **stratigraphic** deposits covering the entire period of occupation, with the most extensive evidence of occupation being a large village with stone-lined
semisubterranean houses dated between 4000 and 3000 B.P.
(2000–1000 B. C.). Archaeological evidence from this site has contributed greatly to understanding of the development and evolution of
the **Aleutian tradition**.

CHARCOAL. Residue resulting from the burning of organic materials. Coke, carbon black, and soot are forms of charcoal, with other forms named for their source material, such as wood. Carbon is important in **archaeological** contexts because it can be tested using radiometric methods to determine the date when a substance burned. *See also* DATING.

CHARNEL HOUSE. Structure specifically constructed for the preparation and storage (either temporary or permanent) of the dead. Many Native American groups of the **Eastern Woodlands** constructed and maintained charnel houses, with several descriptions of these structures appearing in the chronicles of **Hernando de Soto** and other early European explorers. Charnel houses played an important role in preserving the physical remains of deceased ancestors, an important aspect of Native American **religious** beliefs. *See also* BURIAL; SHAMANISM.

CHENOPODIUM BERLANDIERI. A plant species belonging to the genus *Chenopodium*, commonly referred to as goosefoot, lamb's quarter, or pigweed. Belonging to the same family as the beet and spinach, *Chenopodium berlandieri* was an important component of **Woodland** period **subsistence** practices in the **Eastern Woodlands** of North America. Small, starchy seeds were harvested from these plants, with evidence of their consumption by indigenous peoples as early as the **Archaic** period. Research by David and Nancy Asch indicate that this plant was **cultivated** by Early Woodland peoples, and remained an important component of their subsistence practices until the **Mississippian** period.

CHEROKEE INDIANS. A Native American people of the **Southeast** who inhabited the mountainous regions of Tennessee, North and South Carolina, Georgia, and Alabama when first contacted by Europeans. Unlike other Native American groups of the Southeast, the Cherokee are **Iroquoian** speakers, with some scholars suggesting that they were relatively late arrivals in the region. However, Cherokee culture was similar in many respects to that of the Muskogee **Creek** and other **Southeastern** cultures. The Cherokee were village **agriculturalists** who also hunted **deer**, **bear**, and **elk**. During the

17th and 18th centuries, the Cherokee were decimated by smallpox, and other European-introduced **diseases**, as well as **warfare** with colonists and other Native American groups. The Cherokee practiced a republican form of government, and in 1827 established their capital at New Echota in northern Georgia. However, the discovery of gold on Cherokee lands in the 1830s led to the removal of most Cherokees from their eastern homeland on the **Trail of Tears**. Today, the Cherokee are the most populous Native American group in the United States, numbering more than 300,000, with the majority residing in Oklahoma. *See also* SEQUOYAH.

CHERT. An opaque form of cryptocrystalline siliceous rock used for chipped stone implements. Cherts are frequently brown or gray-black, but may appear in a variety of colors. Cherts are similar to flints but are often lighter in color and less pure in silica content. Cherts were a favored **lithic** material for **tool** production by many Native American groups because they are easily flaked and have predictable plains of cleavage. Inferior cherts were often **heat treated** to alter their physical properties and make them easier to manipulate.

CHETRO KETL. One of the largest **Anasazi pueblos** in **Chaco Canyon**. This pueblo was five stories in height, containing over 500 rooms and 12 **kivas**. **Dendrochronological** data indicate that construction on Chetro Ketl was begun around 950 B.P. (A.D. 1000) and it was occupied until approximately 800 B.P. (A.D. 1150). Like the other pueblos in Chaco Canyon, Chetro Ketl is thought to have been abandoned due to the advent of a decades-long drought in the region.

CHEYENNE INDIANS. An **Algonquian**-speaking Native American people who inhabited a large area of the upper Midwest (principally in the present-day state of Minnesota) prior to European contact. Originally village-based **agriculturalists**, increased pressure from the **Sioux** and **Ojibwa** for their traditional territory forced the Cheyenne to move southwest and onto the **Great Plains**. Abandoning precontact cultural practices, the Cheyenne adopted a highly mobile, **horse**-based culture centered upon **bison hunting**. The Cheyenne eventually divided into two groups: a northern group occupying territory along the Platte River, and a southern group centered along the upper Arkansas River. Europeans increasingly encroached upon Cheyenne territory, with several attempts made to place them on reservations in southeastern Colorado. However, antagonized by the massacre of hundreds of unarmed Cheyenne men, women, and children at Sand Creek, Colorado, they resisted further confinement, eventually uniting with the Sioux to defy the U.S. military campaign on the Plains. They participated in the Battle of Little Bighorn in 1876, defeating Custer and the 7th Cavalry. Today there are more than 11,000 Cheyenne, primarily located in Montana and Oklahoma.

CHICKASAW INDIANS. A **Muskogean**-speaking Native American group who occupied territory in present-day northern Mississippi and northwestern Alabama. Considered one of the **Five Civilized Tribes** of the **Southeast**, the Chickasaw were village **agriculturalists**, **hunters**, and **traders**. Their geographic location made the Chickasaw important to French, English, and American **colonial** interests in the region. The conflict between European powers for control of the Southeast led to near-constant **warfare** between the Chickasaw and the **Choctaw**, **Creek**, **Cherokee**, and Shawnee, eventually reducing their ability to resist demands on their territory. In 1834, the Chickasaw were forcibly moved from their homelands to Oklahoma. Today, there are more than 20,000 Chickasaw, with most living in Oklahoma.

CHIEF. Preeminent sociopolitical leader in chiefdom societies. Although the term often has been misapplied to any leader of a Native American society, **anthropologists** use the term to denote the hereditary leader of an intermediately complex society. Native American chiefs received deferential treatment in life and death, with these leaders having access to higher status material goods and a greater degree of control over the sociopolitical decision-making process. *See also* CHIEFDOM.

CHIEFDOM. Anthropological term used to describe a form of sociopolitical organization intermediate between the **tribe** and the **state**. Chiefdoms are societies in which individuals are ranked, usually based on kinship, with these **ascribed** social rankings leading to differential access to resources and a permanent political structure.

Social leadership in chiefdoms is vested in a hereditary **chief** who commonly possesses authority over a social group larger than that of the local community. **Archaeological** evidence suggests that the most sociopolitically complex Native American societies north of Mesoamerica were organized as chiefdoms. The largest chiefdom in North America is thought to have been **Cahokia**.

CHIEF JOSEPH (1732–1794). Preeminent **Nez Perce** leader of the later portion of the 19th century who led his people in resistance to confinement on a reservation in Idaho established by the U.S. government. He defied the United States and led his people on a long journey to the comparative safety and freedom of Canada. The Nez Perce were halted by the U.S. military less than 50 kilometers (30 miles) from the Canadian border and forced to return to the Coleville Reservation in Washington.

CHINOOK INDIANS. Native American peoples of the **Northwest Coast** who spoke a variety of languages of the Penutian family that are known as *Chinook*. They lived along the Columbia River valley, and were famous as **traders**. Their trade contacts were so extensive that their trade language, referred to as Chinook jargon, was the principal lingua franca of Northwest Coast trade. The members of the **Lewis and Clark expedition** were the first Europeans to describe the Chinook (1805). Chinook **religion** focused on salmon rites and guardian spirits, with the **potlatch** playing an important role in the social, ceremonial, and **religious** life of the community. Following a major smallpox outbreak in the early 19th century, the Chinook were vastly reduced in number, with many survivors absorbed into other Northwest Coast groups. Today, there are approximately 1,000 Chinook in Oregon and Washington.

CHIPPEWA INDIANS. *See* OJIBWA INDIANS.

CHITIMACHA INDIANS. Chitimacha-speaking Native American group who occupied a large territory along the lower Mississippi River in the present state of Louisiana when first contacted by Europeans. The Chitimacha were village **agriculturalists** who supplemented their diets with **fishing**, **hunting**, and **gathering**. They are unique among **Southeastern** Native American peoples for their highly complex sociopolitical structure that permitted women to serve in the most politically powerful positions in society, including that of **chief**. The French displaced the Chitimacha after a decade-long struggle for the region. Although they were forced to move away from the Mississippi River valley, the Chitimacha were able to continue to occupy much of their traditional territory. Unlike most other Southeastern peoples, they continue to occupy much of their homeland, with more than 700 Chitimacha presently residing in Louisiana.

CHOCTAW INDIANS. A **Muskogean**-speaking Native American group who occupied territory in southern Mississippi, Louisiana, and west-central Alabama. Considered one of the **Five Civilized Tribes** of the **Southeast**, the Choctaw were village **agriculturalists**, **hunters**, and **traders**. The Choctaw were considered the most prolific agriculturalists of the region, with their agricultural surpluses often used in trade with other Native American groups and Europeans. The Choctaw were important in the **colonial** struggle for the Southeast and were most closely allied with the French until they abandoned their claims to the Southeast. The Choctaw were engaged in near-constant **warfare** with the **Chickasaw**, and **Creek**, and actively resisted American encroachment on their lands. In 1832 a large number of Choctaw were relocated to Oklahoma, with a sizeable group staying behind on the traditional lands in Mississippi. Today there are more than 85,000 Choctaw, with most residing in Oklahoma and Mississippi.

CHORISH CULTURE. Regional **cultural** development considered part of the **Norton tradition** of Cape Krunstenstern in northwestern Alaska. The Chorish culture is the earliest of the **Norton tradition** developments, dated to around 3000 B.P. (1000 B.C.), and is an outgrowth of the earlier **Arctic small-tool tradition**. Chorish culture shows a greater dependence upon the **hunting** of maritime mammals and an abandonment of earlier microblade **tools**.

CHUMASH INDIANS. Native American group of southern **California**. Before European contacts, the Chumash occupied extensive territory along the Pacific Coast. However, European **diseases** and encroachment on Chumash lands greatly reduced their number and territory. They were **hunters** and **foragers** who relied upon both terrestrial and marine food resources. The Chumash are renowned for their elaborate **rock art** carvings and multicolored **pictographs** that depict supernatural myths and **religious** ideologies. At present, approximately 7,500 Chumash reside in California.

CIBOLA. Legendary city of gold sought by Spanish explorers in the **Southwest**. Fueled in part by the fabulous treasures of the conquests of Mexico and Peru and by the firsthand accounts of **Cabeza de Vaca** and Fray Marcos de Niza, **Francisco Vásquez de Coronado** set out in 1540 to conquer Cibola and claim its riches. Coronado and his party conquered the six **Zuñi** pueblos Fray Niza had reported as Cibola, but no gold was found. Coronado and his party ventured across much of the southwest in search of riches, with **Hernando de Alvarado's** side party reaching as far north as Kansas.

CIRCUM-CARIBBEAN CULTURE AREA. Region encompassing the inhabited tropical rainforest islands of the Caribbean. Specific **culture** traits of the aboriginal inhabitants of these islands most closely resemble those of South America, with local groups influenced strongly by mainland groups in South America and Mesoamerica. Most models for the initial settlement of the Caribbean propose that South American peoples migrated northward along the Antilles chain, eventually settling all of the inhabitable islands of the region.

At the time of European contact, most Circum-Caribbean peoples practiced **agriculture**, and supplemented their diets by **hunting, fishing**, and **foraging**. Sociopolitical organization among Circum-Caribbean **cultures** was generally consistent with that of **chiefdoms**, with the presence of ranked social classes, **ascribed** social inequalities, and powerful social elites. Although remnants of the original inhabitants of the Circum-Caribbean **culture area** remain, most of the indigenous cultures of the region were eradicated by **epidemic disease**, **warfare**, and **slavery** following contacts with Europeans.

CLAN. Social group based upon actual or purported descent from a common ancestor. Clan membership can be traced either through male (patriclan) or female (matriclan) lines. Clans are generally exogamous, with marriage within the clan regarded as incestuous. Clan membership is useful in ensuring mutual support and defense as well as mediating disputes over property rights and postmarital residence issues. Some clans express their unity by means of a common emblem, referred to as a **totem**. Most Native American groups maintained some form of social organization that incorporated clans, with these groups serving as major constituent elements of social, political, and **religious** life.

CLIFF DWELLINGS. General term applied to residential structures constructed into the cliffs, caves, and sheltered overhangs of the Four Corners region of the **Southwest**. Many of the cliff dwelling sites, such as **Mesa Verde** and Bandelier, are of **Anasazi** origin. These structures are usually carved into the natural stone, with **adobe** or masonry walls and wooden roofs. Cliff dwellings are considered part of the general **Puebloan** architectural pattern, and were eventually abandoned in preference for multiroom Pueblos during the 15th century.

CLIFF PALACE. One of a number of **archaeological** sites on **Mesa Verde** in southwestern Colorado. Composed of over 150 rooms and 23 **kivas**, Cliff Palace is thought to have supported a resident population of 100–150 people. Built between 750 and 650 B.P. (A.D. 1200–1300), Cliff Palace is the largest site at Mesa Verde, and provides one of the best examples of the **cliff dwellings** of the **Anasazi**.

CLIMAP (Climate and environment monitoring with GPS atmospheric profiling). A scientific research project developed by the National Oceanic and Atmospheric Administration (NOAA) and the World Data Center to evaluate the earth's climate. Using computer modeling, the project seeks to develop detailed climatological information on global climate change during the past 18,000 years. This project is of particular interest to North American **archaeologists** interested in the peopling of the Americas and those researching human responses to environmental change during the past 20,000 years.

CLOVIS CULTURE. Paleoindian culture, dating from 12,000 to 11,000 B.P. (10,000–9000 B.C.), first identified in the 1930s near

Clovis, New Mexico. Additional **archaeological** research indicates that Clovis materials occur throughout much of the North American continent. Clovis **culture** is usually defined by the presence of a distinctive stone **tool** technology featuring **fluted projectile points**. Clovis culture is generally associated with the **hunting** of **megafauna** such as **mammoth** and **bison**. Clovis is the best-defined early culture in North America, but many archaeologists contend that it does not represent the earliest human culture on the continent. *See also* BLACKWATER DRAW SITE; CLOVIS POINT; PRE-CLOVIS CULTURE.

CLOVIS POINT. Specialized stone **tool** utilized by one of the earliest **Paleoindian** groups. Clovis points represent the earliest defined **projectile point** technology in North America and date to approximately 12,000 B.P. (10,000 B.C.). Clovis points indicate a careful and deliberate reduction process, with their most distinctive feature being the removal of long, slender thinning **flakes** along their medial sections. The removal of these flakes produces a highly distinctive finished projectile point with a central channel that archaeologists call a **flute**. *See also* BLACKWATER DRAW SITE; CLOVIS CULTURE; PRE-CLOVIS CULTURE.

CLOVIS SITE. *See* BLACKWATER DRAW SITE.

COCHISE TRADITION. Archaic period, pre**ceramic hunting** and **foraging culture** of Arizona and other parts of the **Southwest** from approximately 10,000 to 1800 B.P. (8000 B.C.–A.D. 150). The Cochise sequence is divided into three distinct stages: Sulpher Spring (10,000–8000 B.P.), Chiricachua (8000–3500 B.P.), and San Pedro (3500–1800 B.P.). The Cochise **tradition** is culturally related to later **Mogollon** and **Hohokam** cultures.

CODY KNIFE. A diagnostic **artifact** type for the Cody cultural complex dating between 9700 and 8000 B.P (circa 7700–6000 B.C.). These **Paleoindian artifacts** are found throughout the **Great Plains** region from Texas to Alberta. Cody knives consist of large, asymmetrically **flaked**-stone tools with a transverse cutting edge and a shoulder on either one or both sides. Technological studies indicate that these objects were used as cutting **tools**, and morphological analyses indicate that they were commonly fashioned from broken **projectile points**.

COILING. A technique used in the production of **ceramics** in which the raw clay is rolled with the hands to form long, slender strands. These individual strands of clay are then placed atop one another in a circular fashion. Coiling begins at the bottom of the vessel and continues until the vessel reaches the desired height. The inner and outer surfaces of the pot are then smoothed. Coiling was one of the predominant techniques employed in the production of ceramics by Native Americans. *See also* ANVIL AND PADDLE TECHNIQUE.

COLBY MAMMOTH SITE. Paleoindian site in Wyoming that contains **Clovis projectile points** in direct association with Columbian **mammoth**. The Colby site dates to approximately 11,000 B.P. (9,000 B.C.), and is one of the largest mammoth kill sites in North America. Evidence from this site also indicates that Paleoindian people cached meat for future consumption.

COLE, FAY-COOPER (1881–1961). American **anthropologist** who received his training at Columbia University (Ph.D., 1914) and went on to found the anthropology program at the University of Chicago in 1929. He conducted ethnographic research in the Philippines and Indonesia, but is important to North American **archaeology** for helping to found the **Society for American Archaeology** and for introducing **dendrochronology** to eastern North America. In addition, he helped lead an archaeological survey of Illinois and major excavations at the Kincaid site. Perhaps Cole had his greatest impact on American archaeology with the training he provided through the University of Chicago's archaeological field school. Many of the students trained in the Chicago field school went on to play prominent roles in North American archaeology.

COLES CREEK CULTURE. *See* TROYVILLE-COLES CREEK CULTURE.

COLONIALISM. Policy by which one nation maintains control over a foreign territory, or colony. The purposes of colonialism include economic exploitation, the creation of new markets, and the extension of the colonizer's way of life beyond its national borders. European nations engaged in the most extensive colonialism in world history during the period from A.D. 1500 to 1900. During this time, Europeans colonized the Americas and Australia, as well as much of Africa and Asia. The Spanish, Dutch, English, and French were all engaged in the colonization of North America. Native Americans were dramatically impacted by European colonialism, experiencing loss of territory, population decline and dislocation, increased **warfare**, forced **acculturation**, and sociopolitical subjugation.

COLONOWARE. Term used to describe low-fired, unglazed, plain earthenware **ceramics** produced in North America during the 17th, 18th, and 19th centuries. Colonoware is produced using indigenous techniques and traditional materials, but takes the stylistic form of European ceramics. **Archaeologists** have found colonoware in both Native American and enslaved African American contexts, suggesting that it was produced by both groups.

COLUMBUS, CHRISTOPHER (1451–1506). Italian-born Spanish navigator who led an expedition across the Atlantic in search of a western sea route to Asia in 1492. Instead of landing in Asia, Columbus landed in the Bahamas. He led three subsequent expeditions of exploration in the Caribbean. Although he is generally credited with being the first European to "discover" the Americas, there is considerable **archaeological** and historical evidence that Scandinavian sailors had reached North America centuries earlier. Traditional historians have credited Columbus with opening up the Americas for European exploration and colonization. However, many contemporary historians, and not coincidentally extant Native Americans, see his expeditions as typifying European brutality, exploitation, and ethnocentrism. *See also* L'ANSE AUX MEADOWS.

COMANCHE INDIANS. Shoshonean-speaking Native American group believed to have originated in the **Great Basin**. They split off from the **Shoshone** and moved onto the **Great Plains** in the 18th century. During the **historic period**, they occupied portions of Colorado,

Kansas, Oklahoma, New Mexico, and Texas. The Comanche were excellent horsemen, using the increased mobility afforded by the European introduction of the **horse** to develop highly mobile **bison-hunting subsistence** practices. They also used their mobility to their advantage during the 18th and 19th centuries, utilizing a quick-strike raiding technique to resist European encroachment on their lands. At present, there are approximately 11,000 Comanche in the United States, with the largest concentration in Oklahoma.

CONJUNCTIVE APPROACH. Theoretical perspective advocated by American archaeologist **Walter W. Taylor** (1948) as an alternative to prior **archaeological** practice. Taylor was frustrated by the failure of archaeologists to make **culturally** meaningful insights, because of what he saw as a myopic preoccupation with **artifact** description. Instead, Taylor proposed that archaeologists study the interrelationships and social contexts of their data in an attempt to reveal the causes of prehistoric culture change. Although most archaeologists did not change their perspectives in light of Taylor's arguments, his views were highly influential in the formulation of **processual archaeology** by **Lewis Binford** and others.

CONQUISTADORS. Any of the military leaders who took part in the Spanish conquest of the Americas in the 16th century. The conquistadors were responsible for considerable loss of life and cultural destruction among the native peoples of the Americas. *See also* ALVARADO, HERNANDO DE; CORONADO, FRANCISCO VASQUEZ DE; DE SOTO, HERNANDO; NARVAEZ, PANFILO DE; OÑATE, JUAN DE PONCE DE LEÓN; OÑATE, JUAN DE.

CONTRACT ARCHAEOLOGY. *See* CULTURAL RESOURCE MANAGEMENT.

COOSA. A major Native American **chiefdom** in the **Southeast** that extended from southeastern Tennessee, across northwestern Georgia, and into east-central Alabama. The province received its name from its capital, Coosa, identified by **archaeologists** as the Little Egypt site located on the Coosawatte River in northwestern Georgia. Coosa was the most populous and sociopolitically complex Native American polity encountered by the expedition of **Hernando de Soto** (1540). Following European contacts, the chiefdom was reduced in both population and sociopolitical importance.

COPPER. Metallic element that occurs naturally in the Great Lakes and parts of the Appalachians. Copper is highly malleable, and was used by many Native American groups for the production of high-status **artifacts**. Although sometimes used to produce items of a utilitarian nature, given its relative scarcity, copper was generally used by Native American artisans to produce a variety of pendants, **beads**, headdresses, **gorgets**, plaques, and other nonutilitarian items. These items are commonly found in the **burials** of high-status individuals.

COPROLITES. Desiccated human feces preserved in the **archaeological** record due to extreme aridity. Because they contain food residues, human coprolites are used to reconstruct diet and **subsistence** activities. Coprolites are most commonly found in dry cave sites and in open-air desert sites. Studies of coprolites have allowed archaeologists to gain insight into the dietary practices of many Native American groups of the **Southwest**, indicating dramatic changes in subsistence practices during the past 12,000 years.

CORDILLERAN. One of two major ice sheets covering much of the North American continent during the **Pleistocene**. Stretching along the mountains of Alaska and British Columbia, the Cordilleran glacial complex would have effectively impeded human penetration into North America along its path. Geologists proposed that an ice-free path (referred to as the **Mackenzie Corridor**) existed between the Cordilleran and **Laurentide** glacial formations, permitting human passage to the south, but contemporary geological research suggests that this corridor would only have been passable before 25,000 B.P. (23,000 B.C.) or immediately after 15,000 B.P. (13,000 B.C.). Research on the date and size of the Cordilleran glacial formation has implications for the initial peopling of the Americas.

CORE. Lithic material from which **tools** and **flakes** are produced. Prepared cores are those that have been initially worked so that the shape of the resulting flakes can be controlled more effectively. Cores can also be used as tools themselves, serving as hammers, choppers, and other scraping tools (referred to as core tools).

CORN. *See* MAIZE.

CORNER-NOTCHED TRADITION. A distinctive style of **projectile point** common in the **Eastern Woodlands** during the early **Archaic** period from 9000 to 8000 B.P. (7000–6000 B.C.). **Artifacts** of this type have characteristic corner notches, where **lithic** materials were removed for **hafting**. This preference in projectile design style is thought to reflect a transition in **hunting** strategy from thrusting spears to **atlatl**-propelled darts.

CORONADO, FRANCISCO VASQUEZ DE (1510–1554). Spanish **conquistador**, explorer, and governor of the Mexican province of Nueva Galicia. Coronado mounted an expedition into the **Southwest** in search of **Cibola**, the legendary seven cities of gold. Instead he discovered the **Zuñi** pueblos of New Mexico. A side expedition under the command of **Hernando de Alvarado** split from the main party, venturing as far north as Kansas.

COUNCIL. Sociopolitical decision-making group common among the Native Americans of the **Eastern Woodlands**. Councils consisted of socially important individuals, usually male lineage heads, who met for the purpose of debating sociopolitical issues, including punishment for criminal offenses and proclamations of **war**. Councils commonly convened their meetings in private, within large semisubterranean **council houses**. Councils were most common among Native American groups lacking powerful **chiefs**, but they also played important advisory roles in those societies in which sociopolitical power was vested in chiefs. The **Iroquois** council was composed of individual chiefs (*sachem*) who met to discuss issues of mutual interest to the individual tribes, with their council decisions requiring unanimous support of all *sachem* before they could be enacted.

COUNCIL HOUSE. Designated meeting place for sociopolitical decision-making councils. Common to Native American societies of the **Eastern Woodlands**, council houses were normally large, semisubterranean structures specifically built for the purposes of council deliberations. These structures served similar purposes as **Southwestern kivas** and the **earthlodges** of the **Great Plains** and Midwest.

COUVADE. Ritual imitation of childbirth by fathers; also referred to as sympathetic pregnancy. This practice is thought to be part of a series of social rituals related to childbirth designed to protect the child from supernatural forces. Such actions assert a man's claims of paternity, while simultaneously tricking harmful spirits into focusing their harmful energies on him rather than the newborn child. The couvade was an important practice for a number of Native American **cultures**.

COWBOY CAVE SITE. Cave site in the Colorado Plateau of Utah. This site is intriguing to **archaeologists** because it contains human occupation from the Early **Archaic** period (8600–1500 B.P. [6600 B.C.–A.D. 450]) as well as an earlier prehuman use by herbivores. These prehuman remains indicate the presence of **bison, mammoth,** camel, **horse**, and sloth, revealing a great deal about the local environment during this period. Human occupation of the cave was not continuous, indicating a series of **cultural** responses to local environmental changes over a period of approximately 7,000 years.

CRADLEBOARD. Wooden frame device constructed to hold a small child. These devices were commonly wrapped with cloth to protect the child from environmental extremes and to ensure that the child would not fall out. Cradleboards were slung over the back so that the child's caregiver could complete necessary tasks while attending to the child. Cradleboards were common among Native American groups of the **Great Plains** and **Southwest**. In addition to their role in protecting the child, they were also used in the production of **artificial cranial deformation** among societies that prized the shape of modified crania.

CRAIG MOUND. *See* SPIRO SITE.

CRANIAL DEFORMATION. *See* ARTIFICIAL CRANIAL DEFOR-MATION.

CREE INDIANS. Algonquian-speaking Native American group who formerly occupied an immense territory along Hudson Bay and St. James Bay in present-day Quebec, Ontario, and Manitoba, Canada. During the **historic period**, one group allied themselves with the **Assiniboine** and moved southwest into **bison** territory, becoming the Plains Cree. Another group remained behind in their traditional territory, becoming known as the *Woodland Cree*. Although a fiercely independent people, the Cree participated in the **fur trade** with the Hudson Bay and North West companies. Both branches of the Cree practiced elaborate **hunting** rituals and observed many taboos regarding the spirits of game animals. Fears of **witchcraft** were also common among the Cree peoples. Like most Native American groups, smallpox and other European-introduced **diseases** vastly reduced their population during the 17th and 18th centuries. At present, the Cree are the largest and most geographically expansive Native American group in Canada, with more than 120,000 in Quebec, Ontario, Manitoba, Saskatchewan, and Alberta. Approximately 10,000 Cree live in the United States, with many residing on a reservation in Montana with the **Ojibwa**.

CREEK INDIANS. Confederation of many **Southeastern** Native American groups, with the majority coming from groups that spoke dialects of **Muskogean**, a branch of the Hokan-Siouan languages. Receiving their name from the English, the Creeks occupied a vast territory in the present-day states of Georgia and Alabama. They were village **agriculturalists**, with **archaeological** evidence suggesting their development out of the late prehistoric and early historic **Mississippian chiefdoms** of the southern Appalachian region. Towns in the Creek Confederacy were divided between the Upper Creeks, those along the Coosa and Tallapoosa Rivers of Alabama, and the Lower Creeks, those living along the Chattahoochee and Flint Rivers of Georgia. There was no overarching governmental structure among the Creeks, with village decisions based on **council** deliberations, and decisions impacting the entire confederacy made in large communal councils. The Creeks played a vital role in the **colonial** struggle for the **Southeast** between the French, Spanish, English, and Americans, with their allegiances constantly shifting to reflect their collective interests. Many Creeks supported the English during the War of 1812, resulting in the First Creek War with the United States (1813–1814). Creek lands in the Southeast were eventually claimed by the United States, with their forced removal to Oklahoma in the 1830s. At present there are more than 50,000 Creeks, with most residing in Oklahoma.

CREMATION. Disposal of the dead by intentional burning. Although there was considerable variation in the **burial** rituals practiced by Native American groups, cremation was a common mortuary practice for the **Archaic** and **Woodland** period groups in the **Eastern Woodlands** and Eastern **Great Plains**.

CROOKS SITE. A **Woodland** period **archaeological** site (1850–1400 B.P. [A.D. 100–550]) in the present-day state of Louisiana representative of a southern variation of the **Hopewell culture** called **Marksville**. The Crooks site consists of a large square **burial** mound with more than 300 individual interments. Burial goods placed with many of these burials indicate that local artisans produced high-status goods based on Hopewellian forms.

CROW CREEK SITE. Archaeological site in central South Dakota located at the junction of the Missouri River with Crow Creek and Wolf Creek. Archaeological evidence from this site indicates that a group of people from the **Central Plains Cultural Tradition** moved to this location after its abandonment by people of the **Middle Missouri Cultural Tradition**. The Crow Creek site was heavily **fortified**, with an exterior **palisade** and a deep moat. Despite these defensive capabilities, the Crow Creek site was overrun by a hostile force around A.D. 1325. Archaeological research at the site revealed the presence of a mass grave containing 486 individuals within the fortification ditch. Paleopathological examination of the human remains indicates that the residents of the Crow Creek site were insufficiently nourished, suggesting that local **warfare** was the result of regional overpopulation and resource depletion.

CROW INDIANS. Siouan-speaking Native American group of the **Great Plains** who call themselves the Absaroka (bird people). Historically affiliated with the **Hidatsa**, the Crow occupied the area around the Yellowstone River of Wyoming and Montana. The Crow were prolific **bison hunters**, with a highly developed **horse** culture. They were also prominent middlemen **traders**, exchanging horses, **bows**, **firearms**, and other items between surrounding Native American groups. The Crow engaged in **warfare** with the **Blackfoot** and **Sioux**, siding with the Americans in the Sioux wars of the 1860s and 1870s. At present there are approximately 10,000 Crow in the United States, with most residing in southern Montana.

CROW KINSHIP SYSTEM. System for reckoning social relations of kinship practiced by the **Crow, Hopi**, and other Native American groups. It is considered a bifurcate merging kinship system, and is associated with societies practicing a particularly strong form of matrilineal descent. In essence, the Crow kinship system treats relatives from one's mother's and father's side in very different ways. Cross cousins from the father's side are equated with members of the parental generation, while cross cousins from the mother's side are equated with one's children's generation. Kinship systems are important to anthropologists because they reveal much about the nature of social life within Native American societies.

CULTIVATION. Deliberate manipulation of the natural environment in order to enhance the propagation of a desired plant species. Cultivation activities include the removal of weeds, as well as the addition of water and nutrients to the soil. Cultivation is considered one of the necessary preconditions for the development of **agriculture**. Native Americans are believed to have cultivated select plant species, such as *Chenopodium berlandieri* and **knotweed**, as early as Late **Archaic** times.

CULTURAL DIFFUSION. The movement of **culture** trait (or ideas) from one society to another. **Archaeologists** adhering to the concept of **culture history** see diffusion as one of the principal processes responsible for the cultural changes visible in the archaeological record. Cultural diffusion was used as a primary explanatory mechanism for many early North American archaeologists in their attempts to explain the widespread elements of material culture.

CULTURAL ECOLOGY. Term devised by American **anthropologist** Julian Steward to describe analysis of the dynamic relationship between humans and their environment. Steward saw **culture** as the primary mechanism by which humans adapted to environmental change, and conversely he saw the environment as the most compelling force shaping human cultures. Cultural ecology, first defined by Steward with the use of ethnographic and **archaeological** data from **Great Basin** cultures (particularly the **Shoshone**), remains an important theoretical underpinning for the work of many North American archaeologists and anthropologists.

CULTURAL EVOLUTION. Theoretical proposition that human **cultures** develop in a manner similar to that of biological organisms. Originally an outgrowth of colloquial theorizing about the nature of human societies, the first frameworks for cultural evolution were unilinear and Eurocentric, with European culture held up as the ideal form of human sociocultural development. Modern perspectives on cultural evolution favor the explicit use of **Darwinian** evolutionary principals in the investigation of human culture change. Cultural evolutionary perspectives are of increasing importance within North American archaeology.

CULTURAL RESOURCE MANAGEMENT (CRM). Government-mandated examination and preservation of **archaeological** and historical sites prior to their development or destruction. Cultural resource management is a comparatively new area of North American archaeology, and it is most frequently undertaken prior to large public works such as road or dam construction. This area of archaeology is primarily concerned with balancing development needs with the preservation and recording of significant cultural resources. Also referred to as contract archaeology, CRM is now the largest single area of employment for North American archaeologists. It is through the efforts of CRM archaeologists that a large number of newly discovered archaeological sites have been recorded.

CULTURE. The learned and nonrandom behaviors, thoughts, and actions shared by humans in a social group. Culture is considered to be the unique set of practices that make one group of people distinct from all other such groups. It includes everything from **religion**, social structure, politics, kinship, **subsistence**, and **language** to architecture and morality. The culture concept is a unique feature of American **anthropology** and has been used to compare and contrast the distinct lifeways of Native American social groups.

CULTURE AREA. A geographic region in which similar patterns of social life predominate among individual **cultures**. **Archaeologists** borrowed this concept from ethnology, using it to refer to geographic areas within which the archaeological record of past societies indicates considerable homogeneity in material culture. North American culture areas generally include the **Arctic**, **California**, **Great Basin**, **Great Plains**, **Northeast**, **Northwest Coast**, **Southeast**, **Southwest**, and **Subarctic** regions.

CULTURE HISTORY. Theoretical perspective in North American **archaeology** with the primary goal of establishing the chronological and spatial dimensions of cultural materials and the social groups that produced them. **Culture** historical perspectives place emphasis on the historical development of cultural practices, attempting to trace the influences of differing cultural traditions upon each other. An overemphasis on culture historical perspectives by North American archaeologists during the first half of the 20th century led **Walter Taylor** to propose the **conjunctive approach**, and later **Lewis Binford** to proffer **processual archaeology**.

CUSHING, FRANK HAMILTON (1857–1900). Pioneering ethnologist who worked primarily among the **Zuñi** in the American **Southwest**. Cushing showed considerable academic promise at an early age, and was named curator of the ethnology department of the National Museum of Washington, D.C. at the age of 19. Brought to the Southwest in 1879 by **John Wesley Powell**, Cummings stayed behind at **Zuñi pueblo** to record the various rituals and ceremonies of the Zuñi. He also examined **archaeological** sites in the Southwest, **Southeast**, and **Northeast**.

– D –

DAKOTA. *See* SIOUX.

DALLES TRADE NETWORK. An extensive **Archaic** period **trade** network centered along an eight-kilometer (five-mile) stretch of rapids on the Columbia River of the **Pacific Northwest**. The Dalles trade network extended throughout the Pacific coast to the **Great Plains**, linking groups from as far away as the present-day states of Alaska and California. Native American peoples gathered at the Dalles to trade, **fish**, and engage in **religious** and social rituals. Items frequently traded among groups participating in the Dalles network included blankets, **beads**, **bison** skins and meat, obsidian, **salmon**, **slaves**, shells, and exotic **lithic** materials. The Dalles trade network continued well after European exploration of the region, eventually linking in trade both Native American and European groups.

DALTON TRADITION. A **cultural tradition** of the **Southeast** and eastern **Great Plains** evidenced by similarities in the production of **projectile points** and other **lithic** materials. Dated from 10,500 to 9900 B.P. (8500 to 7900 B.C.), Dalton materials are commonly non-**fluted projectile points** with characteristic outcurving, concave bases. These items are thought to be multipurpose **tools**, serving as projectile points, knives, saws, chisels, and scrapers. Dalton materials are found throughout the Southeast, and also are found in the eastern Great Plains and southern portions of the **Northeast**. The Dalton tradition is considered a response to the considerable environmental and **subsistence** changes that occurred in the early **Holocene**, during the transition from the **Paleoindian** period to the **Archaic** period.

DANGER CAVE SITE. **Archaeological** site located near Great Salt Lake, Utah, with evidence of human occupation as early as 11,000 B.P. (9000 B.C.). Excavated by **Jesse Jennings**, Danger Cave contains a sequence of short-term occupations that form much of the basis for the identification of the **Desert Archaic tradition**. The Desert Archaic is characterized by cultural adjustments associated with increased aridity and the extreme environmental conditions of the

Great Basin. Preservation of cultural and environmental materials at Danger Cave was excellent, including pieces of leather, string, nets, textiles, **basketry**, millstones, and various **tools** of bone and wood.

DARWINIAN ARCHAEOLOGY. Theoretical approach to the understanding of the **archaeological** record predicated upon the idea that **culture** change can be explained through the explicit use of Darwinian **evolutionary** theory. Also referred to as *selectionism*, Darwinian archaeologists contend that biological and ecological factors are the most important determinants in understanding human behavior. Darwinian theoretical perspectives in North American archaeology are of increasing importance in the understanding of **culture** change among Native American societies.

DATING. The use of scientific techniques to determine the age of an **artifact**, ecofact, or other **archaeological** specimen. Archaeological dating can either be relative (where the age of an object is given in relation to another object, but no specific calendrical date is given for its age) or absolute (where the age of an object is given in relation to a modern calendrics). Relative dating techniques consist of interpretive techniques like **frequency seriation** or **stratigraphic** superposition, while absolute dating techniques include **archaeomagnetic**, **dendrochronology**, **radiocarbon** (both conventional and **accelerator mass spectrometry**), **thermoluminescense**, and other advanced scientific techniques.

DAVIS, EDWIN HAMILTON (1811–1888). Physician and amateur **archaeologist** who, together with **Ephraim Squire**, undertook the mapping and excavation of Native American archaeological sites in the Ohio and Scioto River valleys during the 1840s. Much of our knowledge of the archaeological sites of the Ohio River valley is due to their careful recording. Many of the sites documented by Squire and Davis have since been destroyed, with their records serving as the only evidence of their size and orientation. Despite a large collection of **cultural** materials from his investigations, Davis erroneously considered the large **mounds** and geometric **earthworks** of eastern North America the results of prior occupation of the region by the peoples of Mexico, Central America, or Peru.

DEBERT SITE. Paleoindian site in Nova Scotia dated to approximately 10,600 B.P. (8600 B.C.). Evidence from the Debert site suggests that it was a seasonal encampment, with several small structures with internal hearths and **artifact** clusters on their floors. The Debert site was occupied during the late spring, summer, and early autumn, when local **subsistence** resources were at their most abundant.

DEBITAGE. Lithic refuse produced during the production of flaked-stone **tools**. Debitage differs based on the stage of tool production and the raw material being used, with **archaeologists** using this information, along with the spatial distribution of debitage to reconstruct the tool production process. Many North American archaeological sites, especially those from the **Paleoindian** and **Archaic** periods, lack formal stone tools, with the only direct evidence of human presence at these sites the presence of lithic debitage. Additionally, most sites proposed as evidence of the **pre-Clovis culture** rely on the presence of debitage to infer an early human presence in North America.

DEER. Any of the ruminants of the family Cervidae, found throughout North America. Deer typically have a compact body, a short tail, and long, slender ears, with males having bony antlers that are shed annually. Deer were a source of both food and skins for Native Americans, and after the arrival of Europeans, became important components of **trade**. *See also* FUR TRADE; HUNTING.

DEERSKIN TRADE. *See* FUR TRADE.

DEETZ, JAMES (1930–2000). American **archaeologist** whose research addressed issues of **culture** change at both historic Native American and European colonists. His dissertation, *The Dynamics of Stylistic Change in Arikara Ceramics*, is considered one of the earliest examples of **processual archaeology**. Deetz's research at Plimoth Plantation, California mining communities, and New England graveyards are among his best-known archaeological studies, but he is probably best remembered for his textbooks, *Invitation to Archaeology* and *In Small Things Forgotten*, works that introduced successive generations of American archaeologist students to the discipline.

DELAWARE INDIANS. English name given to a confederation of **Algonquian**-speaking Native American groups who occupied the Delaware River valley and portions of the Atlantic seaboard in the present-day states of New Jersey, Delaware, Pennsylvania, and New York during the 17th century. These people referred to themselves as the Lenni-Lenape, and were composed of three major **clan** divisions: the Munsee (wolf), Unalchachtigo (turkey), and Unami (turtle). They were village **agriculturalists**, but supplemented their diet through **hunting** and **fishing**. During the 17th and 18th centuries, the Delaware were pushed west by European encroachment on their territory, eventually settling in the Susquehanna Valley and portions of Ohio. Later colonial expansion by the United States forced them into Kansas and Texas, and at present there are more than 10,000 Delaware residing in Oklahoma.

DENALI COMPLEX. Group of **archaeological** sites in Alaska dated between 10,500 and 8000 B.P. (8500–6000 B.C.) with **lithic** materials consisting of wedge-shaped **cores** and microblades that show clear stylistic connections with Siberian stone **tool traditions**. Considered part of the **Paleoarctic Tradition**, the Denali complex is thought to be a descendant of the **Nenana complex** and antecedent to the **Northern Paleoindian Tradition**.

DENBIGH CULTURE. *See* CAPE DENBIGH.

DENBIGH FLINT COMPLEX. One of two **lithic tool** complexes of the **Arctic** region dated to approximately 4500–2800 B.P. (2500–800 B.C.). Denbigh flint materials are found from northern Alaska to Greenland, with their producers thought to be the ancestors of contemporary **Inuit** peoples. Denbigh tools are extremely well made, and are indicative of **subsistence** practices centered on aquatic resources and **caribou hunting**. *See also* CAPE DENBIGH.

DENDROCHRONOLOGY. The scientific study of the annual growth ring patterns in trees as a means of **dating** wooden **artifacts**. Changing climatic conditions produce differential growth patterns that can then be used to assess climatological change and produce chronologies. Although dendrochronology can be used in any region where tree samples are sufficient to permit analysis, this technique has proven most valuable for **archaeologists** working in the arid regions of the **Southwest**. *See* ANDREW E. DOUGLAS.

DENTALIA. Small, slender, hornlike "tooth shells" found along the Pacific **Northwest Coast**. The shells were traded as **beads** and wealth itcms among the native peoples of the Northwest Coast and **California** culture areas. Some archaeologists have proposed that dentalia shells were a rudimentary form of money, used as a common currency for economic transactions between peoples of the Northwest Coast and northern **California**.

DEPTFORD CULTURE. Name given to the Early **Woodland** peoples of northwest Florida (circa 4500–900 B.P. [2500 B.C.–A.D. 100]). Deptford sites demonstrate many of the **cultural** changes experienced by contemporary peoples in eastern North America, with evidence of increasing **sedentism**, larger populations, the construction of **burial mounds**, and **subsistence** practices increasingly reliant upon the **domestication** of local plants. Deptford culture is usually divided into two periods (Early and Late). Early Deptford is characterized by the presence of fabric-impressed **ceramics**, while Late Deptford indicates a shift to simple stamped and cord-marked wares.

DESERT ARCHAIC TRADITION. **Cultural** tradition of the **Great Basin** region dated to between 8500 and 3000 B.P. (circa 6500–500 B.C.) that demonstrates adaptation to an increasingly arid environment and emerging desert conditions in the region. Excavations at **Danger Cave**, Utah, by **Jesse Jennings** provided much of the evidence for the definition of the Desert Archaic Tradition. The Desert Archaic Tradition is important for archaeologists because it demonstrates the cultural transitions accompanying the long, slow transition from highly nomadic big-game **hunters** to **sedentary** village **agriculturalists**.

DE SOTO, HERNANDO (1500–1542). Spanish **conquistador** who participated in the conquest of the Inca Empire of Peru with the Francisco Pizarro expedition. He was later named colonial governor of Cuba and given the right to conquer the North American mainland (La

Florida) by Emperor Charles V. In 1539 de Soto sailed from Havana, Cuba, with an expeditionary force of about 600 men, landing near present-day Tampa Bay, Florida. For four years (1539–1543), his party traversed the **Southeast** in search of gold, silver, and other riches, crossing the present states of Florida, Georgia, the Carolinas, Tennessee, Alabama, Mississippi, and venturing as far west as Arkansas, Oklahoma, and Texas. De Soto and his men are credited with being the first Europeans to see and cross the Mississippi River (1541).

De Soto's expedition was not peaceful, with him and his men terrorizing local Native American peoples, seizing food supplies and valuables, burning villages, and killing, maiming, and enslaving villagers. Several pitched battles took place between de Soto's party and local Indian groups, with survivors from his expedition claiming that as many as 10,000 people were killed by his men. Among the longer term effects of his exploration was the introduction of European **diseases** among native peoples.

After exploring the Arkansas River region west of the Mississippi, the party turned back east to the Mississippi. De Soto died of a fever in 1542, and his body was buried unceremoniously in the river to keep his death a secret from the Native Americans whom he had intimidated during his explorations. The remnant of his party, approximately a third of those who began, made its way down the Mississippi River and along the coast, eventually arriving in Veracruz, Mexico (1543). Several detailed chronicles were produced by the survivors of the de Soto expedition, with these works providing a great deal of information on the nature of Native American societies of the Southeast during the middle 16th century.

DIRECT HISTORICAL APPROACH. A particular type of **ethnographic analogy** employed in the interpretation of **archaeological** materials, which holds that ethnographically recorded information from **cultures** in a given region can be used to examine the actions of earlier cultures in that same region. This approach relies on many assumptions, including the notion that recorded ethnographic behaviors (and the rationales shaping those actions) are of a local origin and have continued relatively unchanged. In addition, there is an implication that there was minimal population movement in the past, something that cannot be assumed for the archaeological record of most regions of North America. The direct historical approach was a widely held concept by North American archaeologists working with the **culture historical** framework that predominated in American archaeology until the 1960s.

DISEASE. A pathological condition that negatively affects an organism. A variety of diseases are common to humans, but the specific diseases present in a group are dependent upon a variety of social, environmental, and **subsistence** practices. European-introduced diseases (influenza, measles, smallpox, and so on) dramatically impacted Native Americans, with estimates claiming that Native American populations declined by 80–90 percent as a result or exposure to these diseases. Indigenous peoples had no prior exposure or natural immunities to these diseases, making them far more lethal for Native Americans than they had been for European peoples. Some diseases (tuberculosis and syphilis in particular) were shared by these groups prior to direct contacts, while others may have been passed from Native Americans to Europeans (chargas).

DOGS. Any member of the canine genus Canis, particularly the domestic species, *Canis familiaris*. Dogs were the first animal to be **domesticated** by humans, and are descended from a feral, wolflike ancestor. Dogs accompanied **Paleoindians** into the Americas, and were used by many Native American groups as companions, aides in **hunting**, and occasionally sources of food.

DOMESTICATION. Intentional interference in the natural propagation of a plant or animal species by humans. Domestication results in alterations in the natural life cycle of these organisms so that they may be of greater use to humans. Native Americans domesticated a large number of indigenous wild plants and animals, including **chenopodium**, **knotweed**, **maize**, **beans**, **squash**, and others.

DORSET CULTURE. An outgrowth of the **Arctic small-tool tradition**. People practicing this **culture** occupied the Eastern Canadian **Arctic** from 2500 to 1000 B.P. (500 B.C.–A.D. 1000). The Dorset **culture** is found over a larger area than previous Arctic cultures, suggesting a highly successful adaptation to prevailing environmental conditions. **Archaeologists** have explained the expansion of Dorset culture as a shift in **subsistence** practices from a reliance on **caribou** to **seal** as local environments changed. The material culture of Dorset peoples includes semisubterranean houses, distinctively styled **harpoons**, and an elaborate artistic tradition. Highly detailed carvings of animals and people are common on Dorset sites, suggesting the presence of **shamanic** religious practices.

DOUGLAS, ANDREW E. (1867–1962). American astronomer who developed the modern sciences of **dendrochronology** and dendroclimatology. Although the presence of annual growth-cycle rings in trees was known before his pioneering research, Douglas was able to determine that climatic cycles (particularly sun spot activity) could be revealed in the variable sizes of tree rings. When well-preserved wood samples from **archaeological** sites were compared to living samples, Douglas, with assistance from archaeologist Clark Wissler, determined that master chronologies of environmental changes could be established, and that these chronologies could in turn be tied to absolute dates. *See also* DATING.

DRAPER SITE. Large **Huron** village located in Toronto, Ontario, occupied from A.D. 1400 to 1500. The site was the subject of a large-scale excavation from 1975 to 1976, when it was threatened by the expansion of the Toronto International Airport. Excavations uncovered a large portion of the village, including several large **middens**, a series of **palisades**, and 34 **longhouses**. These large investigations allowed **archaeologists** to understand settlement patterning, community structure, **subsistence** practices, and other areas of daily life for the Huron with much greater clarity than was previously possible.

DRILL. A **tool** used to create a hole in any hard substance. Native Americans produced a variety of drills for working with leather, wood, shell, and stone. Native Americans also commonly recycled worn or damaged **projectile points** into drills. *See also* AWL.

DUGOUT CANOES. A long, narrow watercraft produced by hollowing out a large tree with the controlled use of fire, **adzes**, and other woodworking **tools**. Dugout canoes were the primary watercraft utilized by

Native Americans of the **Eastern Woodlands** and some portions of the eastern **Great Plains**. *See also* CANOE.

D'UKTAI CULTURE. Archaeological culture of northeastern Asia dated between 18,000 and 14,000 B.P. (16,000–12,000 B.C.). D'uktai culture is important to North American archaeology because it is characterized by well-made bifacial **tools** and microblades similar to those found at some early **Paleoindian** sites in Alaska. This evidence supports the prevailing archaeological perspective that the earliest inhabitants of North America were **hunting** groups that migrated into the Americas from northeastern Asia.

DWELLINGS. Native American domestic structures varied based on locally available construction materials and environment. Common Native American dwellings include the **earthlodge, hogan, longhouse, pit house, pueblo, tipi**, and **wickiup**. *See also* ADOBE; ROCKSHELTER.

– E –

EARSPOOLS. Decorative items of stone, **copper**, **ceramic**, or other material placed within a perforation in the earlobe. Considered an extreme form of ear piercing, earspools were a common form of body decoration among many Native American peoples.

EARTHENWARE. Type of **ceramic** produced through firing clay objects at relatively low temperature. Given this low firing temperature, earthenwares are not vitrified, making them more porous and coarse than stoneware and porcelain.

EARTHLODGE. Class of architectural structures constructed by Native American groups of the eastern **Great Plains** Midwest, and the **Eastern Woodlands** that are characterized by semisubterranean interiors and exterior earth coverings. Earthlodges varied greatly in size, and among Plains peoples earthlodges served as domestic structures, but they also played important roles in communal social, political, and **religious** rituals. Eastern Woodlands peoples constructed earthlodges not as domiciles, but as ceremonial structures. These buildings were usually located near the center of villages, with **ethnohistorical** and **archaeological** data indicating that they served as meeting places for community **councils** and as settings for certain **religious** rituals. *See also* COUNCIL HOUSES.

EARTHWORK. Any of a number of distinct types of public structures built by Native Americans through the excavation and embankment of earth. Earthworks were constructed across the North American continent, serving such diverse purposes as **burial mounds**, astronomical observatories, and defensive **fortifications**. The term most commonly appears in the North American **archaeological** literature in reference to the linear and geometrical designs of the **Adena** and **Hopewell cultures**. *See also* ARCHAEOASTRONOMY.

EASTERN AGRICULTURAL COMPLEX. Group of indigenously **domesticated** plant species of the **Eastern Woodlands** prior to the introduction of domesticated **maize** and **beans** from Mesoamerica. Plants forming this **agricultural** complex include **sumpweed** (*Iva annua*), **goosefoot** (*Chenopodium berlandieri*), **sunflowers** (*Helianthus annuus*), little barley (*Hordeum pusillum*), **knotweed** (*Polygonum erectum*), and **maygrass** (*Phalaris caroliniana*). Paleobotanical evidence indicates that Native Americans were collecting these plants as early as 6000 B.P. (4000 B.C.), with signs that many were domesticated by approximately 4000 B.P. (2000 B.C.).

EASTERN WOODLANDS CULTURE AREA. Term used to describe the various Native American groups inhabiting the wooded regions east of the Mississippi River to the Atlantic coast. During the late precontact period, most Native American groups of the Eastern Woodlands were village **agriculturalists** that supplemented their diets with **hunting** and **fishing**. These groups engaged in the construction of **earthworks**, produced exquisite **ceramics**, and engaged in long-distance **trade** networks. Native peoples of the Eastern Woodlands also exhibited high degrees of social differentiation, and are considered by many **archaeologists** to have been the most sociopolitically complex Native American societies north of **Mesoamerica**. The Eastern Woodlands **culture**

area is also frequently subdivided into the **Northeast** and **Southeast** culture areas.

EFFIGY MOUND. An **earthwork** modeled after the general shape of an animal. Effigy **mounds** have been identified in the midwestern United States, with a large number of these structures in Wisconsin and Iowa. The majority of North American effigy mounds were constructed by **Eastern Woodlands** groups between 2500 and 600 B.P. (500 B.C.–A.D. 1400). *See* ZOOMORPHIC.

EFFIGY PIPE. A Native American smoking **pipe** modeled after the general shape of a human or animal. Although many indigenous peoples constructed effigy pipes, they are most commonly associated with the **Hopewell culture** of the Ohio River valley, circa 2100–1500 B.P. (100 B.C.–A.D. 500). *See* ZOOMORPHIC.

EGALITARIAN SOCIETY. A society in which there is a general equality of persons in matters of politics and economics. Although there are no completely egalitarian societies, there are social groups in which there are minimal differences in wealth, power, prestige, and social status. These societies are usually small-scale groups, commonly referred to as **bands**. North American **archaeologists** usually interpret **Paleoindian** and later societies of the **Great Basin** and western **Great Plains** with reference to egalitarian social principals.

ELK. Name given to any of several species of large **deer** native to northern Europe, Asia, and North America belonging to the family Cervidae. The name is most properly applied to the largest member of the Cervidae family, *Alces alces*. Elk were a source of both food and skins for Native Americans, and after the arrival of Europeans, became important components of **trade**. *See also* FUR TRADE; HUNTING.

EPIDEMIC DISEASE. A widespread outbreak of contagious pathogens within a population. Epidemic **diseases** are thought to have dramatically impacted Native American societies as a result of European contacts. Given their reproductive isolation from European and Asian populations, Native Americans lacked the antibodies necessary for protection against common Old World diseases. When Native Americans were exposed to these illnesses, including small pox, influenza, and the common cold, they died in large numbers. Epidemiological studies of "virgin soil" epidemics like those experienced by Native Americans suggest that 80–90 percent of Native Americans died as a result of European-borne diseases.

ERICSSON, LEIF (970?–1020). Norse explorer thought to be the first European to land in North America (circa A.D. 1002). Son of Erik the Red, Leif Ericsson was charged by the Norwegian king, Olaf I, to Christianize the indigenous peoples of Greenland. His ship was blown off course, with his group landing on the Atlantic coast of North America, probably in present-day Nova Scotia. Several Norwegian sagas recount his exploration of these new lands, referred to as Vinland.

ESKIMO. A general term referring to a number of **cultural** groups who, with the closely related **Aleut**, constitute the native population of the **Arctic** and **Subarctic** regions of Greenland, Alaska, Canada, and northeastern Siberia. This designation includes groups more properly referred to as Alutiit, Iglilik, **Inuit**, Inupiat, Nunamiut, Nunivak, Yupik, and others. The name Eskimo was applied to these peoples by Europeans and is thought to derive from a Montagnais word for snowshoes. Although the name Eskimo is favored by Arctic peoples in Alaska, those in Canada and Greenland prefer Inuit. The Eskimo are of Asian origin, like other Native American groups, but they are distinguished by climatic adaptations, blood type differences, and language (**Aleut–Eskimo Linguistic Group**). **Anthropologists** interpret this uniqueness as evidence that Eskimo peoples are relatively recent migrants to North America from northeastern Asia, arriving only during the last 5,000 years.

Although Eskimo groups are distinct in their material culture, **hunting** methods, and **subsistence** practices, they share adaptations to extremely cold, snow- and ice-bound environments, with diets that are heavily reliant upon **caribou**, fish, and marine mammals. Elaborate **harpoons** and seagoing craft (including **kayaks** and **umiaks**) were developed for hunting whales and other large marine mammals, while clothing was produced from caribou and **seal**. Domestic architecture varied seasonally, with snow-block igloos or semisubterranean sod and stone houses used in winter, and animal-skin tents erected in the summer. At present, there are approximately 45,000 Eskimo in Alaska, 20,000 in Canada, 50,000 in Greenland and Denmark, and 1,500 in Siberia.

ETHNOARCHAEOLOGY. A form of **ethnographic analogy** that relies on the use of information from living groups as a source of potential insights to aid in understanding past human action. Ethnoarchaeology centers on the study of contemporary cultures in order to better understand relationships between the production and use of material culture. **Processual archaeologists** saw this practice as providing a new source of interpretive insight into the patterns revealed in the **archaeological** record. North American archaeologists have used ethnoarchaeological studies of Eskimo and Aleutian groups to better understand the nature of Paleoindian **hunting** techniques, **tool** production, and social structure.

ETHNOGRAPHIC ANALOGY. The use of ethnographic information collected from historically recorded **cultures** as a means of interpreting patterning in **archaeological** remains. Building upon the detailed ethnographic descriptions of extant cultures, ethnographic analogies are thought to provide "living" correlates that aid in the understanding of past social life.

ETHNOHISTORY. The study of a **culture's** development and change through the use of written records, oral histories, material culture, **archaeological** remains, and ethnographic sources. Ethnohistorians usually combine the perspectives of **anthropologists** and historians to examine the nature of historical cultural development within a society. Ethnohistorical studies in North America have traditionally addressed the myriad changes that took place in Native American societies after they experienced contact with Europeans.

ETOWAH SITE. Archaeological site near present-day Cartersville, Georgia, that was the center of a large Native American **chiefdom** during the **Mississippian** period, circa 1100–450 B.P. (A.D. 900–1500). Located near the confluence of the Etowah River and

Pumpkinvine Creek, the Etowah site contains at least seven earthen **mounds**, an expansive plaza flanked by residential areas, and a surrounding defensive ditch. Excavations on Mound C, the largest mound at Etowah at more than 18 meters in height (63 feet), suggest that the polity was ruled by **chiefs** who combined their secular administrative duties with those of priestly rituals. A large number of **burials** were also excavated from mound contexts at Etowah, demonstrating dramatic differences in access to exotic artifacts between commoners and elites. Among the most notable **artifacts** recovered from Etowah are elaborate repose **copper** ornaments and carved shell **gorgets**. Etowah had extensive contacts with other Mississippian polities in the **Southeast**, with evidence of **trade** in copper, seashells, and nonlocal **lithic** materials. By the time of **Hernando de Soto's** expedition, Etowah was no longer a dominant town, with present evidence suggesting that the site was abandoned sometime in the middle 16th century.

EVA SITE. Archaeological site located in western Tennessee along an extinct channel of the Tennessee River. The Eva site contains four sealed **stratigraphic** deposits dated as early as 7200 B.P. These early materials relate to a semipermanent Early **Archaic** settlement, with the majority of **artifacts** and **faunal remains** indicating specialized **deer-hunting** activities at the site (including **atlatls** and **bannerstones**). A large number of **burials** recovered from the Eva site suggest that the site was occupied by a stable and somewhat homogenous group of people, with evidence of increased longevity among site occupants. Additional **cultural** materials from the site include **awls**, fishhooks, scrapers, bone **beads**, red **ocher**, and nutstones.

EXCHANGE. Patterns of human interaction that involve the transfer of material goods or services between individuals or societies. Exchange occurs within local communities, between communities, over long distances, and between members of the same **culture** and those from different cultures. Exchange includes transactions carried out for economic reasons such as **trade**, as well as the ceremonial transference of symbolically valuable objects. Exchange networks existed in prehistoric and historic times in North America, linking populations through commercial and social contacts.

EXTINCTION. Biological concept that applies to the termination of a species. Extinction occurs when a species can no longer reproduce itself at replacement level due to an inability to cope with changing conditions in its environment. Most extinctions result from environmental change, but humans are thought to have contributed to the extinction of plant and animal species as well. Through **hunting** and the destruction of natural habitats, **Paleoindians** are thought to have contributed to the extinction of North American **megafauna**. Extinction has also been applied to situations where a human cultural group can no longer pursue its traditional ways of life and thus ceases to exist as an identifiable, autonomous **culture**. *See also* BLITZKRIEG MODEL.

– F –

FAUNAL REMAINS. General term referring to animal remains from **archaeological** sites. Studies of faunal remains reveal much about past environments, site seasonality, and human **subsistence** practices. The archaeological analysis of past human use of animals and plants is normally considered part of the field of faunal analysis. Studies of animal remains from North American archaeological sites provide information critical to the understanding of Native American animal **domestication**, dietary preferences, **subsistence** practices, and human dietary adaptations to environmental change.

FEASTS. Ritual social acts involving the preparation and dispersal of foodstuffs. **Anthropological** evidence from North America indicates that feasts played an important role in the social life of local communities, especially when observing special events like marriages, funerals, and other **religious** observances. **Archaeological** data from **Mississippian** societies in eastern North America demonstrates the importance of feasting rituals to local political economies and sociopolitical relations. Another example of Native American feasts is the **potlatch** of the **Pacific Northwest**.

FEWKES, JESSE W. (1850–1930). American ethnographer and **archaeologist** who pioneered the field of **ethnoarchaeology**. His principal ethnoarchaeological research focused on Tusayan Pueblo and **Mesa Verde** in the **Southwest**. He was also responsible for some of the earliest uses of wax cylinder recording to preserve Native American music and oral history.

FIGURINE. Small stone or **ceramic artifact** modeled after a living creature. Figurines modeled on the human form are considered **anthropomorphic**, while those shaped like animals are **zoomorphic**. Many Native American cultures produced figurines, with these items primarily used in **religious** rituals. Stone figurines from **Cahokia** and other **Mississippian** sites suggest that these artifacts were commonly used in **agricultural** fertility rituals.

FIREARMS. General term applied to projectile-firing weapons. Firearms played an important role in Native American and European interactions, revolutionizing the nature of indigenous **hunting** and **warfare**. These weapons varied from early muzzle-loaded, matchlock, flintlock, and percussion-lock muskets to later breech-loading rifles. Firearms increased the mortality rates of Native American warfare and the ability of indigenous hunters to kill more game.

FIRE-CRACKED ROCK (FCR). Rocks that have been cracked or broken by direct exposure to the heat of a fire. Commonly referred to as FCR, these objects are frequently found in association with **fire-hearths**. The presence of FCR on **archaeological** sites is usually an indicator of pre**ceramic** Native American occupations in the **Eastern Woodlands**. However, FCR has been recovered from Native American archaeological sites in other regions.

FIREHEARTH. An **archaeological** feature containing ash, charcoal, burned rocks, and/or other evidence of an intentionally set, human-controlled fire. Native Americans used hearths to cook food, to warm the interior of their houses, and occasionally for surface-firing **ceramics**.

FISHING. The intentional procurement of fish by humans as a means of **subsistence**. Native American fishers used hook-and-line techniques as well as **fish weirs** and other techniques to catch fish. There is also limited evidence to suggest that some Native American groups in the **Southeast** stocked human-made ponds to ensure the ready availability of fish.

FISH WEIR. A wattled fence placed in a stream to catch fish. These structures made use of natural topography, currents, and tidal actions (depending on their location), and were designed to efficiently capture large numbers of fish. Although most fish weirs were relatively small, some were quite extensive, including the **Boylston Street fish weir** in present-day Boston. *See also* FISHING.

FIVE CIVILIZED TRIBES. Term applied to the **Cherokee**, **Chickasaw**, **Choctaw**, **Creek**, and **Seminole** of the **Southeast**. These groups were seen as more compliant with the American policy of "civilizing" Native Americans, with each having a stable **agricultural** economy, a written constitution, and judiciary and legislative systems based on those of the United States. Reprisals by the U.S. government following the Civil War restricted many of the political freedoms previously enjoyed by these tribes, severely limiting their autonomy in political and judicial matters.

FIVE NATIONS. Confederation of culturally distinct Native American groups composed of the **Mohawk**, Oneida, **Onondaga**, **Cayuga**, and **Seneca**. Also referred to as the **Iroquois** League or **Iroquois Confederacy**, this group eventually expanded to include the Tuscarora and other groups. The Five Nations occupied a territory from the Hudson River to the St. Lawrence River and west to the Genesee River.

FLAKE. A thin, flattened piece of stone intentionally removed from a **core** by chipping with a stone, bone, or antler hammer. **Archaeologists** use the spatial distribution of flakes and their place in the reduction process to reconstruct the sequence of **lithic tool** production. In addition, many archaeological sites lack formal stone tools, with the only direct evidence of human presence at these sites the presence of flakes. *See also* DEBITAGE.

FLINT RUN COMPLEX. A group of **Clovis** sites clustered around a jasper outcrop in the Shenandoah Valley of Virginia. These sites are thought to represent a local population of between 500 to 1,000 people at approximately 8300 B.C. (6300 B.C.). Individual site types in the complex include both residential areas and stone-processing areas.

FLORAL REMAINS. General term referring to plant remains from **archaeological** sites. Studies of floral remains reveal much about past environments, site seasonality, and human **subsistence** practices. The archaeological analysis of past human plant use is normally considered part of the field of paleoethnobotany (also referred to as archaeobotany). Studies of floral remains from North American archaeological sites provide information critical to the reconstruction of Native American plant use and the process of plant **domestication**.

FLOTATION. Technique for recovering small particles of organic materials from **archaeological** soils. Sediments from specific archaeological contexts are immersed in water, and organic particles that float to the surface or sink to the bottom of the flotation tank are collected for additional analysis. Flotation is an essential method for recovering microfloral and microfaunal remains for archaeological analysis. This technique has allowed North American archaeologists to recover microscopic plant remains related to human subsistence practices and allowed them to identify the presence of previously unknown **domesticated** plant species. Flotation has also proved useful in the recovery and identification of fish remains from archaeological contexts.

FLUTE. A characteristic attribute of **Paleoindian projectile points** (especially **Clovis** and **Folsom**), where a thinning **flake** has been removed longitudinally on one or both sides of the **artifact**, resulting in a central concave channel or groove. Flutes allowed projectile points to be hafted securely to spears for use in **hunting**. These characteristics are considered to be diagnostic stylistic traits of the earliest big-game **hunting cultures** in the Americas.

FOLSOM CULTURE. **Archaeological culture** defined by the presence of a distinct type of **fluted projectile point** associated with the hunting of **megafauna**. Known as *Folsom points*, these fluted projectile points have been found in direct association with the remains of several extinct **megafaunal** species, including ancient **bison**. Dated to between 11,000 and 10,000 B.P., the Folsom tradition is thought to have developed out of the earlier **Clovis culture**. Folsom and subsequent research have revealed their presence over much of the North American continent.

FOLSOM POINTS. Distinct type of **fluted projectile point** associated with the **Paleoindian Folsom culture** of North America during the period between 11,000 and 10,000 B.P. These fluted points were first recovered from **archaeological** deposits near Folsom, New Mexico, with subsequent research revealing their presence over much of the North American continent.

FOLSOM SITE. Archaeological site in northeastern New Mexico with evidence of **Paleoindian** presence at approximately 11,000 B.P. Discovered in the 1920s, the Folsom Site is the type site for the **Folsom culture**, and is a location where several **bison** of a presently extinct species were killed and **butchered** by Paleoindian people. This site contains direct association between these **extinct** bison and a distinct type of **fluted projectile point** known as *Folsom points*. These fluted points were given the name *Folsom*, and subsequent research has revealed their presence over much of the North American continent.

FOOD. Native American groups **subsisted** upon a wide variety of plants and animals, with local diets shaped by cultural food preferences, **subsistence** technologies, and locally available resources. **Foraging** groups took advantage of nuts, weeds, grasses, fruits, and roots, as well as local animal species. **Agricultural** groups continued to collect local subsistence resources while fulfilling the majority of their food needs through the **cultivation** of **domesticated** plants. *See also* ACORNS; AGAVE; ANTELOPE; BEANS; BEAR; BEAVER; BISON; CARIBOU; CHENOPODIUM BERLANDIERI; DEER; ELK; FISHING; GOURDS; KNOTWEED; MAIZE; MARSHELDER; MASTODON; MAYGRASS; OTTER; PIÑON SEEDS; PRIMARY FOREST EFFICIENCY; PRONGHORN; QUID; SALMON; SCREWBEAN; SEAL; SQUASH; SUMPWEED; TEOSINTE; TURKEY.

FORAGING. Subsistence regime based on collecting wild plants, **hunting** non**domesticated** animals, and **fishing**. Also referred to as "hunting and gathering," the vast majority of foraging groups are small **band** societies that engage in seasonal migrations to maximize their access to available food resources. Native American societies were foragers for thousands of years prior to the development of **agriculture**.

FORD, JAMES A. (1911–1968). North American **archaeologist** with a primary research interest in the **Southeast**. Ford began his archaeological studies while a high school student, eventually earning a Ph.D. and becoming one of the most important figures in American archaeology. Ford undertook research in Mississippi, Louisiana, and other Southeastern states, and participated in archaeological expeditions to Alaska, Mexico, and South America. He served as a curator at the American Museum of Natural History in New York, and is perhaps best known for his refinement of interpretive methodologies in archaeology, including **stratigraphy**, typology, and **seriation**. His theoretical orientation was largely based in **culture history**, with Ford favoring interpretations of **cultural** developments based on the diffusion of cultural practices from one group to another. His last work, *A Comparison of Formative Cultures in the Americas*, which was published posthumously, presented his perspective on the diffusion of cultural practices among the peoples of the Americas.

FORMATION PROCESSES. Processes of both natural and human origin that affect the present form taken of the **archaeological** record. Cultural formation processes include the deliberate or accidental activities of humans that impact **artifacts** and features after their use, while natural formation processes refer to environmental events that impact the disposition of artifacts and features after their use. North American archaeologist Michael Schiffer has conducted extensive research into the ways in which formation processes affect the temporal and spatial nature of the archaeological record.

FORT ANCIENT CULTURE. Native American **culture** located along the Ohio River valley and its tributaries from approximately 1000 to 350 B.P. (A.D. 900–1600). Fort Ancient was once thought to be a local variant of **Mississippian culture** but is now seen as an independent contemporaneous cultural development. These peoples practiced a mixed **subsistence** regime, with evidence of **agriculture** supplemented by **foraging**. The culture was transformed during the early **historic period**, with an influx of indigenous groups such as the **Delaware**, **Miami**, and Shawnee into the region. Fort Ancient culture is thought to have disappeared in response to European-introduced **diseases** and the **acculturation** of local populations to the cultural practices of immigrant groups.

FORT DE CHARTRES. French fort located on the Mississippi River in Illinois. First constructed in 1720, Fort de Chartres was designed to protect French **colonial** interests in the region against English expansion. The fort was constructed three separate times between 1720 and 1763, and served as the center for French colonial administration of the Illinois country. The fort was transferred to English control at the conclusion of the French and Indian War (1765). The English renamed it Fort Cavendish, finally abandoning it in 1771. **Archaeological** investigations and historical reconstructions at Fort de Chartres have added a great deal to our understanding of the colonial experience of the French, English, and Native Americans on the frontier.

FORTIFICATION. Structure erected to protect a military position, **trade** center, or settlement against attack. Fortifications range from ditches and low walls to high walls with bastions, ramparts, bafflegates, ditches, towers, and other elements of military architecture. Native American sites were frequently fortified during both the prehistoric and **historic periods**. The most extensive fortifications in North America are those found at many large late prehistoric towns in the **Southeast** and **Great Plains** (particularly those of the upper Missouri River region). *See also* PALISADE; WARFARE.

FORT MICHILIMACKINAC. French fort located at the northern tip of Michigan on the south shore of the Straits of Mackinac, where Lake Michigan meets Lake Huron. Constructed in 1715, Fort Michilimackinac was a trading center for the French **fur trade**, linking Europeans and Native Americans from Montreal throughout the Great Lakes region and beyond. The French surrendered the fort to the English in 1761 at the conclusion of the French and Indian War. The English continued to use the fort in much the same way as the French. However, local Native American groups, the **Ojibwa** and **Ottawa** in particular, disliked English trade policies and ultimately participated in an attack on the fort during Pontiac's Rebellion. The English constructed a new fort on Mackinac Island in 1781 and abandoned Fort Michilimackinac. **Archaeological** investigations and historical reconstructions at this and other forts have added a great deal to our understanding of the **colonial** experience of the French, English, and Native Americans on the North American frontier.

FORT ROSS. Russian fort and **trading** post established on the Sonoma Coast of California in 1812. Constructed as a center for sea **otter hunting** and the **cultivation** of wheat and other **agricultural** products needed by Russian settlements in Alaska, Fort Ross allowed the Russians to counter the Spanish **colonization** of California. It also served as a trading post between the Russians and local Native American peoples. In 1841 the Russians abandoned Fort Ross and their California territories. **Archaeological** investigations and historical reconstructions at Fort Ross have added a great deal to our understanding of Russian relations with Native Americans and the colonization of the Pacific Coast.

FOX INDIANS. Algonquian-speaking Native American group who share many elements of **culture** with the **Sauk**. The Fox occupied an area of eastern Michigan, but were forced to abandon this area in the early 17th century due to increased **warfare** with the **Ottawa**. The Fox, together with the Sauk, migrated north across the Straits of Mackinac, eventually settling in present-day Wisconsin. When recorded by Father Claude Jean Allouez in 1667, the Fox were located in the area around Green Bay. The Fox were a potent military force and engaged in near-constant **warfare** with the **Ojibwa** and other groups. The Fox and Sauk banded together for mutual defense, fighting wars against the **Illinois**, **Sioux**, and French. Military incursions by the French dramatically reduced the Fox population, eventually leading to the merging of the Fox and Sauk peoples. During the middle 18th century, the Fox moved into the Illinois territory. They were forcibly removed to lands west of the Mississippi in the 1830s, but returned to reclaim their Illinois lands during the Black Hawk War. After the end of hostilities, the Fox moved west, settling on reservations in Iowa, Kansas, and Oklahoma. At present, there are approximately 5,000 Fox in the United States.

FRANCISCANS. Members of a Catholic **religious** order founded in 1209 by St. Francis of Assisi. Franciscans take vows of extreme poverty, and friars can own no property of any kind, either individually or communally. Franciscans were among the most prominent Catholic missionaries of the colonial period in North America, and their impact on Native American cultures through missionization and the introduction of European **diseases** and material goods was immense.

FREMONT CULTURE. **Archaeological culture** found in present-day Utah and areas of Idaho, Colorado, and Nevada from about 1300 to 600 B.P. (A.D. 650–1350). Deriving its name from the archaeological remains in the Fremont River valley, Fremont culture is considered a variation of the better known **Puebloan** cultures to the south, particularly the **Anasazi**. Unlike the Anasazi, however, Fremont peoples lived in **pit houses**, **wickiups**, and **rockshelters**. Fremont settlements indicate that their social structure consisted of small, multifamily **bands**, with little social distinction between groups. Although they practiced **agriculture**, Fremont peoples remained largely **foragers**, collecting wild **piñon** nuts, rice grass, and various berries, nuts, and tubers, while **hunting deer**, bighorn sheep, rabbits, birds, and fish. Fremont material culture reveals distinctive styles of **basketry**, **ceramics**, leather moccasins, and **anthropomorphic** clay **figurines**. In addition, Fremont sites often contain **zoomorphic** and anthropomorphic **pictographs** and **petroglyphs**. Increased aridity in their traditional territory is thought to have forced the Fremont peoples to abandon their settlements around 600 B.P. and adopt a more nomadic lifestyle.

FREQUENCY SERIATION. Relative **dating** method that uses fluctuations in the proportional abundance (frequency) of **artifact** types within **assemblages** to measure changes in material culture through time. Pioneered in the United States by **A. L. Kroeber**, this type of analysis relies upon the assumption that the popularity of **artifact** types varies through time and that the relative frequencies of these variations can be used to date **archaeological** materials. Archaeologists **James A. Ford** and **James Deetz** produced some of the best-known examples of frequency seriation research. Frequency seriation was extremely important in the early development of cultural chronologies for North American archaeological sites prior to development of **radiocarbon dating**.

FROBISHER, MARTIN (1535?–1594). English explorer who made three voyages (1576, 1577, and 1578) to the **Arctic** in search of the fabled Northwest Passage. He explored Frobisher Bay and Baffin Island, eventually traveling a short distance up the Hudson Strait on his third voyage. The narratives of his voyages (1578) provide some of the earliest descriptions of local Native American groups.

FUR TRADE. Term used to describe the complex economic system linking European **traders** and Native American **hunters** from the 17th century to the 19th century (also referred to as the **deerskin** trade in the **Southeast**). Based on the procurement of animal skins and pelts by Native American hunters and their **exchange** for European trade goods, the fur trade became the primary way in which many Native Americans interacted with Europeans. The fur trade developed in response to increased demand for fur and leather goods in Europe, and had a tremendous impact on Native Americans and animal populations. The fur trade played an important role in the exploration and **colonization** of the interior of North America by Europeans. The impacts upon Native Americans were considerable, including the introduction of large numbers of **firearms** and other trade goods, as well as European **diseases**.

– G –

GARBAGE PROJECT. Study of modern waste disposal designed to investigate areas of consumption and disposal using archaeological methods. Directed by William Rathje, this project focused on issues of food waste, diet and nutrition, recycling, and toxic waste disposal.

Findings from this research are thought to have implications for the study of modern societies and more traditional **archaeological** studies.

GATECLIFF SHELTER SITE. Archaeological site in the Monitor Valley of Nevada containing more than 10 meters (30 feet) of stratified archaeological deposits within a **rockshelter**. Earliest evidence of human occupation at the site dates to approximately 5500 B.P. (3500 B.C.). Excavations by David Hurst Thomas at Gatecliff revealed more than 30 distinct occupations, with excellent evidence of cultural and environmental changes in the region over the past 5,000 years.

GATHERING. The collection of wild foods as a principal means of **subsistence**. Gathering requires an extensive knowledge of edible plants in the local environment as well as knowledge of their seasonal availability. Most gathering societies also supplemented their diets with **hunting**, **fishing**, or both. *See also* FORAGING.

GENDER ROLES. Gender roles and the sexual division of labor among Native American societies varied widely. The general stereotype is that men engaged in **hunting**, **warfare**, and political activities while women engaged in **agriculture**, collecting, child-rearing, **ceramic** production, and other domestic activities. However, like most stereotypes, there is much that this simple dichotomy fails to acknowledge. Among some Native American societies of the **Great Plains** and **Southwest**, alternative genders, commonly referred to as **berdache**, were recognized as being something unique: neither male nor female, nor simply a combination of the two.

Gender roles and the sexual division of labor varied based on the nature of each group's principal means of social organization. Thus, those who favored matrilineality tended to reinforce female roles in **subsistence** practices and recognized property rights through female lines. More patrilineal societies tended to reinforce the social importance of male property ownership and the contributions of males to subsistence. Prominent social positions were commonly filled by males in most Native American societies, but there were societies, like the **Chitimacha**, in which women not only participated in making important social decisions but also served as the preeminent socio-political leaders.

Like most aspects of Native American life, contacts with Europeans had dramatic impacts on the sexual division of labor for indigenous peoples. For the **agricultural** societies of the **Eastern Woodlands**, these impacts were primarily felt in the pressure exerted by the **colonial** Americans for men to take a more active role in farming. This was anathema to most Native American males, since their traditional practices made females responsible for almost all agricultural activities.

GERONIMO (1829–1890). Apache leader who resisted forced removal from lands granted to the Apache in treaties with the United States. Geronimo gained fame in the 1870s by leading a group of Chiricahua Apache warriors in armed resistance against U.S. forces. He eventually began raiding American settlements in Arizona and New Mexico. He was captured by American forces in 1886 and was allowed to settle in Oklahoma. Geronimo's reputation as a warrior and resistance fighter led to great fame.

GHOST DANCE. Religious ritual practiced by Native Americans in the western **Great Plains** in the late 19th century. Developing out of the visions of **Paiute** prophet Wovoka, the Ghost Dance presented a messianic vision of Native American **cultural** revival. The religion preached the return of the dead, the end of the westward expansion of whites, as well as the restoration of Native American lands and cultural **traditions**. The Ghost Dance lasted for five days, with dancers reported to have experienced trances and convulsive shaking. The Ghost Dance spread rapidly among Native American **cultures**, culminating with the Sioux outbreak of 1890 and the subsequent massacre at Wounded Knee on December 29, 1890.

GLACIAL KAME CULTURE. Late **Archaic archaeological culture** of southern Ontario, southern Michigan, northern Indiana, and northwestern Ohio during the period from 3500 to 3000 B.P. (1500–1000 B.C.). Glacial Kame culture is distinguished by a preference for interring the dead in natural **mounds** of glacial gravel. It is believed that these mounds served as territorial markers and were the precursors of a **burial mound** tradition of the Midwest.

GLACIATION. The process through which land becomes covered by sheets of ice (glaciers). The temporal periods during which glaciers form are referred to as *glacials*, while the warmer periods falling between glacial periods are called *interglacials*. During the onset of glaciation, water is bound up in expanding glaciers, causing a corresponding drop in sea levels. It was just such glaciation events that led to the exposure of **Beringia**, allowing humans and animals to pass between northeastern Asia and North America. When climates warmed, the glaciers melted, resulting in higher sea levels and the separation of the Asian and North American continents.

GLADWIN CLASSIFICATION SYSTEM. System proposed by **Harold Gladwin** and Winifred Gladwin for classifying the cultures of the American **Southwest**. In part a response to the **Pecos classification system**, the Gladwin system represented the **cultures** of the Southwest as a dendritic system, with the three major regional cultures (**Anasazi**, **Mogollon**, and **Hohokam**) serving as the roots from which intraregional cultures developed. Geographical areas within these three culture areas were then divided into stems and branches. Relying on the application of culture trait lists, the Gladwin system proceeded from the idea that Southwestern cultures shared a common origin, evolving over time into their historic forms.

GLADWIN, HAROLD S. (1883–1983). Stockbroker turned **archaeologist**, Gladwin had an abiding interest in the prehistory of the North American **Southwest**. After making his fortune in the financial markets, Gladwin turned his interests in archaeology to a full-time pursuit in the 1920s. He conducted excavations at **Casa Grande** in Arizona in 1927, using **ceramics** to create a cultural sequence for the region. His research laid much of the groundwork for understanding the development of the various **culture** groups in the Southwest. Despite his academic contributions, Gladwin advocated pseudoscientific perspectives on the migration of Old World cultures into the Americas, discrediting himself within the professional archaeological community. *See also* GLADWIN CLASSIFICATION SYSTEM.

GODDARD SITE. Native American **archaeological** site located on Penobscot Bay, Maine. This site is considered important because of the presence of a Norwegian silver penny minted between A.D. 1065 and 1080. The Native American context of this **artifact** is dated to the 12th or 13th century, suggesting either direct or indirect contact between the Norse and local Native American peoples. Most archeologists believe this object was **traded** to local people from **Dorset** groups in Labrador or Newfoundland. *See also* L'ANSE AUX MEADOWS.

GOOSEFOOT. *See CHENOPODIUM BERLANDIERI.*

GORGET. A relatively large, flat, or gently curving decorative object of polished stone, shell, or metal, worn around the neck. Native American **cultures** produced an array of gorget forms, with the most common being those of carved shell produced during the **Mississippian** period. These Mississippian carved shell gorgets often contain elaborate engraving and fenestration of an **anthropomorphic** and **zoomorphic** nature. These gorgets are considered part of the **Southeastern Ceremonial Complex**.

GOSHEN COMPLEX. Name given to a distinct **Paleoindian foraging** tradition of the northern **Plains**. Defined by **archaeologist** George Frison based on his research at the **Hell Gap site** in Wyoming, the Goshen complex is contemporaneous with **Clovis**, but appears to have been a distinct **cultural tradition**. Defined largely on the presence of distinctive **projectile points**, known as *Goshen points*, sites related to this cultural complex are dated to between 11,300 and 10,400 B.P. (9200–8400 B.C.).

GOURDS. Any of the approximately 700 species of plants that constitute the family *Cucurbitaceae*. Gourds are annual herbaceous plants native to temperate and tropical areas. This plant family includes melons, **squash**, and pumpkins, all staple foods for Native American **cultures** practicing **agriculture**. In addition to their contribution to Native American diets, gourds were frequently dried and used as containers. Some archaeologists contend that gourd containers may have influenced the development of **ceramic** containers by Native Americans.

GRAVE GOODS. Objects intentionally placed in a **burial**. Also called grave inclusions, mortuary goods, and funerary offerings, grave goods normally consist of **tools**, weapons, food, or other utilitarian or ceremonial objects placed with the deceased. These items are related to the social standing of the deceased and the groups with which they were affiliated in life. In addition, grave goods are interpreted as a representation of **religious** beliefs concerning death and the afterlife. **Archaeologists** attribute much of their knowledge of prehistoric Native American cultural practices to the analysis of human remains and grave goods. However, recent legal developments in the United States have limited archaeological investigations of human burials. *See also* BURIAL; NATIVE AMERICAN GRAVE PROTECTION AND REPATRIATION ACT.

GREAT BASIN CULTURE AREA. Geographic area composed of the various local environments that lie between the Sierra Nevada and Rocky Mountains in the present-day states of Nevada, Utah, western Colorado, southeastern Oregon, southern Idaho, western Wyoming, eastern California, as well as northern Arizona. This region is characterized by extreme variations in altitude, rainfall, temperature, and vegetation. During the late **Pleistocene**, it had greater rainfall and possessed a greater density of plant and animal species. **Archaeological** evidence of **Paleoindian** occupation indicates that camels, wild horses, and **mammoth** were common in this region. By 10,000 B.P. (8000 B.C.), local environments resembled more closely their modern counterparts.

Native American groups living in the Great Basin were generally small and seasonally mobile. Some groups in the southeast portion of the Great Basin practiced limited horticulture during the period from 1000 to 600 B.P. (A.D. 1000–1350). These peoples, commonly referred to as **Fremont** and Virgin River **Anasazi**, cultivated **maize**, **beans**, and **squash**, and lived in sedentary communities. However, climate change in the region forced them to adopt a more mobile lifestyle. During the **historic period**, the Great Basin was home to the Chemehuevi, **Comanche**, Kawaiisu, **Pauites**, **Shoshone**, **Utes**, Washo, and other groups. These peoples exhibited remarkable linguistic uniformity, with most speaking closely related dialects of the **Uto-Aztecan language family**.

GREAT PLAINS CULTURE AREA. A largely treeless grassland extending from the Mississippi River valley west to the Rocky Mountains, and south from present-day Manitoba, Saskatchewan, and Alberta to central Texas. The earliest evidence of human occupation of the Great Plains are **Paleoindian** sites (circa 12,000 B.P. [10,000 B.C.]) related to big-game **hunting**. By about 7500 B.P. (5500 B.C.), regional **cultural** adaptations demonstrate a reduced reliance upon **megafauna** (primarily **bison**) and an increase in **foraging** activities. Between 2500 and 350 B.P. (500 B.C.–A.D. 1600), marked differences in **subsistence** regimes between eastern and western Plains groups develop, with eastern Plains groups adopting sedentary, village **agriculture**. Eastern Plains peoples began to construct **fortified** villages and semisubterranean **earthlodges**. These eastern agricultural groups are considered ancestral to the modern **Arikara**, **Hidatsa**, **Mandan**, **Pawnee**, **Wichita**, and other groups. Western Plains groups continued as mobile foragers, and with the introduction of the **horse** they became focused on **bison** hunting as their primary subsistence activity. These groups became increasingly mobile, with the **tipi** serving as their primary domestic structure. These nomadic groups of the western Plains are considered ancestral to the modern **Blackfoot**, **Crow**, **Cheyenne**, **Comanche**, **Sioux** (Dakota), and other groups. Other well-known Great Plains peoples include the Comanche, **Kiowa**, Sioux, Pawnee, and **Blackfoot**.

Many contemporary stereotypes of Native Americans are drawn from the cultural practices of Great Plains peoples, including **tipi**s, feathered headdresses, and the Plains horse culture. However, many of these practices were not long-standing regional cultural traditions, but were brought about as a result of both direct and indirect contact with Europeans.

GREAT SUN, THE. Title of the preeminent social leader among the **Natchez Indians** of the **Southeast**. Simultaneously serving as **chief** and priest, the Great Sun was considered divine, receiving extreme social deference from commoners. The Great Sun was carried on a litter, resided in a secluded structure atop a **mound**, and possessed the power of life and death over his subjects. Such deference apparently did not end with the death of the Great Sun, with descriptions of the **burial** ritual of **Tattooed Serpent** indicating that his funerary rite included sacrificial retainers to serve him in the next life. Descriptions of the Great Sun's power over Natchez social, political, economic, and **religious**

affairs are frequently used as a source of ethnographic analogies for the prerogatives of social elites during the **Mississippian** period.

GREEN CORN CEREMONY. Religious ceremony practiced by Native American groups of the **Eastern Woodlands** to celebrate the annual harvesting of **maize** crops. The ceremony was the most important community ritual for most Native American groups of the Eastern Woodlands, and was held in the ceremonial ground located near the center of the village. Included in the rituals constituting the green corn ceremony were a series of dances, games, and the relighting of community fires by local priests. This ceremony was a time of ritual purification of the community, for settling past disputes between community members, and for giving thanks to the gods for the gift of maize.

GREEN RIVER CULTURE. Regional variation of the **Central Riverine Archaic tradition** along the Ohio and Green Rivers in present-day southern Indiana and northern Kentucky. Dated to between 5000 and 4000 B.P. (3000–2000 B.C.), the Green River peoples lived in large, semisedentary communities and produced large shell **middens**. **Subsistence** practices were based upon the collection of locally available plants, supplemented by **hunting**, **fishing**, and the **gathering** of freshwater mussels. **Archaeological** evidence from the Indian Knoll site, the best-studied Green River site, indicates that their society was largely **egalitarian**; however, **burial** evidence suggests that some form of social ranking may have been present.

GRIFFIN, JAMES BENNETT (1905–1997). Prominent American **archaeologist** whose research centered on the prehistory of the **Eastern Woodlands**. Griffin was one of the foremost North American **ceramic** analysts, with his research forming much of the basis for the regional prehistories of the Midwest and **Southeast**. He advocated the use of advanced statistical techniques and emerging scientific methods in archaeological studies. He was among the first North American archaeologists to employ **radiocarbon dating**, and spectrographic analysis and neutron activation analysis of archaeological materials. Griffin also made major contributions to North American archaeology by training numerous students during his nearly 40 years of research and teaching at the University of Michigan.

GROUND STONE. General term used to refer to stone **tools** that have been modified through grinding. Also used to describe the surface appearance that results from pounding stones against each other during the processing (especially grinding) of seeds or other plant material. **Manos**, **metates**, and mortars and pestles are the most common types of ground stone **artifacts**, but **axes**, **pipes**, and **beads** are also commonly found on North American **archaeological** sites.

– H –

HAFTING. The attachment of a stone **blade** to a shaft or handle through the use of binding elements such as string or sinew. Hafted tools are more efficient than their unhafted counterparts and are capable of being used for a much wider variety of productive tasks.

HAIDA INDIANS. Indigenous people of the **Northwest Coast** who resided on the Queen Charlotte Islands, British Columbia, and portions of Prince of Wales Island in southeast Alaska. The Haida speak a Nadene language, and are closely related to the **Tlingit** and **Tsimshian**. Haida **subsistence** was based on the gathering of wild plants, **hunting**, and **fishing**. They practiced matrilineal descent, and were organized into **clans** that belonged to either the Raven or Eagle moieties. These matriclans were the basic landowning and ceremonial units of Haida society, with **chiefs** selected from the most prominent clans. Each lineage and clan also had its own totemic marker that was commonly carved into house posts and decorative "totem poles." Like most groups of the Northwest Coast, the major Haida social ceremony was the **potlatch**. The Haida continue to be known for their woodworking craftsmanship and decorative arts. At present, there are approximately 4,000 Haida living in the United States and Canada.

HALLUCINOGENS. Substances that produce dramatic alterations to perception and profound psychological effects. Normally associated with dreams, schizophrenia, or **religious** visions, hallucinogens distort perceptions, thoughts, and emotions. Many Native American peoples cultivated or collected naturally hallucinogenic substances for use in religious rituals. Rather than being used for recreation, **to-bacco**, mescaline, and other substances played a role in **shamanic** rituals where altered states of consciousness were thought to be necessary for contact with supernatural forces.

HAMMERSTONE. A rounded, largely unmodified stone used as a hammer. Hammerstones were used to break open nuts and other extremely hard objects and were also employed in the production of **flaked**-stone **tools** from **cores**.

HARDAWAY SITE. A multicomponent Native American **archaeological** site located in the present state of North Carolina. The site's principal importance lies in its rich deposits dating to the Early **Archaic** period (circa 10,500–9000 B.P. [8500–7000 B.C.]). Previous research at the site indicates that Hardaway was a base camp utilized by seasonally mobile **foraging** groups.

HARPOON. Composite **tool** used by seafaring Native American peoples of the **Arctic**, **Subarctic**, and **Northwest Coast** to **hunt** whales and other large sea mammals. Harpoons consist of a spearlike shaft, fitted with a detachable barbed point that is fastened with a cord for retrieval. Hunters attempted to sink several harpoon points into a whale or other prey, with each point attached to a long cord and a flotation device (commonly an inflated sealskin). These flotation devices restrained the animal's movement, eventually forcing it to the surface where it could be killed with spears, lances, and other weapons.

HAURY, EMIL W. (1904–1992). Pioneering **archaeologist** of the American **Southwest**. Haury received his undergraduate education in anthropology from the University of Arizona and his Ph.D. from Harvard. After completing his doctorate, he returned to Arizona, where he served as the director of the Arizona State Museum and as a faculty member in the Department of Anthropology at the University of Arizona. Haury conducted extensive archaeological investigations at **Point of Pines** and other important sites in Arizona and northern Mexico. His field research led him to construct one of the most complete culture histories of the Southwest, linking historic peoples of the region to prehistoric archaeological cultures. He is most closely associated with the archaeological record of the **Mogollon** peoples of the Southwest. Haury is also notable for his advocacy of new scientific techniques in archaeology, including **dendrochronology**.

HAYNES, C. VANCE, JR. (1928–). Archaeologist and geoscientist whose career has primarily focused on improving our understanding of **Paleoindian** cultures. Known for his detailed **stratigraphic** excavations at **Blackwater Draw**, Sandia Cave, and other Paleoindian sites, Haynes has attempted to answer a series of questions regarding the earliest human occupation of the Americas. Haynes is considered one of the strongest advocates of the view that **Clovis** peoples were the first humans to migrate into the Americas across the **Bering Land Bridge**. His views also contributed to the development of **Paul S. Martin's Blitzkrieg model** for human settlement in the Americas.

HEAD-SMASHED-IN BUFFALO JUMP. Archaeological site located in the Porcupine Hills of southwestern Alberta, Canada, considered one of the earliest, largest, and best-preserved **bison jump** sites in North America. Consisting of a series of cliffs 10–18 meters (approximately 30–60 feet) in height, Head-Smashed-In was used by Native Americans of the **Great Plains** to procure bison as early as 5700 B.P. (3700 B.C.). A series of rock **cairns** above the cliffs are thought to have been used to drive bison toward the edge. This location continued to be used as a bison jump until the 19th century, with thousands of bison herded over the edge of these cliffs. Archaeological evidence for the processing of these animals includes **butchering** stations, meat caches, cooking pits, and areas of discarded bison bone.

HEARTH. *See* FIREHEARTH.

HEAT TREATMENT. Process that improves the suitability of **lithic** raw materials to be used in the production of **tools** by exposing them the heat of a fire. Heat-treated lithics have more controllable cleavage patterns, but the durability of the material may be compromised in the process.

HELL GAP SITE. Paleoindian site in southeastern Wyoming excavated by George Frison. This site is best known for the presence of a unique style of **projectile point**, known as the Hell Gap point, that is similar to Plano and **Agate Basin** projectile points. These remains are interpreted as forming the **Goshen Complex**, believed to be either a **lithic tradition** intermediate between **Clovis** and **Folsom** or simply a local variation of Clovis. This complex is dated to approximately 11,000 B.P. (9000 B.C.).

HICKORY NUTS. Small, egg-shaped nuts produced by any of 15 separate species of deciduous trees found in North America that belong to the walnut family. These nuts contain large, sweet-tasting, edible seeds that were a staple food by many Native American groups, particularly those of the **Archaic** period **Eastern Woodlands**.

HIDATSA INDIANS. Native American people of the eastern **Great Plains** who occupied territory along the upper Missouri River in the present-day state of North Dakota. A **Siouan**-speaking culture, the Hidatsa were **sedentary** village **agriculturalists** who grew **maize**, **beans**, and **squash**. Although they also participated in annual **bison** hunts, they were primarily sedentary peoples. Hidatsa social organization was based on matrilineal **clans**, but age-grade secret societies were also vital to social life. These groups included the Black Mouths, a male military society, as well as the Goose and White Buffalo Cow societies for females. The principal **religious** ceremony was the **Sun Dance**. The Hidatsa maintained close cultural ties with the **Mandan** and **Arikara**. These groups were to dominate trade relations with Europeans in the eastern Plains, becoming increasingly wealthy while serving as middlemen in the **trade** with western Plains nomadic groups. In the 19th century, European-introduced **diseases** and increased warfare with the **Dakota** diminished the role of the Hidatsa in regional trade networks and reduced their number. At present, more than 1,500 Hidatsa reside on the Fort Berthold reservation in North Dakota.

HISTORICAL ARCHAEOLOGY. **Archaeological** research directed toward the analysis of historically documented **cultures**. Historical archaeology in North America is primarily focused on archaeological remains related to the European colonization of the continent. These efforts include research on European settlements and postcontact Native American sites.

HISTORIC PERIOD. Temporal period following European contacts with Native American peoples. Since Native American peoples lacked writing, these contacts resulted in the first written documentation of indigenous cultures. However, as many scholars argue, Native Americans had oral histories and long periods of **cultural** development even without the recording of these events in written form.

HOE. An **agricultural tool** used to loosen soils prior to the planting of seeds. Native American hoes were commonly made from stone or **bison** scapulae. The presence of hoes on **archaeological** sites provides evidence that the site's occupants practiced agriculture.

HOGAN. Traditional domestic structure of the **Navajo** (Dené) peoples of the **Southwest**. A hogan is a circular wooden building with a domed roof, usually oriented with the doorway facing the rising sun. The exterior of the structure is commonly covered with mud or sod, with a small opening in the roof to vent smoke from a central hearth.

HOHOKAM. Group of Native American peoples who occupied territory in the northern Sonoran Desert of south-central Arizona and northern Mexico from approximately 2300 to 600 B.P. (circa 300 B.C.–A.D. 1400). Considered one of the three major prehistoric **cultural** traditions of the **Southwest** (the others being the **Mogollon** and **Anasazi**), major Hohokam settlements were clustered along the Gila and Salt Rivers. The Hohokam were previously thought to have been migrants from Mexico given similarities in architecture and material **culture**, but recent **archaeological** research suggests that they developed out of local **hunting and gathering** groups with extensive **trade** contacts with Mesoamerican groups to the south. The Hohokam are perhaps best known for their complex irrigation **canals** that channeled water from the highlands to their fields in the valley floor. The **agricultural** practices of the Hohokam, centered upon the cultivation of **maize**, **beans**, and **squash**, would not have been possible without these extensive canals. Around 600 B.P. (A.D. 1350), the Salt and Gila River valleys were abandoned, with an accompanying collapse of the Hohokam cultural tradition. Reasons for this abandonment are still under investigation. The **Pima** and **Papago** peoples are considered to be the most closely related extant culture groups to the Hohokam.

HOLMES, WILLIAM HENRY (1846–1933). Pioneering **archaeologist**, **anthropologist**, geologist, and artist whose career was largely devoted to the prehistory of the **Southwest**. His studies of the Southwest began with a series of landscape paintings of canyons and **cliff dwellings**. Holmes turned his interests to archaeology in the 1870s while employed by the United States Geological Survey. Holmes developed a keen interest in Native American **ceramics**, eventually accepting a position with the **Bureau of American Ethnology** (BAE) at the Smithsonian Institution. Holmes eventually served as the chief of the BAE from 1902 to 1909, completing some of the earliest BAE publications. During his later years, Holmes returned to art, becoming the first director of the National Gallery of Art, where he served from 1920 to 1933.

HOLOCENE. The current geological epoch that began at the end of the **Pleistocene** epoch, around 10,000 B.P. (8000 B.C.). The Holocene is generally characterized by a warmer climate than that of the preceding Pleistocene.

HOPEWELL CULTURE. Archaeological cultures of the **Eastern Woodlands** centered primarily along the Ohio and Illinois River valleys. Flourishing during the Middle **Woodland** period, between roughly 2100 and 1500 B.P. (circa 150 B.C.–A.D. 450), Hopewell sites are characterized by the presence of **earthen mounds** and complex, geometric **earthworks**. Rather than a single, unified **culture**, however, the Hopewell are commonly seen as a number of individual culture groups that shared commonalities in material culture and economic, social, and **religious** practices. The Hopewell peoples practiced a variety of **subsistence** practices, including horticulture and **foraging**. They were excellent potters and metalworkers, producing a variety of elaborate and highly ornate items. Hopewellian groups were linked through a series of long-distance **trade** relationships, which archaeologist Stuart Struever has referred to as the Hopewell **interaction sphere**. These interactions included trade relations linking groups as far away as the Gulf of Mexico, the eastern Rockies, southern Canada, and throughout the **Eastern Woodlands**. The Hopewell share many similarities with the **Adena**, with these cultural traditions partially overlapping both temporally and geographically.

HOPEWELL INTERACTION SPHERE. *See* JOSEPH R. CALD-WELL; HOPEWELL CULTURE.

HOPI INDIANS. Uto-Aztecan–speaking western **Puebloan** peoples of the American **Southwest**. Considered to be descendants of the prehistoric **Anasazi**, the Hopi occupy a series of **pueblo** settlements on mesas in northern Arizona. The oldest of these settlements is a Hopi village named Oraibi, which has been occupied since 800 B.P. (1150 A.D.). The Hopi are sedentary **agriculturalists**, growing **maize**, **beans**, **squash**, melons, and cotton. They are also pastoralists with a large number of sheep. The Hopi are a matrilineal society, with a strong matriclan structure. Hopi **religious** life centers on the secret practices of individual **kivas**, with their most important rituals including the use of elaborate masks and costumes for the impersonation of **kachina** spirits. The Hopi continue to be recognized as outstanding weavers, potters, and artists. At present, more than 6,000 Hopi reside in Arizona and New Mexico.

HORSE. Common term applied to a member of the species *Equus caballus*. Although horses were once indigenous to North America, they were extinct in the Americas by 10,000 B.P. (8000 B.C.). The horse was reintroduced to North America by Europeans, and eventually became an important draft animal and means of transportation for many Native American societies. Horses had their most dramatic impact on the native cultures of the **Great Plains**, where they led to the development of the highly mobile **bison-hunting** cultures of the **historic period**.

HRDLICKA, ALES (1869–1943). Pioneering physical **anthropologist** of Czechoslovakian birth who immigrated to the United States in 1881. Hrdlicka was trained as a physician, but the developing field of academic anthropology captivated his intellectual interests. After receiving advanced training in physical anthropology at the Ecole d' Anthropologie in Paris, he returned to the United States to pursue research at the American Museum of Natural History (AMNH). While at the AMNH, he participated in several major anthropometric studies of Native Americans in the **Southwest** with Fredric Ward Putnam. Hrdlicka later became curator of physical anthropology at the National Museum of Natural History at the Smithsonian Institute. During his subsequent 40 years at the Smithsonian, he compiled one of the largest collections of human physical remains in the world and completed extensive analyses of these remains.

Based on the results of his research, Hrdlicka became convinced that the first Native Americans originated in Asia and migrated across the Bcring Strait. However, he was also certain that indigenous peoples had not been in the Americas for more than a few thousand years. He spent much of his career debunking claims for great antiquity of Native Americans in the New World, effectively chilling research into the earliest occupations of the Americas for decades. It was not until he examined **archaeological** evidence from the **Folsom site** that he acknowledged the scientific possibility of earlier occupations.

HUNTING. The intentional pursuit of a nondomesticated animal for the purpose of procuring **subsistence** resources. Hunting involves active means of capturing or killing the prey on the part of the hunter. Native Americans engaged in hunting for subsistence purposes from their initial migration into the Americas. However, the **archaeological** record indicates that hunting contributed a decreasing percentage of Native American diets with the later development of **agriculture**.

Archaeologists reply upon the direct evidence of animal remains in the archaeological record as well as the presence of specific **tools** for knowledge on group specific hunting practices. **Ethnohistoric** documents, **ethnographic analogies**, **ethnoarchaeology**, and archaeological sites (like **Olsen-Chubbuck**) provide valuable information on the nature of Native American hunting. Hunting practices also varied considerably by region, with caribou and elk the major focus of hunting activities in the **Subarctic**, while **deer** were the primary focus of hunting in the **Eastern Woodlands**, and **bison** on the **Great Plains**. Among coastal groups of the **Arctic**, **Northwest Coast**, and Subarctic, hunting practices also included maritime mammals such as whale and **seal**.

Hunting technologies also varied by region and temporal period. The earliest hunting culture of North America, **Clovis**, is seen as an adaptation to the hunting of **megafauna** with large, hand-thrown spears. The development of the **atlatl** by later groups is suggestive of changing hunting practices, with emphasis on smaller species and hunting techniques adapting to greater distance between the hunter and prey. The use of the **bow and arrow** also represented a major transition in both hunting techniques and prey species, with an increase in smaller prey animals (birds, rabbit, and so on). The introduction of **firearms** by Europeans also altered the nature of Native American hunting, with the emphasis slowly changing from a subsistence activity to an economic activity with the advent of the **fur trade**.

HUNTING AND GATHERING. *See* FISHING; FORAGING; GATHERING; HUNTING.

HUPA INDIANS. Athabascan-speaking Native American group of northwestern **California** who occupy territory along the Trinity River. The Hupa, given their location, were also highly influenced by Native American groups of the **Northwest Coast** culture area. They were primarily **fishers, hunters**, and gatherers, and maintained elaborate **religious** rituals enacted by powerful **shaman**. Among the most important of their rituals was the World Renewal Ceremony, an annual ritual that was thought to purge the village from negative energy and protect the Hupa from impending disasters. The Hupa were also engaged in a series of complex **trade** relations with neighboring groups, trading **acorns, baskets**, salt, and other locally available resources for **deerskins, dentalia** shells, **tobacco**, and other materials. Although the Hupa were negatively impacted by European contacts, especially during the California gold rush, they have maintained control over much of their traditional territory and continue to reside in California's Hoopa Valley. At present, there are more than 2,000 Hupa residing in California.

HURON INDIANS. Iroquoian-speaking Native American group indigenous to the Georgian Bay and Lake Ontario regions. The Huron were village **agriculturalists** who resided in large domestic structures occupied by multiple matrilineally related nuclear families. The principal agricultural products of the Huron consisted of **maize, beans, squash, sunflowers**, and **tobacco. Hunting, fishing**, and wild plant gathering also provided supplements to local agricultural **subsistence** practices. Social organization consisted of individual matri**clans**, with clan elders constituting **councils** that advised local

chiefs. Women were especially influential in Huron political decision, with the most influential women of the clan selecting their political leaders. During the **historic period**, the Huron competed with elements of the **Iroquois Confederacy** for control of the northeastern **fur trade**. As a result of these conflicts, most historic Huron villages erected massive defensive **palisades**. Invasions by the **Iroquois** into Huron territory during the mid-17th century devastated the Huron, forcing them to abandon their homelands and migrate westward. At present, approximately 4,000 Huron (also referred to as the Wyandots) reside in Oklahoma.

HYPSITHERMAL. *See* ALTITHERMAL.

– I –

ICEHOUSE BOTTOM SITE. Archaeological site located along the Little Tennessee River in western Tennessee. Research by Jefferson Chapman at the site indicates the presence of noncontinuous occupations ranging in age from 9000 to 1500 B.P. (7000 B.C.–A.D. 450). Although the site revealed much about the transition from the Early to Middle **Archaic** periods in the **Eastern Woodlands**, the most important aspect of the site is one of the earliest dates for the presence of **maize** in the region. **Accelerator mass spectrometry dating** (AMS) indicates that maize was present at Icehouse Bottom as early as 1900 B.P. (A.D. 100), suggesting that maize may have been cultivated in the Eastern Woodlands much earlier than previously thought.

ICONOGRAPHY. The artistic representations and decorations (signs and symbols) found on objects of material culture. These elements are thought by cognitive **anthropologists** to have overt ideological meanings of both a social and **religious** nature. Iconographic elements may include representations of deities, mythological persons or creatures, and abstract geometric designs. Among the most common forms of iconography among Native American peoples were **anthropomorphic** and **zoomorphic petroglyphs** and **pictographs**, including numerous depictions of **Kokopelli**. Additionally, items belonging to the **Southeastern Ceremonial Complex** are decorated with elaborate iconographic images.

ILLINOIS INDIANS. Confederacy of **Algonquian**-speaking Native American groups, including the Cahokia, Kaskaskia, Michigamea, Moingwena, Peoria, and Tamaroa. These groups were indigenous to portions of Wisconsin, Illinois, Iowa, and Missouri when first recorded by Jacques Marquette and Louis Jolliet in the 17th century. The Illinois were village **agriculturalists** who supplemented their diets with **hunting**, **fishing**, and **gathering** activities. During the 18th century, they were engaged in a series of conflicts with the **Sioux**, **Fox**, and **Iroquois**, which vastly reduced their population. The assassination of Chief Pontiac in 1769 by a Kaskaskia led to an intensification of **warfare** among these groups, with the Illinois nearly exterminated in the process. By the early 19th century, the remaining Illinois migrated west of the Mississippi. Descendants of this group presently reside in Oklahoma.

ILLNESS. *See* DISEASE.

INTERACTION SPHERE. A cultural, economic, and information **exchange** network linking several individual cultures. Interaction spheres are composed of patterned social relationships centering on the exchange of **trade** items, ritual knowledge, or other similar social transactions. *See* HOPEWELL INTERACTION SPHERE.

INUIT. Group of closely related Yupik- and Inuktitut-speaking peoples of the **Arctic culture area**. Occupying territory stretching from the Pacific coast of Alaska, across the Canadian Arctic, to the eastern coasts of Quebec, Labrador, and Greenland, the Inuit are descendants of prehistoric **hunting** peoples who were among the last people to immigrate to the Americas from northern Asia. Inuit peoples developed specialized technology and **cultural** adaptations to the **hunting** of whales, **seals**, fish, and **caribou**. In addition, several physiological traits exhibited by the Inuit indicate their adaptation to **subsistence** practices high in animal fats and cholesterol. Social organization among the Inuit tends to prioritize the nuclear family, but strong bonds of reciprocity and resource sharing link both relatives and non-biologically related persons.

Like other Native American peoples, the Inuit were profoundly impacted by European contacts, with their population severely reduced as a result of European-introduced **diseases**. Inuit subsistence and economic practices were also negatively impacted by competition from European commercial **fishing**. At present, there are more than 5,000 Inuit people residing throughout Canada. *See also* ESKIMO; THULE TRADITION.

IOWA INDIANS. Siouan-speaking groups of the upper Midwest and Great Lakes region that exhibit a combination of **Eastern Woodland** and **Plains** culture traits. Also referred to as the Ioway, the Iowa are thought to have once been a component of the Winnebago, along with the Omaha, Oto, and Ponca. The Iowa were village **agriculturalists** who subsisted primarily on **maize**, **beans**, and **squash**. They also supplemented their diet with seasonal migrations designed to procure **beaver**, **bear**, **bison**, and other plant and animal resources not available in their village locales. During the 17th century, many Native American groups were forced westward, encroaching on the Iowa territory. The **Sauk**, **Fox**, **Kickapoo**, and **Ojibwa** engaged the Iowa in **warfare** over **hunting** territories during the 17th and 18th centuries. Losses from war, coupled with the effects of European-introduced **diseases**, further reduced the ability of the Iowa to preserve their territorial integrity. By 1824, the Iowa ceded all their lands in the present-day states of Iowa and Missouri and were later allocated reservation lands in northeastern Kansas. The majority of Iowa people, approximately 2,000, reside in Kansas, Nebraska, and Oklahoma.

IPIUTAK CULTURE. Predominant **culture** type of the Bering Strait between Siberia and Alaska at approximately 1900–1300 B.P. (A.D. 50–650). Thought to be descended from earlier **Denbigh flint complex** groups, Ipiutak peoples were **foragers** whose **subsistence** practices centered upon **caribou hunting**. Ipiutak culture is best known for exceptionally well-carved **ivory artifacts**.

IROQUOIAN CONFEDERACY. Social and political alliance of individual **Iroquoian**-speaking Native American cultures from upper New York that played a major role in the early history of European

colonization of the **Northeast**. Also known as the *League of the Haudenosaunee*, the five original members of the confederacy were the **Mohawk, Oneida, Onondaga, Cayuga**, and **Seneca**, with the **Tuscarora** joining in the early 18th century. Iroquois tradition contends that the confederacy was founded in the late 16th century, and was built upon the ideas of Hiawatha. The rationale for the formation of the confederacy is thought to have been the mutual protection of its members from invasions by other Native American peoples and Europeans. Political decisions within the confederacy were democratic, with unanimity required before decisions were finalized. By the early 17th century, the Iroquois were the region's dominant indigenous power. During the American Revolution, divisions arose among the members of the Iroquois Confederacy with the Oneida and Tuscarora siding with the Americans and the rest of the league allied with the English. The Iroquois aligned with the English were defeated in 1779, putting an effective end to the confederacy. Archaeologists have spent a great deal of time examining the multiethnic nature of the confederacy as evidenced by **archaeological** remains from Iroquoian sites.

IROQUOIAN LANGUAGE FAMILY. Linguistic family consisting of 16 distinct Native American **languages**. Iroquoian languages were spoken in and around the eastern Great Lakes and in portions of the Middle Atlantic and Southeast. Most of the Iroquoian languages have become extinct; however, **Mohawk, Oneida, Onondaga, Cayuga, Seneca, Tuscarora**, and **Cherokee** continue to be spoken. Languages in the Iroquoian family share distinct grammatical complexities, making them distinct from other language groupings in North America.

IROQUOIS. Any member of a cultural group united to form the **Iroquois Confederacy** or, more broadly, any speaker of an **Iroquoian language**.

IROQUOIS KINSHIP SYSTEM. System for reckoning social relations of kinship practiced by the **Iroquois** and other Native American peoples. It is considered a bifurcate merging kinship system, and is associated with societies practicing a loose form of matrilineal descent that also recognizes paternal familial contributions. In essence, the Iroquois kinship system treats relatives from one's mother's and father's side in very different ways. The terms for siblings are extended to parallel cousins, but cross cousins are given a different term. Cross cousins on the father's side are also equated with those on the mother's side. In addition, children use the same term for their father and their father's brother, and the same term for their mother and their mother's sister.

IRRIGATION. The artificial supply of water to land through direct human intervention. Irrigation can consist of elaborate constructions such as check dams, canals, and reservoirs, as well as simple systems of hand irrigation where pots are filled with water and then dumped where needed. Irrigation allows increased crop yields by providing supplemental water to **agricultural** fields. The most extensive irrigation systems found in North America were constructed by indigenous groups of the **Southwest**. The **Hohokam** were the most prolific users of irrigation, constructing extensive canals to channel water to their fields.

IVORY. Variety of hard, white dentin formed in the tusks of elephants, walruses, and **mammoths**. It is highly prized for its luster, durability, and suitability for carving. Ancient Native Americans used ivory for the production of a wide range of utilitarian and nonutilitarian **artifacts**. The Ipiutac culture is among the best-known ivory-using groups. The **Inuit** and other peoples of the **Arctic** and **Subarctic** culture areas continue to produce exquisitely carved ivory **artifacts**.

– J –

JAKETOWN SITE. Archaeological site located in northwestern Mississippi thought to have been a regional **trade** center during the Late **Archaic Poverty Point** period (circa. 3500–1400 B.P. [1500–600 B.P.]). Archaeological remains at the site consist of a deep, stratified **midden** and significant standing earthen architecture. Although believed to be related to a later occupation of the Jaketown site by **Mississippian** peoples (circa 850–450 B.P. [A.D. 1100–1500]), there are two large, flat-topped rectangular **mounds**, with additional mounds having been impacted by the construction of a highway through the site. The largest mound at the site, Mound B, has a base of 45 meters by 60 meters (150 feet by 200 feet) and a height of 7 meters (23 feet), and a projecting ramped stairway on its eastern side.

JAMESTOWN. First permanent English settlement in North America. Named for King James I, Jamestown was founded in May 1607 on a peninsula in Virginia's James River. The rise of Williamsburg as the center of political and economic life in Virginia led to the decline and abandonment of Jamestown. Coastal erosion eventually converted the Jamestown Peninsula into an island in the 18th century. **Archaeological** investigations at Jamestown have revealed much about the early English **colonial** presence in North America and relations with local Native American groups.

JASPER. Opaque, fine-grained form of chert characterized by a dark red color (although other colors are common). Polished to a fine luster, Native Americans used jasper to produce a range of ornaments and utilitarian **artifacts**. Well-crafted **zoomorphic** figurines of jasper are common at the **Poverty Point site**.

JEFFERSON, THOMAS (1743–1826). The third president of the United States and principal author of the Declaration of Independence. Jefferson is considered important to the prehistory of North America because he pioneered **archaeological** investigations into several mounds on his Virginia property. Having been trained in the scientific method, Jefferson applied these techniques to the analysis of prehistoric **earthworks** along the Rivanna River. Through the use of detailed notes related to the provenience of each **artifact**, Jefferson was able to recognize the **stratigraphy** of these **mounds** and infer their order of deposition. His investigations showed conclusively that these mounds were the result of Native American construction and not evidence of lost civilizations. Jefferson published his findings in his *Notes on the State of Virginia. See also* MOUND BUILDER CONTROVERSY.

JENNINGS, JESSE D. (1909–1997). American **archaeologist** who worked at various times in the Midwest, **Southeast, Southwest,**

Great Basin, and **Great Plains**, as well as in Guatemala and American Samoa. He completed his Ph.D. at the University of Chicago in 1943, served as a naval officer in World War II, and returned after the war to work for the National Park Service and later the University of Utah. Although he conducted archaeological research in a variety of settings, his research at **Danger Cave** in Utah and subsequent research on the **Fremont culture** provide his most enduring archaeological legacies.

JERUSALEM ARTICHOKE. Member of the **sunflower** family (*Helianthus tuberosus*) native to North America and **domesticated** as a food source by Native American peoples. The plant is a coarse, branched perennial normally 2–3 meters (7–10 feet) in height. The edible portion of the plant consists of underground tubers of various shape, size, and color. The Jerusalem artichoke was a staple of many Native American diets.

JESUITS. Members of a Roman Catholic **religious** order called the *Society of Jesus*. Originally organized by St. Ignatius of Loyola in 1534, the Jesuits were a missionary group that actively promoted the Counter-Reformation in Europe. They were the most active Christian missionaries in the Americas from the 16th to 18th centuries. Jesuit missions were established throughout French Canada and across the French and Spanish Midwest and **Southeast**, with this order converting tens of thousands of Native American people to Christianity. These missionary efforts were to have dramatic impacts on the indigenous peoples of North America, many of which have been examined **archaeologically**. The Jesuit order was abolished by Pope Clement XIV in 1773, but was later restored by Pope Pius VII in 1814. The Jesuits remain the single largest male religious order within the Catholic Church.

JICARILLA INDIANS. *See* APACHE.

JONES-MILLER SITE. Paleoindian **bison kill site** in Colorado associated with the **Folsom** culture and dated to approximately 10,000 B.P. (8000 B.C.). The site is notable for the presence of remains from more than 300 **bison** in an ancient arroyo. Analysis of these animals indicated that the majority were cows with nursing calves, suggesting that these animals were killed in the late fall. **Archaeological** remains from the Jones-Miller site and available ethnographic information suggest that individual Folsom groups coalesced into large social groups to engage in organized and coordinated collective bison **hunts**.

– K –

KACHINAS. Ancestral spirits of the **Pueblo** Indians consisting of more than 500 individual spirit beings. Kachinas are important elements of **Southwestern religious** beliefs, serving as intermediaries between humans and the supernatural. Each Pueblo community had its own unique kachinas that lived with them for half the year. Various **religious** ceremonies featured humans dressed as kachina spirits, with each kachina impersonator wearing an elaborately carved wooden mask that transformed them into literal kachina spirits. Kachinas were also frequently depicted in small wooden doll-like figures that were used to educate children on appropriate social behaviors and religious beliefs.

KAYAKS. Specific type of **canoe**like watercraft characterized by a pointed bow and stern and the absence of a keel. Kayaks are propelled through the water through the use of a double-bladed paddle. Canoes were used for **fishing** and **hunting** by the **Inuit** and other **Arctic** groups. Kayaks are constructed with an interior frame of wood or whalebone, and were covered by sealskins coated with fat for waterproofing. They are exceptionally stable watercraft and can be righted easily without taking on water when rolled over.

KENNEWICK MAN. Skeletal remains of a human male discovered in 1996 along the banks of the Columbia River near Kennewick, Washington. **Radiocarbon** analysis of these remains indicated that they dated to more than 9000 B.P. (7000 B.C.), making this individual one of the oldest humans ever recovered **archaeologically** in North America. Additional research by archaeologists and physical **anthropologists** suggested that this individual's cranial characteristics were not consistent with those of present-day Native Americans, suggesting to some that Kennewick man may not have been a Native American or was of a markedly different physical type than that of present Native American peoples. Given the repatriation requirements of the **Native American Grave Protection and Repatriation Act (NAGPRA)**, the U.S. Army Corps of Engineers prepared to return these remains to the Umatilla, the traditional Native American occupants of the land where the remains were discovered. Since the remains of Kennewick man hold unparalleled research potential for scholars interested in the earliest peopling of the Americas, archaeologists challenged this repatriation. Eight scientists sued for the right to conduct additional scientific investigations of the Kennewick materials before they were to be returned to the Umatilla. A recent court decision permitted further testing of the Kennewick remains before any repatriation could take place. It is thought that more complete analysis of the Kennewick man's remains will improve our understanding of early population dynamics in ancient North America.

KENSINGTON RUNE STONE. A slab of sedimentary rock bearing an inscription in the ancient runic language found on a Minnesota farm in 1898. Translation of the inscriptions state that the stone was carved by a group of Vikings in A.D. 1362. However, most archaeologists reject the stone's authenticity based on inaccuracies in the runic symbols and a questionable **archaeological** provenience. *See also* PSEUDOARCHAEOLOGY.

KICKAPOO INDIANS. Algonquian-speaking Native American group who were indigenous to the Great Lakes region of the Upper Midwest. Closely related to the **Sauk** and **Fox**, the Kickapoo moved to the south following European contacts, forcibly displacing the **Illinois** and **Miami**, and residing along the Wabash River of Illinois and Indiana. The Kickapoo were village **agriculturalists** who engaged in seasonal **bison hunting** expeditions in the eastern **Great Plains**. They were hostile to European encroachments on their lands, and fought with the French against the English. Later, they joined other Midwestern Native American groups against the United States during both the Revolutionary War and the War of 1812. The Kickapoo eventually ceded their lands east of the Mississippi River and moved to lands in present-day Missouri and Kansas. In the 1850s a large group of Kickapoo moved to a reservation in the Santa Rosa Mountains in Mexico. Smaller groups continue to reside in Kansas and Oklahoma, with a present population for both groups estimated to be less than 1,500.

KIDDER, ALFRED V. (1885–1963). Pioneering American **archaeologist** who excavated numerous sites in the American **Southwest** and Central America. Kidder received his Ph.D. from Harvard University in 1914, becoming one of a handful of American archeologists to have earned a doctorate at the time. He conducted several archaeological expeditions in the Southwest for the Peabody Museum at Harvard, and was eventually named director of research at the **Pecos Pueblo** ruins for the Phillips Academy. Kidder's research at Pecos is generally credited with being the first large-scale systematic **stratigraphic** archaeological excavation in North America, and constituted the largest professional investigation of its time. Research at Pecos also led Kidder to write the first systematic archaeological study of the prehistory of any North American region, *An Introduction to the Study of Southwestern Archaeology*. Kidder's work at Pecos also led to his formulation of the **Pecos classification**, a chronological arrangement of prehistoric Southwestern cultures beginning with early **Basketmakers** and ending with the historic **Pueblo** cultures. By the late 1920s, Kidder turned his interest to the prehistoric Maya, working in Mexico and Guatemala for the remainder of his archaeological career. Kidder was later criticized by **Walter Taylor** for not addressing questions of culture change and causality in his research. Despite this criticism, Kidder remains one of the most important figures in the history of North American archaeology.

KILL SITE. An **archaeological** site related to the specific activities involved in the killing and **butchering** of large game animals. The **Jones-Miller** and **Colby Mammoth** sites are good examples of North American kill sites. *See also* BUTCHERING STATION.

KIMMSWICK SITE. Archaeological site located near present-day St. Louis, Missouri, related to **Paleoindian hunting** activities. Investigations at the Kimmswick site revealed the presence of **mastodon** remains with a **Clovis point** imbedded in its leg, highly suggestive of intentional human hunting of this animal. Additional Paleoindian **tools** and a possible ground sloth hide tent were also recovered, leading investigators to believe that Paleoindian people camped at Kimmswick.

KING SITE. Archaeological site located near Rome, Georgia, with evidence of an extensive occupation during the middle 16th century. The King site is primarily important because excavations revealed the remains of more than 200 individual burials, many with evidence of damage from metal edged-weapons. This evidence, when coupled with the recovery of a sword from the King site consistent with those carried by members of the **Hernando de Soto** expedition, led scholars to suggest that these remains are direct evidence of conflict between **Southeastern** native peoples and Europeans. However, recent research has questioned the European origins of these wounds.

KINSHIP. The most elemental principle for organizing individuals into social groups. Kinship systems establish social relationships between individuals through genetic inheritance, marriage, or other shared group membership (including **clans**). Kinship plays a major role in determining a person's potential marriage partners and defines those with whom sexual relations would be considered incestuous based on specific culturally accepted norms. In Native American societies, kinship determined not only with whom one was considered a relative, but also postmarital residency rules and other essential social practices.

KIOWA INDIANS. Kiowa-Tanoan–speaking Native American group who occupied the southern **Great Plains** during the **historic period**. The Kiowa were a **foraging** society that migrated onto the Plains from their traditional homeland in western Montana during the 17th century. The introduction of the **horse** encouraged the Kiowa to become increasingly mobile, with specific cultural adaptations developing around **bison hunting**. Social status within Kiowa society was based on hierarchical classifications, with individuals of high status having distinguished themselves in **warfare**. The Kiowa practiced the **Sun Dance** ritual, and believed that dreams and visions provided **religious** connections to supernatural powers. The Kiowa successfully resisted American encroachment on the southern Plains until the 1860s, eventually signing the Medicine Lodge Treaty and moving to a reservation in Oklahoma. At present, more than 5,000 Kiowa live in Oklahoma on lands they share with the **Comanche**.

KIVA. Subterranean or semisubterranean structure constructed by the **Puebloan** peoples of the **Southwest** as a chamber for male **religious** and political ceremonies. Most kivas have a small hole in the floor, called a *sípapu*, which served as a link between the world of humans and the supernatural. Although primarily used for ritual ceremonies, kivas were also used for political meetings and informal socializing. The earliest round kivas are thought to be developed out of the circular **pithouses** of the earlier **Basketmaker culture**.

KLAMATH INDIANS. Penutian-speaking Native American group who occupied portions of the high plateau of northern California and south-central Oregon when first encountered by Europeans. Closely related to the **Modoc**, Klamath **subsistence** primarily centered upon **fishing** and the collection of wokas and other marshy plant species. The Klamath were seasonally mobile, scattering during the spring and summer months and coalescing in large **earthlodges** during the fall and winter. The Klamath territory was severely limited by treaties with the United States, with most Klamath forced to reside on lands in Oregon. At present, more than 3,000 Klamath reside in Oregon.

KNEBERG (LEWIS), MADELINE D. (1903–1996). Influential **archaeologist** and physical **anthropologist** who, along with her longtime companion and husband Thomas M. N. Lewis, worked in the **southeastern** United States. Madeline Kneberg Lewis received her training in archaeology from **Fay Cooper Cole** at the University of Chicago. She later served as the director of the archaeological research laboratory for the Tennessee Valley Authority, and was instrumental in both the development of the anthropology program at the University of Tennessee and the founding of the Tennessee Archaeological Society.

KNIGHT MOUND GROUP. **Archaeological** site located in Calhoun County, Illinois, dated to the Middle and Late **Woodland** periods (circa

2300–1500 B.P. [350 B.C.–A.D. 450]). The Knight Mound Group is considered important because it has yielded some of the most elaborate **ceramic anthropomorphic figurines** of the **Hopewell** tradition.

KNOTWEED. Common name for *Polygonum erectum*, a starchy-seeded plant that was one of the major components of the **Eastern Agricultural Complex**. Paleobotanical evidence indicates that Native Americans were collecting knotweed as early as 6000 B.P. (4000 B.C.), with indications that it was **domesticated** by 4000 B.P. (2000 B.C.).

KODIAK TRADITION. Southern derivation of the **Ocean Bay tradition** from 6000 to 1000 B.P. (4000 B.C.–A.D. 950) in the Kodiak Islands of the south Alaskan Peninsula in the north Pacific Ocean. Also known as the *Kachemak*, the Kodiak tradition is composed of groups engaged in sea mammal **hunting, salmon fishing,** and **caribou** hunting. Primarily known for **artifacts** made of slate, including *ulu* and lance blades, Kodiac peoples demonstrate expanding populations and elaborate **burial** rituals, including the presence of human trophy skulls.

KOKOPELLI. Anthropomorphic figure that appears frequently in **Southwestern** art. Thought to represent a deity or a long-distance trader, Kokopelli appears in hundreds of **pictographs** throughout the region. Commonly depicted as a humpbacked flute player, some scholars believe this figure may represent **Mesoamerican** long-distance traders known as *pochteca*.

KOLOMOKI SITE. Woodland period **archaeological** site located in southwest Georgia, with occupation related to the **Swift Creek** and **Weeden Island cultural traditions** (1600–1000 B.P. [A.D. 350–950]). Kolomoki contains eight earthen **mounds**, with the largest more than 17 meters (56 feet) in height. There is also a large village associated with the mounds, but to date it has received far less archaeological investigation that the surrounding mounds. However, it is considered likely that based on the size of the site and its mounds, Kolomoki was one of the largest and most important Woodland period sites in the **Southeast**.

KOSTER SITE. Archaeological site located in Greene County, Illinois, on the Illinois River. The Koster site was occupied for almost 10,000 years with 26 identified living surfaces. Major occupations of the site date to 8500, 7000, and 5250 B.P. (6500, 5000, and 3,300 B.C.). Excavations at Koster revealed the importance of deeply buried archaeological deposits and, given their extensive nature, provided a great deal of the information on the daily life of **Archaic** peoples. The site also provided evidence of one of the earliest house structures presently known in North America and extensive **trade** networks that spanned the entire **Eastern Woodlands**. Research at Koster by the Center for American Archaeology and Northwestern University between 1968 and 1979 also helped to train hundreds of professional archaeologists and avocationalists.

KROEBER, ALFRED LOUIS. Pioneering American **anthropologist** who studied at Columbia University under **Franz Boas**, and received the second Ph.D. in anthropology granted in the United States. He conducted ethnographic fieldwork among the **Arapaho** and among various **California** Native American groups. Kroeber studied **archaeological** collections at the Phoebe Hurst Museum, eventually helping to found the Department of Anthropology at the University of California, Berkeley. Kroeber was one of the most influential figures in the early development of American anthropology, and played a major role in advancing the uniquely American four-field approach to anthropology. Kroeber was interested in the historical development of native peoples, and recognized the importance of archaeology to this process. While working on **Zuñi** sites, Kroeber devised more precise archaeological field methods and used **seriation** as a means of examining **artifact** change through time.

KWAKIUTL INDIANS. Algonquian-Wakashan–speaking Native American peoples of the **Northwest Coast** of Vancouver Island and the mainland of British Columbia. Also called the Kwakwaka'wakw, the term Kwakiutl has become the standard term applied to the more than 30 independent groups in their region. Although they did not share a larger political affiliation, these groups did share a common **language** and **cultural** practices. They were semisedentary, **subsisting** on maritime and terrestrial plant and animal resources. Their social organization was highly **stratified**, with social position inherited through both lineage and **clan** (*numaym*) membership. Social position could be altered, however, through the practice of the competitive **potlatch**. Like other groups of the Northwest Coast, the Kwakiutl have a tradition of elaborate woodcarving, including highly stylized **totem poles**. **Franz Boas** conducted extensive research on the Kwakiutl. At present, the Kwakiutl number more than 4,500.

– L –

LABRET. A decorative ornament inserted into a perforation in the lip. Labrets were a form of personal adornment worn by numerous Native American groups.

LACE SITE. **Archaeological** site located near the L'Anguille River in east-central Arkansas. Excavations by Dan Morse at the Lace site indicate that it was most probably a base camp for **Dalton** peoples approximately 10,000 B.P. (8000 B.C.). This site is located in the same vicinity as the **Brand** and **Sloan** sites.

LAKE FOREST TRADITION. Late **Archaic cultural tradition** associated with the pine and hardwood forests of the Great Lakes and dated to approximately 5200–3000 B.P. (3200–1000 B.C.). Closely resembling the contemporary **Maritime Tradition**, Lake Forest peoples were mobile **foragers** who **subsisted** on seasonally available terrestrial and maritime resources. This tradition is primarily an inland adaptation, with social organization consisting of small **bands** that occupied permanent territories and a fixed seasonal migratory round. There are two recognized variants of the Lake Forest Tradition, the **Laurentian** and the **Old Copper culture**.

LAMOKA CULTURE. Late **Archaic cultural tradition** dated from approximately 4500 to 3800 B.P. (2500–1800 B.C.) in New York state and adjacent areas of the **Northeast**. Lamoka peoples were mobile **foragers** who tended to favor locations near lakes, streams, or swamps. William Ritchie coined the **culture historical** term Archaic to describe Lamoka culture.

LANGUAGES. At the time of first contact with Europeans, Native American peoples of North, Central, and South America spoke more than 1,000 distinct languages. These individual languages belong to more than 100 unique language families, with the major groups consisting of **Aleut–Eskimo, Algonquian, Athabaskan,** Caddoan, **Iroquoian, Muskogean,** Penutian, **Salishan,** and **Uto-Aztecan.** One of the major **cultural** impacts of European **colonialism** was the decline in indigenous population and the concomitant **extinction** of many Native American languages. This process of language loss was exacerbated during the 19th century with the U.S. and Canadian governments adopting educational policies that were designed to eliminate native languages. Despite these earlier efforts, more than 300 languages continue to be spoken by Native American peoples of North America. Ongoing efforts designed to preserve Native American languages are underway, with many focused on teaching Native American youths their group's **traditional** language.

L'ANSE AMOUR. **Archaeological** site in southern Labrador, Canada, with evidence of the earliest presently known **burial mound** in North America, dated to 7500 B.P. (5500 B.C.). Excavated by James Tuck, the L'Anse Amour site is associated with the **Maritime Archaic tradition,** and consists of a low, circular pile of rocks covering a child's grave. At the time of the interment, the body was covered with **ocher** and wrapped in skins, and a variety of **grave goods** were placed in the burial pit.

L'ANSE AUX MEADOWS. **Archaeological** site located on the northern tip of Newfoundland with evidence of a Norse (Viking) occupation during the late 10th century. Believed to be related to the Vinland **colonization** efforts of **Leif Ericsson,** archaeological excavations at L'Anse aux Meadows by Helge Ingstad and Anne Stine Ingstad confirmed the Norse presence more than five centuries before the expedition of **Christopher Columbus.** Although occupied for only a few years, this settlement did result in the earliest recorded substantiated contacts between Europeans and Native Americans (whom the Norse referred to as *Skraelings*).

LAUREL CULTURE. **Archaeological** culture of the upper Great Lakes region, particularly northern Minnesota, dated to the middle

Woodland period (2100–1300 B.P. [150 B.C.–A.D. 650]). Analysis by archaeologist James Stoltman indicates that Laurel peoples did not participate in the contemporary **Hopewell interaction sphere**, but were instead inwardly focused **foraging** societies with seasonal migratory patterns within their local territory. Predominant **subsistence** resources consisted of wild rice, moose, and **beaver**. In addition, toggle-headed antler **harpoons** at Laurel sites indicate that **fishing** was also an important subsistence activity. Laurel sites possess the earliest **ceramics** found in their area, a type of plain and dentate-stamped grit-tempered pottery. Laurel peoples also constructed small **burial mounds** for the interment of their dead.

LAURENTIAN TRADITION. Late **Archaic** period **cultural tradition** of the northeastern United States and southeastern Canada dated between 6000 and 3000 B.P. (4000–1000 B.C.). The Laurentian tradition is considered to be an interior extension of the Late **Archaic Lake Forest** cultural tradition of the lower Great Lakes and upper St. Lawrence Valley. Present evidence suggests that Laurentian peoples practiced a **foraging subsistence** pattern with major contributions from **beaver**, **deer**, fish, and rabbit. Laurentian is defined by **artifact assemblages** that include ground slate points and *ulu* knives, and bone **projectile points**.

LAURENTIDE ICE SHEET. Primary glacial mass covering northern and eastern North America during the **Pleistocene** epoch (1.6 million–10,000 years ago). During the period of maximum **glaciation**, the Laurentide ice sheet reached a thickness of 2,500–3,000 meters (8,000–10,000 feet), covered an area of more than 13 million square kilometers (5 million square miles), and reached as far south as Kansas (37°N latitude).

LEHNER SITE. Archaeological site located in southern Arizona on the San Pedro River, with evidence of **Paleoindian** activities. **Clovis projectile points** and cutting and scraping **tools** dating to approximately 11,000 B.P. (9000 B.C.) were found at the site along with one of the earliest **firehearths** discovered in North America. **Stratigraphic** analysis indicates that the site was a shallow watering hole that attracted **megafauna**. Archaelogists surmise that Paleoindian peoples most probably ambushed these animals as they came to drink.

LEWIS AND CLARK EXPEDITION (1803–1806). Expedition designed to explore the land and peoples purchased by the United States from France in the Louisiana Purchase. Headed by Meriwether Lewis and William Clark, this expedition also sought an efficient overland route to the Pacific Ocean. Their journey helped strengthen American claims to the Oregon territory, and provided the first detailed information on many Native American groups of the West.

LINDENMEIER SITE. Archaeological site located in the foothills northeast of Fort Collins, Colorado, with evidence of **Paleoindian** occupation by **Folsom** peoples at approximately 11,000 B.P. (9000 B.C.). First excavated by a series of avocationalist archaeologists, H. H. Roberts of the Smithsonian Institution led professional investigations at the site in the 1930s. Unlike other Folsom sites, the Lindenmeier site is not a kill site, but a base camp. **Lithic** remains at Lindenmeier suggest that the site was occupied by a series of distinct but interacting groups that shared similar social organization and **subsistence** strategies.

LITHIC. Consisting of or pertaining to stone or rock. Since lithics provided the primary materials from which Native American peoples constructed their **tools**, archaeologists devote a great degree of their attention to the analysis of the raw material from which these tools were made. By classifying these materials based on geological and geographical features, researchers can determine the presence of non-local raw materials and finished goods in archaeological assemblages. Such studies have implications for the reconstruction of **trade** networks and **cultural** contacts. In addition, lithic studies frequently focus on the steps necessary for the production of stone tools and the manner in which finished tools were used. *See also* BLADE; CORE; FLAKE; MICROWEAR ANALYSIS.

LITTLE EGYPT SITE. Archaeological site located along the Coosawatte River in northwestern Georgia thought to be the paramount town of **Coosa**, a major **Mississippian** period town described in the chronicles of the **Hernando de Soto** expedition. Coosa was the most populous and sociopolitically complex Native American polity encountered by de Soto's expedition. Subsequent European descriptions of Coosa indicate that it had declined precipitously in population and sociopolitical importance following contact with de Soto's party.

LITTLE ICE AGE. Period of unusually cold temperature in the Northern Hemisphere that lasted from the 14th century to the 18th century. The Little Ice Age followed the **Medieval Climate Optimum** and preceded the development of present-day climatic conditions. **Archaeological** remains dating to this period indicate a series of **cultural** adaptations to these changing climatic conditions.

LITTLE SALT SPRING SITE. Archaeological site in Sarasota County, Florida, that consists of a spring-fed sinkhole that served as an oasis during the **Pleistocene**, when sea levels were greatly lower than modern levels. Little Salt Spring sink contains evidence of human occupation by **Paleoindian** peoples from approximately 12,000 to 9000 B.P. (10,000–7000 B.C.), with a later occupation by **Archaic** peoples from 6800 to 5200 B.P. (4800–3200 B.C.). Underwater archaeological research at the site revealed the presence of archaeological materials to a depth of more than 26 meters (85 feet). A ledge within the sinkhole contained the remains of a giant land tortoise that was killed and cooked by humans. A wooden stake used to kill the tortoise produced a **radiocarbon** date of 12,000 B.P. (10,000 B.C.).

LONGHOUSE. Traditional domestic architecture of the **Iroquoian** peoples. Longhouses were large, multifamily dwellings that were typically 55–67 meters (180–220 feet) in length, thus the term *longhouses*. They were constructed of a wooden framework of posts and cross-members that was given an exterior covering of bark. Interior divisions of space consisted of a series of discrete partitions within the longhouse for use by individual families.

LOST TRIBES OF ISRAEL. One of the **cultural** groups suggested during the 18th and 19th centuries to have built the large pre-Columbian **earthworks** of North America. At the height of the **mound builder controversy**, several groups (Phonecians, Atlantians, and the Lost

Tribes of Israel) were proposed to have built the large earthen **mounds** found throughout the **Eastern Woodlands**. Since most Europeans and Americans felt that indigenous peoples were incapable of producing such monumental architecture, several fictional accounts for their origins were proposed. Excavations by **Cyrus Thomas** for the **Bureau of American Ethnology** helped prove the Native American origin of these structures.

LOVELOCK CAVE. **Archaeological** site in Humbolt County, Nevada, located near an extinct lake, consisting of a limestone cave approximately 46 meters deep and 11 meters wide (150 feet deep by 35 feet wide). Archaeological research in the cave during the 1920s revealed a series of human occupations between 9000 and 150 B.P. (7000 B.C.–A.D. 1800). The extreme aridity of the local environment helped to preserve a range of **artifacts** that would normally have perished, including **basketry**, blankets, sandals, and highly detailed duck decoys.

LOWER SONORAN AGRICULTURAL COMPLEX. **Agricultural subsistence** practices that developed in the **Southwest** with the addition of **squash**, tepary bean, lima bean, jack bean, and panic grass to the previously cultivated plants of the earlier **Upper Sonoran agricultural complex**. The lower Sonoran agricultural complex is presently dated to approximately 2800 B.P. (800 B.C.).

LOWIE, ROBERT HARRY (1883–1957). Pioneering American **anthropologist** who was one of the leaders of the anti**evolutionism** movement in American anthropology. Of Austrian birth, Lowie's family immigrated to the United States when he was 10. Lowie studied under **Franz Boas** and Clark Wissler at Columbia University, and was a contemporary of **A. V. Kidder**. Lowie studied the **Crow**, **Shoshone**, and other Native American groups of the **Great Plains**, pioneering what he called *salvage ethnography*. After completing his Ph.D., Lowie took a position at the University of California, Berkeley, where he worked with **A. L. Kroeber** to build the Department of Anthropology. Although primarily a cultural anthropologist, Lowie was interested in the information that **archaeology** could provide on historical **cultural** development.

– M –

MACAW. Any of about 18 species of large tropical New World parrots belonging to the genera *Ara* and *Anodorhynchus*, with long tails, large sickle-shaped beaks, and brilliant plumage. Macaws are easily tamed and kept as pets, with **archaeological** evidence from **Paquime** indicating that scarlet macaws (*Ara macao*) were imported in large numbers into the **Southwest** from **Mesoamerica**. It is thought that they were used in local **religious** ceremonies and their feathers **traded** to other groups in the region.

MACKENZIE CORRIDOR. Wide unglaciated passage believed to have extended southwest along the eastern side of the Canadian Rockies during the last major North American **glaciation**. This inland ice-free corridor followed the Mackenzie River basin into the heart of North America, and is thought to have provided a possible route for human migration into the continent during the **Paleoindian** period. Geological data indicate that the corridor was passable during two separate periods: between 36,000 and 24,000 B.P. (34,000–22,000 B.C.), and again from 17,000 B.P. (15,000 B.C.) until the present.

MAHICAN INDIANS. Algonquian-speaking Native American peoples of the upper Hudson River valley above the Catskill Mountains. Consisting of five major social divisions, the Mahicans were village **agriculturalists**, governed by hereditary **chiefs** (*sachem*) and an elected **council**. The Mahicans were profoundly affected by European trade, and in 1664 persistent **warfare** with the **Mohawk** over the control of European **trade** forced the Mahicans to move to Massachusetts. They later migrated to Indiana, and eventually moved to Wisconsin, where they presently number about 1,000.

MAIZ DE OCHO. Variety of **maize cultivated** by Native American groups of the **Southwest**. It was given the name *maiz de ocho* because it has eight rows of kernels. It is well adapted to the dry conditions of the Southwest and produces large kernels that are easier to mill than other varieties of maize. Recent studies indicate that *maiz de ocho* may have been cultivated in the Southwest by as early as 3000 B.P. (1000 B.C.).

MAIZE. A large, **domesticated** species of American grass (*Zea mays*), widely **cultivated** as a staple food by Native American peoples. Maize is the domesticated form of a wild grass, teosinte (*Zea mays parviglumis*), indigenous to the western Sierra Madre Mountains of Mexico. **Archaeological** research by **R. S. McNeish** established an early sequence for the domestication of maize, with recent botanical analysis indicating that teosinte was first domesticated in the Balsas River drainage of Mexico 6000–5000 B.P. (4000–3000 B.C). Once domesticated, maize became an important staple food source for many Native American peoples, eventually becoming the single most important **agricultural** product in the Americas. Maize was commonly processed into flour with the use of a handheld stone grinder (**mano**) and a shallow, concave stone surface (**metate**).

MAKAH INDIANS. Wakashan-speaking Native American peoples of the **Northwest Coast** who occupy the Cape Flattery area of the Olympic Peninsula of Washington state. Makah **subsistence** consisted of complex **foraging**, with whales, **seals**, and other marine mammals providing a major source of food and other resources. Whaling was of tremendous importance to the Makah, with whale hunts providing not only much needed food, but also a spiritual connection to the sea and a source of male social status. Much of our knowledge of precontact Makah culture was provided by **archaeological** research at the **Ozette site**, a Makah village destroyed by a mudslide in the late 14th century. At present, more than 1,800 Makah reside in the state of Washington.

MAMMOTH. Any of various large, hairy, extinct elephants of the genus *Mammuthus*. The most common North American mammoth was the Columbian Mammoth (*Mammuthus columbi*), which was a descendant of *Mammuthus meridionalis*, the ancestral mammoth that entered North America via **Beringia** approximately 1 million B.P. The Columbian mammoth ranged from Alaska and the Yukon, across the midwestern United States, and south into Mexico and Central America. Standing almost four meters (14 feet) at the shoulder, and weighing 8–10 metric tons, the Columbian mammoth consumed approximately 260 kilograms (700 pounds) of vegetation a day and had a natural life expectancy of 60 to 80 years. **Archaeological** evidence indicates that **Paleoindians** hunted mammoth in many areas of North America, with several scholars, including **Vance C. Haynes** and **Paul S. Martin**, suggesting that overhunting by humans and environmental changes accompanying the **Holocene** emergence led to the eventual **extinction** of the mammoth.

MANDAN INDIANS. Siouan-speaking Native American group of the **Great Plains** who traditionally lived along the middle Missouri River in present-day North Dakota. Prior to European contacts, the Mandan were **agriculturalists** who constructed large **earthlodges** and **fortified** villages. They primarily **subsisted** on **maize**, **beans**, pumpkins, and **sunflowers**, but supplemented their diet by **hunting bison** and other animals. They had a series of elaborate social and **religious** rituals, including the **Sun Dance** ceremony. Their society was matrilineal, with matri**clans**, age-grade warrior societies, and women's societies adding additional levels of social integration. The Mandan played a major role in assisting the **Lewis and Clark expedition** and were a favorite subject of artist **George Catlin**, who portrayed many aspects of Mandan social life in a series of paintings. During the early contact period, the Mandan controlled **trade** with Europeans on the eastern Plains, but increased **warfare** and European-introduced **diseases** (especially smallpox) greatly reduced their numbers. By the mid-19th century, they allied themselves with the **Arikara** and joined them on the Fort Berthold reservation. At present, there are approximately 1,500 Mandan in North Dakota.

MANO. Handheld cylindrical stone used in conjunction with a **metate** to grind **maize** and other grains. Manos were used for a variety of crushing and grinding purposes, but **archaeologists** can often use these items to identify the specific plants being eaten by past groups.

MARITIME ARCHAIC TRADITION. **Archaic** period **cultures** of the Atlantic Coast of Maine, Nova Scotia, and Labrador that shared many cultural practices during the period from approximately 9000 to 3000 B.P. (7000–1000 B.C.). Also referred to as the Maritime Tradition, the Maritime Archaic is characterized by groups engaged in the **hunting** of large sea mammals during the summer and elk, **caribou**, moose, and other large land animals during the winter. Maritime

Archaic peoples migrated seasonally to take advantage of the local availability of these resources. Evidence from **burials** at Maritime Archaic sites such as **L'Anse Amour** and **Port aux Choix** indicates that these people performed elaborate **burial** rituals involving the covering of the deceased in red **ocher**. These people were also engaged in long-distance **trade** networks that connected them to peoples in other regions of North America. **Archaeological** research indicates that groups in the Maritime Archaic tradition are the **Red Paint People** of early archaeological lore.

MARKSVILLE CULTURE. Archaeological culture of the lower Mississippi River valley and adjacent areas of the Gulf Coast dated to between 1950 and 1550 B.P. (A.D. 1–400). Marksville culture is very similar to that of the **Hopewell culture** of the Ohio and Illinois River valleys, with parallels in **burial mound** architecture and the presence of exotic **trade** goods. Nonlocal trade items found at Marksville sites include **copper** panpipes, **earspools**, **beads**, bracelets, stone platform **pipes**, mica and **ceramic anthropomorphic figurines**, marine shells, freshwater pearls, and greenstone celts. Marksville **subsistence** practices were based upon intensive **foraging**, with some indications that **maize** horticulture may have been present as well. Although there are many similarities between Marksville and Hopewell traditions, present interpretations favor the view that Marksville was a local **cultural** development based on previous local **Archaic** and **Woodland** practices with the selective adoption of traits introduced from the Hopewell.

MARPOLE CULTURE. Archaeological culture of the **Northwest Coast** indigenous to portions of Vancouver, San Juan, and Gulf Islands during the period from approximately 2400 to 1500 B.P. (400 B.C.–A.D. 400). Marpole society was characterized by social ranking, with marked differences in both the quality and quantity of **burial** goods placed with the dead reflecting the individual's social status in life. **Artificial cranial deformation**, a practice usually reserved for social elites among Northwest Coast peoples, is also present in Marpole burial populations. Marpole peoples were complex **foragers** who resided in permanent villages, although there were regular seasonal migrations designed to capture large numbers of **salmon** during the spring.

MARSHELDER. Edible plant indigenous to North America with the taxonomic classification of *Iva xanthifolia*. This plant was eaten by Native Americans of the **Eastern Woodlands** at least as early as the **Archaic** period. Ethnobotanical evidence indicates that marshelder was **domesticated** by Native American peoples as early as the **Woodland** period.

MARTIN, PAUL SIDNEY (1899–1974). American **archaeologist** who worked primarily in the **southwestern** United States. Martin received his Ph.D. in **anthropology** in 1929 from the University of Chicago. He held positions at the Colorado State Museum (1928–1929) and the Field Museum of Natural History (1929–1974). Martin's primary field research focused on the development of **Mogollon** culture and its relation to the other major cultural traditions of the Southwest. He was also instrumental in the formation of the **Blitzkrieg model** for **Paleoindian** settlement in North America.

MARTIN'S HUNDRED. Historic plantation settlement founded by English settlers along the James River in colonial Virginia in 1619. Originally an 81-square-kilometer (20,000-acre) settlement, Martin's Hundred contained a fort and a small town. The settlement was almost completely destroyed by Native Americans in 1622 and never recovered its previous prosperity. Excavations at the site by Ivor Noël Hume revealed much about the early **colonial** English presence in North America.

MAST FOREST TRADITION. Cultural tradition of the late **Archaic** period of southern New England from 4700 to 3200 B.P. (2700–1200 B.C.). This tradition indicates cultural adaptations to forested environments, with large numbers of pestles and grinders indicative of **subsistence** practices centered upon **acorns** and other nuts. **Deer**, small mammals, and fish were also important components of the diet of Mast Forest peoples. Evidence of increased **warfare** during this period has also been identified at Mast Forest sites in New York.

MASTODON. Any of several large, **extinct** mammals of the genus *Mammut* that lived worldwide 24 million–10,000 B.P. (8000 B.C.).

Although similar to modern elephants, mastodon had unique dentition and other physical characteristics that made them distinct from other *Proboscidea*. Mastodon were closely related to **mammoth**, and both were indigenous to North America. The most common species of mastodon in North America, *Mammut americanum*, became extinct at approximately 10,000 B.P. Some paleontologists and **archaeologists** believe that human **hunting** and environmental changes during the **Holocene** emergence were responsible for their extinction.

MAXWELL, MOREAU SANFORD (1918–1998). American **archaeologist** whose primary research areas were the **Arctic** and **Subarctic**. He earned his Ph.D. in anthropology at the University of Chicago in 1949, having interrupted his studies in order to serve as a U.S. Navy pilot during World War II. He conducted excavations in the Great Lakes region of the **Eastern Woodlands**, including **Aztalan** and **Fort Michilimackinac**. He later moved to Michigan State University, where he continued his studies of the Arctic with archaeological research on Ellesmere and Baffin Islands.

MAYGRASS. Common name for an edible plant species (*Phalanx caroliniana*) indigenous to North America. Maygrass was first **domesticated** by Native Americans during the **Archaic** period. Although a common wild plant in southern North America, archaeobotanical evidence indicates that maygrass was cultivated well outside its natural habitat after its domestication. Maygrass was part of the **Eastern Agricultural Complex**, and had several adaptive advantages as a food source, including resistance to cold and a short growing season. Given its relatively quick growth cycle, maygrass is thought to have served as an early summer food for Native Americans, providing a reliable food source until other plant species could mature.

MCKEAN COMPLEX. Series of **archaeological** sites on the **Great Plains** related to the middle **Archaic** (circa 4900 B.P. [2900 B.C.]), with evidence of increased **subsistence** reliance upon plant foods. The McKean complex includes increasingly specialized **tools** for the processing of plant foods. These changes represent a shift in subsistence practices from a dependence on **bison hunting** to the **gathering** of wild plants.

MCKEITHEN SITE. An early **Weeden Island** site in northern Florida dated between 1750 and 1250 B.P. (A.D. 200–700). Representing a residential village, the McKeithen site has three earthen **mounds** and a horseshoe-shaped ring **midden** surrounding a cleared central plaza. The mounds at the site contained a mortuary structure, a **charnel house**, and a domestic structure respectively. Archaeologist Jerald Milanich interprets the site's development as representing the growth and decline of a powerful "big personage" society and heightened sociopolitical complexity. *See also* BIG MEN.

MCKERN, WILLIAM CARLETON (1892–1988). American **archaeologist** who conducted research in the western and midwestern United States. McKern received his Ph.D. from the University of California, Berkeley, and spent the majority of his professional career as curator, and later director, of the Milwaukee Public Museum (1915–1958). He was a specialist in **petroglyphs**, but his principal contribution to North American archaeology came with his development of the **Midwestern Taxonomic Method** (also known as the *McKern Classification system*), a complex system for **artifact** classification.

MCNEISH, RICHARD STOCKTON (1918–2001). American **archaeologist** who specialized in the early occupation of the Americas and the transition from **foraging** to **agricultural subsistence** practices. Receiving his Ph.D. in **anthropology** from the University of Chicago in 1949, McNeish is perhaps best known for his detailed studies of subsistence practices in the Tehuacan Valley of Mexico, which provided the seminal data on the domestication of **maize**. McNeish's research also addressed the earliest occupation of the Americas, focusing on sites throughout North, South, and Central America. McNeish was an advocate of the **pre-Clovis hypothesis**, using evidence from sites like Pendejo Cave to argue that Native Americans had been on the continent since 40,000 B.P.

MEADOWCROFT ROCKSHELTER. Large **rockshelter archaeological** site in southwestern Pennsylvania thought to contain evidence of early **Clovis** occupation in northeastern North America. Excavated by James Adavasio, Meadowcroft has yielded evidence of multiple occupations dating from 12,000 to 750 B.P. (10,000

B.C.–A.D. 1200). Lower levels at the site contain **pre-Clovis** materials that have been dated to be as old as 19,000 B.P. (17,000 B.C.); however, these dates are extremely controversial. At present, there is little agreement among archaeologists concerning the earliest occupation of the rockshelter.

MEAD SITE. Archaeological site near Fairbanks, Alaska, with evidence of a **Paleoindian** occupation dating to approximately 13,000 B.P. (11,000 B.C.). The Mead site is one of a group of related sites in the Tanana Valley. Located on a ridge overlooking a marshy valley, **artifacts** and **faunal remains** suggest that this site was used for the seasonal **hunting** of swan and other migratory fowl. This evidence is cited as confirmation of an ice-free corridor between Alaska and the rest of the North American continent used as a flyway by migratory birds during this period. *See also* MACKENZIE CORRIDOR.

MEDICINE BUNDLE. Cloth or leather pouch containing ritual objects thought to have supernatural power by Native Americans of the **Great Plains**. Medicine bundles were commonly filled with a variety of unusual natural materials such as eagle feathers, stones, and pigments. The **Crow** and other Plains groups believed that these bundles possessed great spiritual power and could be dangerous to those who handled them without the necessary sacred knowledge. *See also* RELIGION.

MEDICINE MAN. *See* SHAMAN.

MEDICINE WHEEL. Large stone circles found on the **Great Plains** that are thought to relate to special **religious** rituals. Some medicine wheels are more than 12 meters (40 feet) in diameter, while others are arranged in **anthropomorphic** shapes. The Big Horn Medicine Wheel in Wyoming consists of a central **cairn** surrounded by a circle of stones, with lines of cobbles radiating out from the central cairn to the surrounding circle. This wagon wheel–like arrangement gave these structures their names. The majority of medicine wheels are found in the present Canadian province of Alberta.

MEDIEVAL CLIMATE OPTIMUM. Period of unusually warm temperature in the Northern Hemisphere that lasted from the 10th century to the 14th century. Also referred to as the Medieval Warm Period, during this time the Norse (Vikings) took advantage of ice-free seas to colonize Greenland and other outlying lands of the far north. The Medieval Climate Optimum was followed by the **Little Ice Age**, a period of global cooling that lasted from the 14th century until the 18th century, when current climatic conditions developed.

MEDITHERMAL. Period of environmental stability in North America that developed following the **Altithermal**, during the period from 5000 to 3000 B.P. (3000–1000 B.C.). The Medithermal was characterized by a decrease in mean temperatures and an increase in moisture in the Northern Hemisphere. These changes are reflected in **palynology** studies that indicate a concomitant increase in woodland and grassland environmental zones.

MEGAFAUNA. Large land mammals indigenous to North America during the **Pleistocene** era. Consisting primarily of herbivores such as **mammoth**, **mastodon**, **bison**, **horses**, tapirs, camels, and other large mammals, the vast majority of North American megafauna became **extinct** during the late Pleistocene era (circa 10,000 B.P.). Archaeologists and vertebrate paleontologists are divided on the precise causes of the mass extinction of North American megafauna. Some scholars believe that humans played a direct role in these extinctions. Following the work of **Paul S. Martin**, these researchers see **Paleoindian hunting** strategies as leading to the depletion of local **megafauna** populations and eventually their complete extinction. However, other scholars contend that climate change during the **Holocene** emergence played a critical role in these extinctions. Evidence of similar megafaunal extinctions in Europe, Asia, and Australia during the late Pleistocene support the view that climate change played the principal role in the extinction of North American megafauna. *See also* BLITZKRIEG MODEL.

MEN. *See* GENDER ROLES.

MENOMINI INDIANS. Algonquian-speaking peoples who originally resided in Wisconsin and Michigan. The Menomini were village **agriculturalists** who supplemented their diet through **foraging**.

Like other groups of the Great Lakes region, the Menomini were negatively impacted by migrations into their traditional territories by groups from the east following European colonization. However, unlike the **Winnebago** and other groups, the Menomini were able to accommodate these pressures by seeking alliances with the more militarily powerful **Ojibwe** and **Huron**. During the European settlement of the Great Lakes region, the Menomini were able to successfully avoid relocation through the efforts of Chief Oshkosh, and today possess many of the lands controlled by their precontact ancestors. At present, there are more than 7,000 Menomini, with the majority residing in Wisconsin.

MESA SITE. Archaeological site in Alaska that possesses evidence of early **Paleoindian** occupation at approximately 13,000 B.P. (11,000 B.C.). **Artifacts** at the Mesa site are similar to **Clovis projectile points**, and some archaeologists use evidence from Mesa and other Alaskan sites to argue for an indigenous North American origin for Clovis cultures. The precise relationships between these early Alaskan peoples and Paleoindian groups in other areas of North America are presently unclear.

MESA VERDE. Mountainous region of southwestern Colorado, north of the San Juan basin that has evidence of more than 1,000 prehistoric **archaeological** sites. Mesa Verde's environment is unique in the **Southwest**, and is characterized by increased vegetation and abundant water sources. The majority of the archaeological sites at Mesa Verde were occupied by **Anasazi** groups during the period from 1950 to 650 B.P. (A.D. 1–1300). Occupations of Mesa Verde are notable because of their inaccessible locations along cliff edges, and their unique masonry construction. The numerous communities within Mesa Verde supported a large **agricultural** population, considered by archaeologists to have far exceeded that of **Chaco Canyon** or other Anasazi regions. The cliff-sheltered settlements at Mesa Verde are thought to have been a response to increased **warfare** in the region, and the need for greater protection by local groups. Although individual sites at the Mesa Verde could be quite large, there is little evidence to suggest the presence of social stratification among the local population. By the late 13th century, the majority of sites in Mesa

Verde were abandoned, with available evidence suggesting that this abandonment was related to a long-lasting drought and a corresponding collapse in agricultural productivity.

MESOAMERICAN CULTURE AREA. Geographic and **cultural** region extending south and east from central Mexico to include parts of Guatemala, Belize, Honduras, and Nicaragua. In pre-Columbian times, Mesoamerica was inhabited by a series of unique cultures, including the Olmec, Maya, Toltec, Aztec, and others. The cultures of Mesoamerica are thought to have impacted those of North America principally through **trade** and **exchange** and the introduction of Mesoamerican **domesticated** plants.

METATE. A shallow, concave stone used in conjunction with a **mano** to grind **maize**, other grains, and pigments. Manos and metates were used for a variety of crushing and grinding purposes, but archaeologists can often use these items to identify the specific plants being eaten by past groups.

MIAMI INDIANS. **Algonquian**-speaking Native American group originally indigenous to portions of northern Illinois, Indiana, and Ohio. Closely related to the **Illinois**, the Miami were composed of six autonomous **bands**. They were village **agriculturalists** who resided in longhouses within **fortified** villages. Following massive population losses due to European-introduced **diseases**, the **Midewiwin society** became an increasingly important component of Miami **religious** life. During the 1820s, they were relocated to eastern Kansas and merged with the remnants of the Illinois. Following the Civil War, they moved to Oklahoma, where more than 2,000 Miami continue to reside.

MICA. Any of a group of chemically and physically related aluminum silicate minerals, common in igneous and metamorphic rocks, characteristically splitting into flexible sheets. Mica naturally occurs in the southern Appalachian Mountains, and was mined and **traded** with groups throughout the **Eastern Woodlands**. **Woodland** peoples, particularly the **Hopewell**, used mica in the production of high-status, nonutilitarian **artifacts**. Biotite, a black or dark green variety of **mica**, was also used by many Native American groups for the production of decorative ornaments.

MICMAC (MI'KMAQ) INDIANS. Algonquian-speaking Native American groups of eastern Canada, including the maritime provinces of Nova Scotia, New Brunswick, Prince Edward Island, and the Gaspé Peninsula of Quebec. The Micmac were seasonally mobile **foragers** who **hunted caribou**, moose, and small game during the winter, and **fished, gathered** shellfish, and hunted whales, **seals**, and porpoises in the summer. Foraging territories were controlled by individual family groups, with groups claiming access to these areas, and their **subsistence** resources, based upon ancestral claims. The Micmac were early allies of the French, but they later allied themselves with the English. More than 15,000 Micmac presently reside in Canada.

MICROWEAR ANALYSIS. Detailed analysis of **archaeological lithics** using advanced microscopy in an effort to determine the uses of these **artifacts**. Evidence of a **tool's** use can be found in the form of polish, striations, breakage, or minor flaking. Comparisons are made between the microscopic use-wear patterns found on archaeological materials with those from experimental uses to infer the functions of lithic tools.

MIDDEN. Refuse heap, usually found near domestic structures, that contains organically enriched sediments indicative of a human presence. These accumulations of debris are often deposited in **stratified** deposits that are useful for **archaeological dating**.

MIDDLE MISSOURI TRADITION. Cultural tradition found in northwest Iowa, southwest Minnesota, and southeast South Dakota, from approximately 1050 to 450 B.P. (A.D. 900–1500). The Middle Missouri Tradition is characterized by increased dependence upon the cultivation of **domesticated** plants and more sedentary populations. The predominant **subsistence** practice of Middle Missouri Tradition peoples was horticulture, with widespread **cultivation** of **maize, beans**, pumpkin, and **squash**. Surplus foodstuffs were stored in large bell-shaped **storage pits** under the floors of individual houses. Middle Missouri Tradition peoples also supplemented their diets through **bison hunting** and the **gathering** of wild plants.

MIDEWIWIN SOCIETY. Native American term for the Grand Medicine Society, a secret **shamanic** society among the **Chippewa, Miami, Ojibwa, Ottawa,** and **Potawatomi** during the 18th and 19th centuries (although there is evidence that it predates the arrival of Europeans). Primarily a mystical healing society, the Midewiwin (also spelled Midewin and Medewiwin) were sorcerers, jugglers, and tricksters, and were both men and women. The Midewiwin consisted of a small number of initiates, with four defined levels of power among members based on the stages of spiritual knowledge they had mastered. Each member owned a sacred **medicine bundle** made of otter skin that contained a number of sacred objects. There was also a tradition of recording their knowledge and sacred formulas on birch bark in a form of hieroglyphic writing that only other members of the society could decipher. Objects associated with this society, including sacred Migiis shells (*Cypraea moneta*), have been found in numerous earthen **mounds**, many predating European contact by centuries. Since these shells are only indigenous to the South Pacific, their presence in prehistoric North America remains controversial.

MIDWESTERN TAXONOMIC METHOD. Analytical framework devised by **William C. McKern** (1930) to systematize the analysis of **archaeological** materials. Based on the identification of formal similarities between **artifact assemblages**, this system (also known as the *McKern System*) was built upon four basic units of classification: focus, aspect, phase, and pattern. McKern's goal was to create a system that could be used by archaeologists working separately to classify and compare their materials. The Midwest Taxonomic Method was not particularly successful and was only adopted by a small number of archaeologists working in the **Eastern Woodlands**.

MIMBRES. The final period of the **Mogollon** culture in the **Southwest**, from the ninth to the 13th century. Mimbres is well known for distinctive **ceramic** bowls painted with black-on-white designs featuring **anthropomorphic** and geometric designs. During the Mimbres period, domestic architecture changed to multistoried pueblos organized around central plazas. As with the **Anasazi** and **Hohokam** cultural traditions, Mogollon culture (and Mimbres) came to an end in the early 13th century. Although the reasons for the disappearance of this **cultural tradition** are debated, most archaeologists see prolonged drought as the primary reason for this decline.

MISSISSIPPIAN CULTURE. Term denoting both a temporal period (1050–400 B.P. [A.D. 950–1500]) and a **cultural tradition** in the North American **Southeast** and Midwest. Considered the penultimate cultural florescence in all of North America north of Mexico, Mississippian culture is characterized by the presence of large cities such as **Cahokia** and **Moundville** with local populations in the tens of thousands, and a highly complex sociopolitical organization. Mississippian cultures constructed large earthen **mounds** that frequently served as supportive platforms for **chief's** houses, **charnel houses**, and other political and **religious** structures. Mississippian material culture also frequently included well-crafted shell tempered **ceramics**, **anthropomorphic** and **zoomorphic** figurines, monolithic stone **axes**, wall trench structures, and exotic, nonlocal **artifacts** of **copper** and shell. The quantity and variety of exotic materials found at major Mississippian sites have led several scholars to infer that these societies had craft specialization. Mississippi **subsistence** practices were based upon the intensive **cultivation** of **maize**, **beans**, **squash**, **sunflowers**, and other cultigens.

One of the most important features of Mississippian cultures is heightened sociopolitical complexity. Characterized most commonly as complex **chiefdoms**, sociopolitical status in Mississippian societies was hereditary. These hereditary, **stratified** social positions brought dramatic differences in access to material wealth and subsistence resources. Social leadership was normally vested in one matrilineage, with the position of chief passed within this family from one generation to the next. Political elites at the largest Mississippian cities expanded their control over resources by constructing alliances with smaller communities on their periphery through economics, ideology, and **warfare**. The resulting polities were frequently geographically expansive, but were difficult to maintain for long periods of time. Our knowledge of Mississippian societies is derived primarily from **archaeological** research, but some firsthand descriptions of these societies are found in early European documents such as the chronicles of the **Hernando de Soto** expedition. However, there are indications that the largest Mississippian cultures began to decline prior to the arrival of Europeans in North America.

MODOC INDIANS. Penutian-speaking Native American group indigenous to the area south of the Cascade Range in south-central Oregon and northern California. The Modoc were complex **foragers** who shared many **cultural** practices with groups of the **Northwest Coast culture area**. The Modoc were forcibly removed from their homeland in the 1860s, with many Modoc resisting this relocation, leading to the Modoc War of 1872–1873. The Modoc were eventually subdued and relocated to reservation lands in Oklahoma. In the early 20th century, the U.S. government returned the Modoc to Oregon, where at present they number approximately 500.

MOGOLLON CULTURE. One of the major prehistoric **cultural traditions** of the American **Southwest**. Residing in what is now southeastern Arizona and southwestern New Mexico between 2150 and 750 B.P. (200 B.C.–A.D. 1200), the Mogollon peoples began as complex **foragers**, but became increasingly dependent upon **domesticated** plants with the introduction of **maize** into the region from **Mesoamerica**. With a greater dependence upon **cultivated** plants, the Mogollon began to construct larger, more permanent stone houses and public structures. The Mogollon produced distinctive corrugated **ceramics** in brown and red and pottery decorated with black-on-white **anthropomorphic** and **zoomorphic** designs. As with the **Anasazi** and **Hohokam**, the Mogollon culture declined during the 13th century in response to a long-lasting, region-wide drought.

MOJAVE INDIANS. Yuman-speaking Native American groups of the Mojave Desert of eastern California and western Arizona, and the lower Colorado River region. Mojave peoples practiced diverse **subsistence** practices, with those along the Colorado engaged in **agriculture** and those in more desert environments engaged in **foraging**. Social organization was based around individual patrilineal families, with small groups coalescing into seasonally occupied settlements. There are more than 2,000 Mojave in Arizona.

MOHAWK INDIANS. Iroquoian-speaking Native American groups indigenous to the upper Hudson Valley and St. Lawrence River region of New York and southern Ontario. The Mohawk were the easternmost member of the **Iroquois Confederacy**. The name Mohawk was applied to these peoples by neighboring **Algonquian** groups and later adopted by Europeans. These people refer to themselves as *Kanien'kehake*, which means "the flint people." These groups were traditionally village **agriculturalists** who supplemented their diets with **foraging** activities. Like other Iroquoian groups, the Mohawk constructed multifamily **longhouses** within large **fortified** villages. Given their geographic proximity to European colonists, the Mohawk were heavily impacted by **disease**, **trade**, and missionization during the **historic period**. The Mohawk are also noted for their distinctive hairstyle. At present, more than 20,000 Mohawk reside in the United States and Canada.

MOIETY. One of two distinct social groups in a society. Moieties represent the division of society into two discrete social groups based on **kinship**. Moieties were common to many Native American societies, and provided a mechanism for organizing large-scale social labor efforts such as canal construction or earthen mound building.

MONKS MOUND. Largest earthen **mound** at the **Cahokia** site and also the largest Native American earthen construction north of Mexico. Given its name from an occupation of the site by Trappist Monks in the historic period, Monks Mound was constructed by **Mississippian** peoples between 950 and 650 B.P. (A.D. 1000–1300). Although there has been some modification to the mound through erosion, Monks Mound is presently more than 30 meters (100 feet) in height, with a base covering more than 5.6 hectares (14 acres). Monks Mound possesses several distinct construction episodes, with four identifiable mound terraces. The mound was crowned with a series of buildings, including elite residences and other structures of **religious** and political significance.

MONTAGNAIS INDIANS. **Algonquian**-speaking Native American group indigenous to the St. Lawrence and James Bay region of present-day Quebec and Labrador, who are also referred to as the Innu. The

Montagnais were migratory **foragers** who were primarily organized into small, closely related **bands**. The Montagnais were major participants in the **fur trade** with the French, and used their French allies to counter their **Iroquois** and **Mohawk** enemies for supremacy in the St. Lawrence Valley. At present, more than 15,000 Montagnais reside in Quebec and Labrador.

MOORE, CLARENCE BLUMEFIELD (1852–1936). Avocational **archaeologist** who conducted numerous investigations of archaeological sites throughout the **Southeast**. A wealthy Philadelphian, Moore began his archaeological research at the age of 40. He is remembered for both his archaeological investigations and his unique mode of transportation, a private steam-powered paddleboat, the *Gopher*. Although his field investigations were often lacking from a methodological perspective, he published the results of his excavations in a series of profusely illustrated volumes. The majority of his collection was donated to the Academy of Natural Sciences in Philadelphia, and was eventually sold to the Museum of the American Indian.

MOOREHEAD, WARREN KING (1866–1939). Early American **archaeologist** who worked primarily in the Midwest and **Northeast**. Moorehead served as director of the Peabody Foundation for Archaeology at Phillips Academy in Andover, Massachusetts, from 1912 through 1920. During this time he conducted numerous excavations at sites in the Mississippi, Ohio, and Scioto River valleys.

MORGAN, LEWIS HENRY (1818–1881). American lawyer and amateur **anthropologist** who had both personal and professional interests in **Iroquoian** groups, especially the **Seneca**. Morgan was intrigued by **kinship** and became one of first scholars to formally classify Native American kinship system (*Systems of Consanguinity and Affinity of the Human Family*, 1871). He was also intrigued by the importance of **clans** to social organization in a number of societies. Based on these particular areas of research, Morgan developed a unilineal **evolutionary** framework for the development of human societies (*Ancient Society*, 1877). He suggested that all human cultures developed along the same path of savagery, barbarism, and civilization. Morgan's research was very influential during the late 19th and early 20th centuries, and played a vital role in the development of the social theories of Karl Marx and Frederick Engels.

MOUND. Earthen structure produced through the intentional piling of soil, shell, or other materials in a location. Mounds were used by Native American groups for **burials**, as substructures for buildings, as locational markers, and for **religious** reasons. Earthen mounds are the most visible evidence of Native American occupation in many areas, especially in the **Eastern Woodlands**.

MOUND BUILDER CONTROVERSY. Spirited debate among scientists and nonscientists concerning the **cultural** origins of the mound builders of ancient North America. Largely a 19th-century debate, the Mound Builder Controversy was predicated on the widespread belief among Americans of European descent that Native Americans lacked the intellectual and cultural capabilities necessary to undertake the collective labor necessary to construct large **earthworks**. Antiquarians proposed a large number of potential prehistoric inhabitants responsible for **mound** construction, including Phonecians, Egyptians, Vikings, and even the **Lost Tribes of Israel**. The development of a more scientific archaeology in the United States during the late 19th century led the Smithsonian Institution's **Bureau of American Ethnology**, under the direction of **Cyrus Thomas**, to conduct investigations into the cultural origin of mound builders. The results of these investigations, published as the 12th *Annual Report* of the Bureau of American Ethnology (1894), provided conclusive evidence that Native Americans were responsible for the construction of these mounds.

MOUND CITY SITE. Archaeological site located on a terrace above the Scioto River north of Chillicothe, Ohio. Consisting of a rectangular **earthwork** enclosing more than five hectares (13 acres), Mound City contains 24 earthen **mounds**. Constructed between 2150 and 1450 B.P. (200 B.C.–A.D. 500), this site provided much of the archaeological data that initially defined the **Hopewell** tradition.

MOUNDVILLE SITE. Major **Mississippian** period settlement located along the Black Warrior River in west-central Alabama. Occupied from approximately 950 to 550 B.P. (A.D. 1000–1400), at its height, Moundville was the second-largest Native American city north of Mexico. Covering more than 120 hectares (300 acres), Moundville was surrounded by a large wooden **fortification** with a central plaza and 26 mounds constructed inside this protective barrier. Moundville is believed to have been the political and **religious** center for a major Mississippian **chiefdom** along the Black Warrior River. Marked differences in the quantity and quality of **burial** goods, as well as the location and size of domestic structures, suggest that Moundville society was highly stratified, with dramatic social distinctions between elites and commoners.

MUMMY CAVE SITE. Rockshelter site on the Shoshone River in Park County, Wyoming. Mummy Cave was occupied from approximately 9300 to 400 B.P. (circa 7300 B.C.–A.D. 1580). Consisting of 38 discrete strata, **archaeological** materials in the cave represent occupations by peoples of several distinct **cultural traditions**. The most significant materials from Mummy Cave relate to the **McKean Complex** of the **Plains Archaic tradition**. Materials recovered from Mummy Cave include materials of wood, hide, and feathers, as well as a wide variety of **lithic tools** and faunal remains. An exceptionally well-preserved **burial** within the cave, dated to 1200 B.P. (circa A.D. 750), provided the impetus for giving the site its current name.

MURRAY SPRINGS SITE. Archaeological site located near the **Naco** and **Lehner** sites in Arizona and occupied during the **Paleoindian** period at approximately 11,000 B.P. (9000 B.C.). Excavations revealed the remains of several butchered **mammoths** and **bison** in association with **Clovis projectile points** and a mammoth-bone shaft wrench or spearthrower. Murray Springs is also important to archaeologists because **artifact**s from the site were found in identifiable activity areas.

MUSKOGEAN LANGUAGE FAMILY. Native American language family consisting of several individual languages spoken by groups indigenous to the **Southeast**. Major languages in this family include **Choctaw**, **Chickasaw**, **Creek**, Alabama, Koasati, Hitchiti, and **Apalachee**.

– N –

NACO SITE. **Archaeological** site located near the **Lehner** and **Murray Springs** sites in southeastern Arizona during the **Paleoindian** period at approximately 11,000 B.P. (9000 B.C.). Naco is unusual because a large number of **Clovis projectile points** were found in direct association with a single **mammoth** skeleton. It is believed that this mammoth was ambushed by a large number of hunters, fled the attack, and died later from its injuries.

NAMU SITE. **Archaeological** site located at the mouth of the Namu River on the coast of British Columbia. Occupied from approximately 9100 to 450 B.P. (7100 B.C.–A.D. 1500), the Namu site contains more than three meters (10 feet) of archaeological deposits. Namu has revealed much about Native American cultural adaptations during its 9,000-year occupation. Archaeological evidence from Namu indicates the blending of Paleo-Arctic and Paleoplateau cultural traditions at approximately 7000 B.P. (5000 B.C.).

NARVAEZ, PANFILO DE (1470?–1528). Spanish explorer and soldier who helped conquer Cuba in 1511 and led an expedition to **southeastern** North America in 1527. Having been granted the lands of Florida by Emperor Charles V in 1526, Narvaez led an expeditionary force of 300 men to explore this territory. He landed on the west coast of Florida near present-day Tampa Bay in April 1528. A series of natural disasters, skirmishes with Native Americans, and other tactical mistakes led to the party's devastation, with the four surviving members of the expedition constructing rafts and sailing for Mexico. This group, including **Cabeza de Vaca**, eventually reached a Spanish settlement in Mexico in 1536.

NATCHEZ INDIANS. Native American groups formerly located on the lower Mississippi River near present-day Natchez, Mississippi. The Natchez speak a **Muskogean** language and are **culturally** related to other Muskogean Native American groups in the **Southeast**. The Natchez were village **agriculturalists** who cultivated **maize, beans, squash,** and other plants. They also supplemented their diet with **foraging** activities. During the late prehistoric and early **historic periods,**

the Natchez were organized into a complex **chiefdom**, with stark hereditary social divisions between elites and commoners. The preeminent social position in Natchez society was that of the **Great Sun**, a divine chief who held considerable power over his subjects. *See also* TATTOOED SERPENT.

NATIVE AMERICAN GRAVE PROTECTION AND REPATRIATION ACT (NAGPRA). A U.S. federal law that regulates the control of Native American human remains, **burial goods**, and other items of **cultural** patrimony excavated on federal lands or in publicly funded **archaeological** collections. Passed by Congress in 1990, NAGPRA is designed to facilitate the repatriation of certain human remains and funerary objects from museum and university collections to Native American tribes. NAGPRA was initially designed to ensure that remains affiliated with modern Native American peoples could be returned for reburial, without them being subject to additional scientific analysis. The implementation of this legislation has been difficult, and has led to several disagreements between archaeologists and Native Americans, including the controversy involving **Kennewick man**.

NAVAJO INDIANS. Athabaskan-speaking Native American groups, also known as the *Dene*, who resided in the **Southwest** at the time of European contact. The Navajo migrated to the Southwest from the Canadian plains during the early 13th century. Prior to their arrival in the southwest, the Navajo were migratory **foragers**, but they quickly adopted **agricultural** practices from **Puebloan** groups. After European contacts, the Navajo also adopted sheep, goat, and cattle herding. Navaho social organization centers upon matri**clans** with a tradition of strong female-centered domestic leadership. Navajo domestic structures, **hogans**, are generally scattered across the landscape, with little of the nucleation present at Puebloan settlements. Navajo **religion** includes animistic elements, and is notable for strong fears of witchcraft and an avoidance of the dead. At present the Navajo are one of the largest Native American groups, with more than 200,000 residing in New Mexico, Arizona, and Utah.

NEEDLE. Small, slender, rodlike **tool** used for sewing. Native American weavers used bone needles to produce tailored clothing, blankets, **tipi** coverings, and a variety of other needlecrafts.

NEGATIVE PAINTING. Method for creating decorative designs on unfired **ceramics** in which the background elements of the design are covered with wax and then colored paint is applied to the foreground design. When fired, the wax melts, resulting in a light-colored outline surrounding the foreground design. Negative painting was used frequently by Native American groups of the **Southeast** during the **Mississippian** period.

NELSON, NELS CHRISTIAN (1875–1964). American **archaeologist** who immigrated to the United States from Denmark. Nelson's initial archaeological research involved the **stratigraphy** of **shell mounds** of the San Francisco Bay area, but he conducted additional research in the **Southeast** and **Southwest**, as well as Europe and Asia. His most enduring contribution to American archaeology is his work at Tano Pueblo in New Mexico, where he perfected his stratigraphic excavation methods.

NENANA COMPLEX. Series of **archaeological** sites in the **Arctic** and **Subarctic** regions dated between 12,000 and 8000 B.P. (circa 10,000–6000 B.C.) characterized by lanceolate bifacial **projectile points** and other **lithic** materials similar to those of **Paleoindian** groups of the **Plains** and **Southwest**. Also referred to as the Northern Paleoindian tradition, the Nenana complex is thought to represent one of the earliest human occupations of eastern **Beringia**. The **Mesa site** is the best-known example of a site belonging to the Nenana complex.

NET SINKER. Grooved or perforated stones tied to the periphery of a **fishing** net to aid its sinking. Also referred to as net weights and sinkers, these objects frequently survive in the **archaeological** record, while the nets to which they were attached have decomposed.

NEW ARCHAEOLOGY. *See* PROCESSUAL ARCHAEOLOGY.

NEWARK SITE. Large complex of geometric **earthworks** located in Licking County, Ohio. The Newark site is thought to be the largest and most complex earthwork complex in North America. Built by **Hopewell** peoples between 1850 and 1550 B.P. (100 B.C.–A.D. 400), the Newark earthworks originally covered more than 10 square kilometers (four square miles). When originally mapped by **Ephraim G. Squire** and **Edwin H. Davis** in the 1840s, the earthworks at the Newark site included a series of large circles and squares connected by low earthen walls to a large octagonal enclosure. Much of the Newark site has been lost to modern land modification, including the construction of a golf course at the center of the site.

NEZ PERCÉ INDIANS. Native American groups of the Snake River region of central Idaho, western Oregon, and western Washington who speak a **language** belonging to the Sahaptian-Chinook branch of the Penutian language family. The cultural practices of the Nez Percé were similar to those of other groups of the **Plateau culture area**, with subsistence practices centering on **fishing** and the **gathering** of terrestrial plant resources. The introduction of the **horse** into Nez Percé society encouraged many groups to adopt the migratory **bison-hunting** practices of western **Plains** cultures. The Nez Percé were forced to cede much of their territory to the United States in 1855, but the discovery of gold on their land led to additional territorial pressures. This constant pressure by American settlers for the Nez Percé to cede more lands eventually led to the Nez Percé War of 1877, where Chief Joseph led a group resistant to the loss of additional territory. Following their defeat, many Nez Percé were placed on the Coville Reservation in Washington; however, the majority reside on their main reservation in Idaho. At present, there are more than 4,000 Nez Percé in the United States.

NODWELL SITE. **Huron** village site in Ontario, Canada, occupied during the late 13th and early 14th centuries. Excavations at the Nodwell site revealed the presence of a large, **fortified** village with 12 individual **longhouses**. This site is important because it contains an excellent record of domestic occupation and represents one of the most complete excavations of a Huron community from this time period.

NOOTKA INDIANS. Wakashan-speaking Native American peoples of Vancouver Island, British Columbia, and coastal Washington. Consisting of a loose confederacy of more than 20 individual groups, the Nootka were coastal **foragers** who **subsisted** primarily by **salmon fishing**. Culturally related to the **Kwakiutl** and other groups of the **Northwest Coast culture area**, the Nootka participated in seasonal whale **hunts** and practiced the **potlatch**. The Nootka resided in large wooden houses, and were accomplished woodworkers. They practiced a seasonal settlement pattern, with their principal villages occupied during the winter. Each village was sociopolitically independent, with an individual's social position largely related to one's clan affiliation. At present, there are more than 5,000 Nootka in Canada and the United States.

NORTHEAST CULTURE AREA. Large forested region that extends from the Atlantic coast across the Appalachians to the Mississippi Valley, and from the Great Lakes to the Ohio River valley. Groups indigenous to the Northeast practiced a variety of **subsistence** practices from migratory **foraging** to village-based **agriculture**, with almost all of these peoples participating in the **hunting** of **deer** and other large terrestrial mammals. Groups located along the Atlantic coast relied upon **fishing** and shellfish collecting. Given its considerable size and environmental diversity, the Northeast culture area was home to a variety of distinct culture groups, including the **Abenaki**, **Cayuga**, **Delaware**, **Huron**, **Illinois**, **Menomini**, **Micmac**, **Mohawk**, Narragansett, **Ojibwe**, **Oneida**, **Onondaga**, **Potawatomi**, Shawnee, **Seneca**, and numerous others. The major languages of this region included **Algonquian** and **Iroquois**. Domestic architecture varied from temporary single-family structures (wigwams) to large, permanent multifamily structures (**longhouses**). Early contacts between European colonists and Northeastern groups had profound effects on indigenous peoples of this region. The increasing European presence, territorial expansion, introduced **diseases**, and **trade** relations were believed to have played a role in the westward movement of these peoples during the 17th and 18th centuries.

NORTHERN ARCHAIC TRADITION. **Cultural** period in the **Arctic** dated to between 6500 and 1000 B.P. (4500 B.C.–A.D. 950).

Considered a contemporary **cultural tradition** with the coastal **Ocean Bay tradition**, the Northern Archaic is an interior development characterized by the adoption of practices from **Archaic** peoples to the south. Northern Archaic sites show a series of cultural adaptations to both **taiga** and **tundra** environments, with **subsistence** practices centered on the **hunting** of terrestrial mammals and fresh water **fishing**. Cultural materials diagnostic of the Northern Archaic consist of side-notched **projectile points** and a variety of chipped stone **tools**, although microblades appear to be absent. The Northern Archaic is thought to have provided the basis for the development of later northern **Athabaskan** cultures.

NORTHERN PALEOINDIAN TRADITION. *See* NENANA COMPLEX.

NORTHWEST COAST CULTURE AREA. Narrow geographic region stretching almost 3,200 kilometers (2,000 miles) along the Pacific coast of North America from southeastern Alaska to northern California, including the coastal islands. Bounded on the east by the Cascade Mountains and on the west by the Pacific Ocean, the Northwest Coast culture area averages approximately 80 kilometers (50 miles) in width. The predominant terrestrial environment of the Northwest Coast consists of thick temperate-zone rain forests of Douglas fir, cedar, spruce, and hemlock. These forests supported a variety of game animals for Native American peoples, including **deer**, moose, elk, **bear**, mountain goat, sheep, fox, mink, and **beaver**. Coastal marine resources were also important to local diets, with the majority of meat supplied by the **hunting** of whale, **seal**, sea lion, porpoise, sea otter, numerous fish species, and shellfish.

Given the tremendous biotic diversity of their natural environment, Northwest Coast societies were capable of supporting large social groups without the need for **agriculture**. These cultures are collectively considered to be the most sociopolitically complex **foragers** in the Americas, and among the most complex in the world. Most groups were seasonally mobile, with the winter months spent in large coastal villages. With the abundant natural resources at their disposal, Northwest Coast groups developed hereditary social ranking, with one's social position related to that of their family and **clan**. During the **historic pe-**

riod, a traditional social and **religious** ceremony, the **potlatch**, became a way of augmenting one's social position. The best-known groups of the Northwest Coast include the **Bella Coola**, **Chinook**, **Haida**, **Kwakiutl**, **Nootka**, **Salish**, Tillamook, **Tlingit**, and **Tsimshian**.

NORTON TRADITION. Archaeological tradition found at sites in Alaska from 3000 to 1200 B.P. (1000 B.C.–A.D. 750) with material **assemblages** typically containing flaked-stone **tools** similar to the **Denbigh Flint complex**, but with the addition of **ceramics**, oil lamps, and elaborate **ivory** carving. **Ipiutak** is the best-known example of the Norton tradition.

NUNAMIUT ESKIMO. Indigenous North American peoples who occupy the northern foothills and adjacent plain of the Brooks Mountains in northern Alaska. They inhabit an inhospitable environment, with long winters and bitterly cold temperatures. These peoples are specialized **hunters** who follow migratory **caribou** herds in the fall and spring. Based on their **subsistence** practices, the Nunamiut are more heavily dependent upon meat than any other extant **culture** group. **Lewis Binford** conducted **ethnoarchaeological** studies among the Nunamiut in order to learn the details of their **hunting**, processing, and food-storage techniques. Binford took the results of these studies and applied them to the interpretation of prehistoric hunting groups.

– O –

OBSIDIAN. Volcanic glass formed by the rapid cooling of lava. Obsidian is a fine-grained material that can be easily modified into sharp-edged tools. Obsidian naturally occurs in the Rocky Mountains of western North America and was mined by native peoples in this region to produce **tools** and as a **trade** material. Obsidian from the Rocky Mountain region is found throughout North America, with its presence noted in **archaeological** contexts in the Ohio and Mississippi River valleys.

OBSIDIAN HYDRATION DATING. Archaeological dating technique applied to **obsidian tools** to determine their date of manufacture.

This dating technique involves measuring the amount of water absorbed by exposed surfaces on an obsidian tool to determine its age. If the hydration rate is known for the particular type of obsidian being tested, measurements of the hydration layer are used to calculate an absolute date for the **artifact**.

OCEAN BAY TRADITION. Archaeological culture of the Aleutian islands of Alaska during the period from 7500 to 3800 B.P. (5500–1800 B.C.). During this period, the Aleutian climate was warmer and drier than at present, with archaeological evidence that Ocean Bay peoples lived in small, skin tents. The location of Ocean Bay sites and **artifacts** recovered from these sites suggest that these people were engaged in the procurement of marine resources. **Tool** kits from the beginning of this period contain microblades, **harpoons**, fishhooks, and **projectile points** related to the acquisition of a variety of fish and marine mammals for **subsistence** purposes. Later Ocean Bay peoples (circa 6000 B.P. [4000 B.C.]) relied upon ground slate projectile points and knives, abandoning the production of microblade tools. These later Ocean Bay peoples also changed their housing styles as well, replacing skin tents with semisubterranean, sod-covered houses.

OCHER. Form of naturally occurring iron oxide that ranges in color from yellow to brown and red. Red ocher was a highly prized skin pigment used by many Native American cultures for body decorations during **religious** ceremonies. *See also* RED PAINT PEOPLE.

OJIBWA. Algonquian-speaking Native American peoples of the Great Lakes region (primarily along Lake Huron), also known as the *Chippewa* and the *Anishinaabe*. The Ojibwa were seasonally migratory, practicing both horticulture and **foraging subsistence** activities. After the arrival of Europeans, the Ojibwa became involved in a series of conflicts with the **Iroquois** for control of the Great Lakes **trade**. During the 17th and 18th centuries, they migrated into Michigan, Wisconsin, western Ontario, and Manitoba. During the late 18th century, they also moved into portions of the northern **Great Plains** in portions of the Dakotas, Montana, and Saskatchewan. The Ojibwa maintained close **cultural** and linguistic relationships with the

Potawatomi. At present they are one of the most populous native nations, with more than 150,000 Ojibwa in the United States and Canada. *See also* MIDEWIWIN.

OLD BERING SEA STAGE. Cultural period that forms a portion of the **Thule culture** of the **Arctic**, dated between 2250 and 1150 B.P. (200 B.C.–A.D. 800). Related to a general shift in **subsistence** practices to the **hunting** of sea mammals along the Arctic coast, the Old Bering Sea stage is notable for the presence of **kayaks** and **umiaks**. **Artifact assemblages** show a preference for ground slate **tools** and a decline in the production of flaked-stone tools. The Old Bering Sea stage is also identified by the presence of gravel tempered **ceramics**, and bone and antler **harpoon** points, **projectile points**, fish spears, and walrus scapula shovels.

OLD COPPER CULTURE. **Archaeological** culture of the Keweenaw Peninsula and Isle Royale of Lake Superior, during the late **Archaic** period, approximately 5000–3000 B.P. (3000–1000 B.C.). The Old Copper culture derives its name from the prominence of **copper tools** at its sites. Among the first North American groups to adopt the use of copper, Old Copper peoples mined pure copper from deposits in the Lake Superior region. They produced tools from this material and **traded** it to other groups throughout the **Eastern Woodlands**. Lacking the ability to smelt copper **artifacts** to form tools, Old Copper peoples produced lanceolate **projectile points**, crescent knives, awls, fishhooks, **harpoons**, **needles**, bracelets, **beads**, and other objects from copper through cold hammering. The development of trade networks related to the exchange of Old Copper artifacts is believed to have revolutionized cross-cultural interactions during the Late Archaic period.

OLSEN-CHUBBOCK SITE. **Bison** kill site in Colorado related to the activities of a Plains **Paleoindian** group. Dated from 11,000 to 8000 B.P. (9000–6000 B.C.), **archaeological** investigations of the Olsen-Chubbock site have revealed the presence of **Folsom**, Cumberland, and other **fluted projectile points** in association with bison. Olsen-Chubbock is one of the most famous Paleoindian **bison jump** sites, with evidence that humans drove more than 200 bison off a cliff at this site. Such large-scale **hunting** required extensive planning and coordination among hunters, suggesting that several individual Pale-oindian groups may have cooperated at Olsen-Chubbock. Some scholars have suggested that the hunting practices evidenced at Olsen-Chubbock played a direct role in the reduction of bison populations on the **Great Plains**.

OÑATE, JUAN DE (1595–1626). Spanish explorer who led an expedition from New Spain (Mexico) into the **Southwest**. Oñate claimed the territory of New Mexico for the Spanish crown and established a small settlement at San Juan. In 1601 he led an expedition in search of **Francisco Coronado's Quivara** on the southern Plains, crossing portions of the modern states of Texas, Oklahoma, and Kansas. In 1605 he led an expedition along the Colorado River all the way to the Gulf of California. Oñate's adventures in the Southwest were popularized by Gaspar de Villagrá, one of his lieutenants, in a book entitled *Historia de la Nueva México*.

ONEOTA COMPLEX. Widespread **archaeological** manifestation found from eastern Kansas, Nebraska, and the Dakotas to the western Great Lakes, and from southern Manitoba to southern Missouri, during the period from 1050 to 300 B.P. (A.D. 900–1650). The Oneota complex has been alternately defined as a series of closely related **ceramic** styles and as the prehistoric antecedent of the historic **Siouan**-speaking peoples of this region, including the **Iowa**, Kansa, **Missouri**, **Osage**, Quapaw, Winnebago, and other groups. However, some scholars believe that the Oneota were possibly **Algonquians**, more closely related to the **Illinois** and **Miami**.

ONION PORTAGE SITE. Archaeological site located along the Kobuk River in western Alaska with evidence of human occupation as early as 9600 B.P. (7600 B.C.). This site is located near a river crossing favored by **caribou** during their seasonal migrations, and it possesses evidence of human **butchering** of caribou at a very early date. The earliest **artifacts** found at the Onion Portage site belong to the Akmak culture, and bear a remarkable similarity to tools found in the Aleutian Islands and in Northern Japan during the same period. This evidence supports present models for Native American migrations into the Americas across the **Bering Land Bridge**.

ONONDAGA INDIANS. Also referred to as the *Onoda'gega*, *Onon-takeka, or Onondagaono (People of the Hills)*, the Onondaga were one of the original members of the **Iroquoian Confederacy**. Located in central New York, the Onondaga were considered the geographic and political center of the confederacy. Although they were the smallest member of the confederacy, the Onondaga were the traditional "fire-keepers" for the Grand Council of the Iroquois Confederacy and the "keepers of the **wampum**," important ceremonial responsibilities. Onondaga social organization was based upon individual matrilineages and matri**clans**. Males selected from each matrilineage held positions of authority within the community, with a strong tendency toward democratic decision making. The Onondaga supported neutrality during conflicts between the English and French, as well as during the American Revolution. Despite their neutrality, the Americans attacked the Onondaga based upon suspicions that they secretly supported the English. Following the American Revolution, the Onondaga were forced to sign treaties that reduced their lands in New York to a mere 30 square kilometers (approximately 7,300 acres) near present-day Syracuse, New York. Many Onondaga moved with other members of the Iroquois Confederacy to lands on the Grand River in Ontario, while others remained on their lands in central New York. At present, the Onondaga are involved in legal efforts to have additional lands returned to them in New York. More than 1,500 Onondaga presently reside in New York, with several hundred more living in Ontario.

OPTIMAL FORAGING THEORY. Model of human **subsistence** practices borrowed from biology that attempts to understand the decisions motivating cultural food preferences among **foraging** groups. Optimal foraging theory helps **archaeologists** identify the factors critical in shaping past dietary choices. **Archaeologists** have applied aspects of optimal foraging theory to the study of foraging groups in almost all North American **culture areas**.

OSAGE INDIANS. Siouan-speaking Native American groups of the Piedmont and Ozark plateaus of western Missouri, northwestern Arkansas, and southeastern Kansas, primarily along the Osage and Missouri Rivers. The Osage were seasonally nomadic and practiced a mixed **subsistence** regime consisting of **bison hunting, foraging**, and village horticulture. Osage social organization was based on patrilineal **clans** with a strict moiety division. Individual clans lived together in a section of each village, with each clan having representation in a village council. However, males from both moieties filled the two most important sociopolitical positions in Osage society. The introduction of the **horse** greatly increased the mobility of the Osage, permitting them to become increasingly involved in professional bison hunting. The Osage became central players in **trade** with Europeans in the south-central **Great Plains**, emerging as important middlemen in trade between Europeans and Native American groups of the interior and western Plains. Osage lands in Arkansas and Missouri were taken by the U.S. government in the early 19th century, with a reservation for the Osage established in southeastern Kansas. At present there are more than 10,000 Osages, with most residing in Kansas and Oklahoma.

OSCEOLA (1804–1838). Seminole military and political leader who played a major role in the resistance to forced removal of Native American peoples from their lands in Florida. Osceola led his forces against the U.S. military during the Second Seminole War (1835–1842). He was captured by American forces while attempting to reach a peace agreement and was imprisoned at Fort Moultrie, South Carolina, where he died of malaria.

OSHARA TRADITION. Name given by archaeologist Cynthia Irwin Williams for the **Archaic** period of the northern **Southwest** between 7500 and 1350 B.P. (5500 B.C.–A.D. 600). The Oshara Tradition possesses evidence of changes in **projectile point** technology, seasonal mobility, and **subsistence** practices. Evidence suggests an increase in contributions to local diets by **chenopods**, amaranths, grasses, **sunflowers**, dropseed, cacti, rabbit, and mule **deer**. This period is characterized by decreased mobility and a preference for base camps that permitted the year-round exploitation of a fixed group of resources.

OSSUARY. Receptacle for collecting the bones of the dead. Many Native American groups of the **Eastern Woodlands** placed human remains in ossuary deposits associated with earthen **mounds**. Ossuaries have also been found in association with **charnel houses**, with these deposits thought to represent the periodic cleaning of these structures to make room for more remains.

OTTAWA INDIANS. Algonquian-speaking Native American groups that inhabited the northern shore of Lake Huron when first contacted by Europeans. There are close **cultural** and linguistic connections between the Ottawa and the **Ojibwa** and **Potawatami**. The Ottawa became important **trading** partners of the French during the 17th century, eventually allying themselves with the French and **Huron** against the **Iroquois**. Incessant **warfare** with the Iroquois over control of trade in the eastern Great Lakes forced the Ottawa to relocate to the west, with some groups moving as far as the Mississippi River. At present there are more than 10,000 Ottawa living in southern Ontario, northern Michigan, and Oklahoma.

OTTER. Any of several aquatic, carnivorous, web-footed members of the weasel family. The North American otter (*Lustra canadensis*) is found from northern Alaska and Canada into the southern United States. The North American otter is typically 70–90 centimeters (2–3 feet) in length and weighs from four to 10 kilograms (10–25 pounds). Otter fur is thick and glossy brown, and is highly valued. Native Americans made use of the otter as a source of food and skins, but the arrival of Europeans made these animals an important resource for exchange. *See also* FUR TRADE.

OWASCO TRADITION. Cultural tradition of the **Northeast**, particularly the Finger Lakes region of New York. The Owasco tradition dates to approximately 1150–550 B.P. (A.D. 900–1400) and is seen by many archaeologists as representative of proto-**Iroquoian** cultural practices. **Owasco** sites are generally large **palisaded** villages, containing domestic **longhouses**, with evidence of an increasing reliance upon **agricultural subsistence** practices.

OZETTE SITE. Archaeological site located along the Pacific Coast of the Strait of Juan de Fuca in present-day Washington state. Positioned on a steep, forested slope above the tidal shore, the Ozette site represents a 15th-century **Makah Indian** village that was destroyed by a massive mud slide around 459 B.P. (A.D. 1491). The anaerobic environment of the mud covering the site helped to preserve six individual wooden houses and a range of organic **artifacts** that would not have survived under normal environmental conditions, including artifacts of wood, basketry, and cloth. The remarkable preservation of the cultural materials at Ozette has allowed archaeologists to understand the nature of **Northwest Coast** village life with far greater clarity than previously afforded.

– P –

PACIFIC NORTHWEST CULTURES. *See* NORTHWEST COAST CULTURE AREA.

PAIUTE INDIANS. Numic-speaking (**Uto-Aztecan language family**) Native American groups who occupied portions of Utah, Arizona, Nevada, Oregon, and California. Traditionally divided into northern and southern branches, both groups were primarily migratory **foragers** who subsisted on wild plant foods and small game. The Northern Paiute also participated in seasonal **bison** hunts and were more heavily influenced by groups from the **Great Plains**. After the introduction of the **horse**, the Northern Paiute became increasingly mobile, constructing **tipis** and following migratory bison herds. The Southern Paiute constructed temporary brush shelters called **wicki-ups**, used rabbit-skin clothing, and made woven **baskets**. Both groups were very loosely organized in terms of sociopolitical organization. The Paiutes were dramatically impacted by European contacts during the 19th and 20th centuries, especially during the Mormon migration into Utah in the 1850s and 1860s. As a result of the increasing European presence, the Paiutes experienced a reduction in their territory, with most forced to abandon traditional foraging practices. At present there are more than 8,000 Paiutes in the western United States, with many residing on the Paiute reservation in southwestern Utah.

PALEO-ARCTIC TRADITION. Term used to describe the earliest well-documented human occupation of the **Arctic** region, dated between 10,000 and 7000 years B.P. (8000–5000 B.C.) and primarily defined by distinctive **lithic tools**, including microcores, microblades, and small bifaces. Sites such as **Onion Portage** helped to define the Paleo-Arctic tradition as a series of **cultural** adaptations to rising sea levels and a loss of earlier coastal environments. Although the Paleo-Arctic tradition precedes the **Arctic small-tool tradition**, there is little **archaeological** evidence available at present to link the two cultural **traditions**. Recent research on the **Kodiak tradition** of southwestern Alaska suggests that it developed out of the earlier Paleo-Arctic tradition.

PALEOINDIAN. The earliest prehistoric human **cultures** of the Americas. Presently dated from approximately 13,000–9000 B.P. (11,000–7000 B.C.), Paleoindian cultures are distinguished by a series of lithic **tools** and **fluted projectile points**, including **Clovis**, **Folsom**, and others. Prevailing views suggest that Paleoindian peoples lived in small **hunting bands** that entered North America from eastern Siberia via the **Bering Land Bridge**.

PALISADE. Defensive barrier formed by placing vertical posts side by side around a settlement. Palisades were one of the principal means of fortification for Native American sites of the **Eastern Woodlands** and eastern **Great Plains**. Given the complexity of their construction and the amount of resources devoted to their creation and maintenance, palisades are thought to be general indicators of the relative importance of **warfare** to local groups.

PALYNOLOGY. Scientific analysis of plant spores and pollen in order to reconstruct past environments and climates. Pollen is extremely durable and survives well in **archaeological** sediments, revealing much about past **subsistence** activities and local environments.

PAPAGO INDIANS. Uto-Aztecan–speaking peoples of the desert region of southern Arizona and northern Sonora, Mexico. Closely related **culturally** and linguistically to the **Pima**, both groups are thought to be the historic descendants of the **Hohokam**. The Papago were semi-sedentary **agriculturalists** who occupied a series of small, dispersed villages along the San Pedro, Santa Cruz, and Altar Rivers. They practiced **irrigation** agriculture, cultivating **maize**, **beans**, cotton, and the giant saguaro cactus. The Papago also collected salt from small desert lagoons and **traded** it to other groups. The Papago had little contact with Europeans until the late 17th century, allowing them to retain much of their **traditional** culture. In 1848 the United States gained control of Arizona, with the newly established Mexican border traversing Papago lands. Most of the Papago moved to the United States in the late 19th century; however, some groups remained in Mexico. At present, there are approximately 7,500 Papago on reservations in southern Arizona.

PAQUIME SITE. Extensive **archaeological** site located in the Sonoran Desert in the Mexican state of Chihuahua. Also called Casas Grandes, Paquime is thought to have been the most important social, political, and economic center in the region during the period from 750 to 525 B.P. (A.D. 1200–1425). Paquime was linked in a complex **trade** network with other sites in the **Southwest**, forming what has been called the Paquime **interaction sphere**. Located on the boundary between **Mesoamerica** and the Southwest, Paquime became a center for the trade of **copper, macaws**, shell, **turquoise**, and other finished goods.

PAWNEE INDIANS. Caddoan-speaking Native American groups who occupied the Platte River valley in south-central Nebraska and northern Kansas. The Pawnee were a confederacy composed of four independent groups, each with its own village. The Pawnee were village **agriculturalists** who cultivated **maize**, **beans**, and **squash**, and supplemented their diet with **foraging** activities. These groups also engaged in seasonal **bison** hunts as well, providing them with much needed meat and **bison** skins. Each group constructed dome-shaped **earthlodges** in their permanent villages, but used **tipis** while engaged in the seasonal bison hunt. Social ranking was an important aspect of Pawnee society, with distinctive statuses for **chiefs** and **shaman**, the most important social positions. The Pawnee maintained generally good relations with the United States, with many Pawnee men serving as cavalry scouts. Pawnee lands in Nebraska and Kansas were ceded to the United States in the 19th century, with most Pawnee moving to a reservation in Oklahoma. Presently, there are more than 2,500 residing in Oklahoma.

PECKING. Process used in the manufacture of durable stone **tools** from granular stone by hammering the stone with a hammerstone. Native American stone bowls, **manos**, and **metates** were commonly produced through the pecking technique.

PECOS CLASSIFICATION. Chronological framework for the prehistory of the **Southwest** devised by **A. V. Kidder** at the **Pecos Conference** of 1927. This classification system divided **Anasazi culture** into eight temporal units based on styles of architecture and **ceramics**. When first developed, it was expected that the Pecos classification would be applicable to the entire Southwest, but additional **archaeological** research indicated that it was of limited geographic and cultural applicability. Although changes have been made to the Pecos classification system, it still provides the basis for contemporary chronological divisions of Anasazi culture.

PECOS CONFERENCE. **Archaeological** conference organized by **A. V. Kidder** at the **Pecos Pueblo** ruins near Santa Fe, New Mexico, in 1927 with the purpose of bringing together scholars working in various areas of the American **Southwest** to establish common terminologies and research priorities. The Pecos Conference provided an important opportunity for scholars to share the results of their research and plan future archaeological investigations. It was also at this conference that Kidder proposed the **Pecos classification**. The Pecos Conference continues to be held annually in the Southwest.

PECOS PUEBLO. **Archaeological** site located on a rocky knoll near the Pecos River, near the boundary between **cultural** groups of the southern **Great Plains** and **Puebloan Southwest**. Occupied from 1150 to 122 B.P. (A.D. 800–1838), Pecos Pueblo was settled by Puebloan groups from the Rio Grande Valley. The local environment has fertile soils, a reliable water supply, adequate wood, and abundant plants and animals, making it highly suitable for human occupation. The site expanded dramatically around 650 B.P. (A.D. 1300), with architectural additions indicative of defensive **fortifications**. The residents of Pecos were Tiwa-speaking village agriculturalists, who also engaged in extensive **trade** with both Puebloan and nomadic Plains groups. This trade helped make Pecos Pueblo an important regional center. **Francisco Coronado** visited Pecos Pueblo in 1540, with the Spanish establishing a mission in the town in 1618. The Pecos mission was destroyed in the Pueblo Revolt of 1680 but was reestablished by the Spanish in 1693. Raids by the nomadic **Apaches** and **Comanches**, together with epidemic **disease**, decimated the local population in the 18th and 19th centuries, with the pueblo eventually abandoned in 1838.

PEÑASCO BLANCO. Spanish for "white cliff," this **archaeological** site is a large, oval-shaped **pueblo** in **Chaco Canyon** overlooking the confluence of Chaco and Escavada washes. Occupied from approximately 1050 to 850 B.P. (A.D. 900–1100) Peñasco Blanco contains more than 150 surface rooms and extends for three or four stories in height. The site also contains two great **kivas** within the central plaza and two more outside. This site is also associated with a series of **pictographs** that some **archaeoastonomers** believe record a supernova in A.D. 1054 and a visit by Halley's Comet in A.D. 1066.

PEQUOT INDIANS. Algonquian-speaking Native American group who were closely related to the **Mohegan**, and who occupied southern Connecticut and Rhode Island when first encountered by Europeans. They were village **agriculturalists** who planted **maize**, **beans**, squash, **tobacco**, and other plants. They also supplemented their diets with aquatic resources, principally **fish**. The Pequot were not one of the largest Native American groups of the **Northeast**, but they were excellent warriors who defended their territories against larger groups, particularly the **Mohawk**. In1637, the Pequot engaged in a series of military engagements with American colonists (termed the Pequot War), which led to a drastic reduction in their population and the enslavement of the vast majority of those who survived. Although there are only slightly more than 1,000 Pequot, with most residing in Connecticut, they have become one of the wealthiest Native American groups in the United States.

PETROGLYPHS. Carving, scratching, or pecking in natural rock surfaces that express artistic or **religious** meanings. Native American petroglyphs commonly depict **anthropomorphic** and **zoomorphic** figures as well as abstract, geometric symbols.

PHASE. **Archaeological** term defined by Gordon Willey and Philip Phillips as "the practicable and intelligible unit of archaeological study." Phases are commonly defined by archaeologists as spatially and temporally unique archaeological **assemblages** that are distinct from all those that precede and follow it.

PHILLIPS, PHILLIP (1900–1994). Pioneering American **archaeologist** who shifted his professional interests from architecture to archaeology following the stock market crash of 1929. Phillips received his training in archaeology from Alfred Tozzer at Harvard University, focusing on the prehistory of the **Southeast**. He worked with **James Griffin** and **James Ford** for more than a decade on the archaeological survey of the lower Mississippi alluvial valley. Phillips went on to conduct archaeological research throughout the Southeast, specializing in the analysis of carved shell from the **Southeastern Ceremonial Complex**. Perhaps his greatest contribution to American archaeology was the publication of *Method and Theory in American Archaeology* with **Gordon Willey**. This book attempted to bring concordance to archaeological methodology and terminology, and provided one of the earliest cultural syntheses for the **Eastern Woodlands**.

PHYTOLITHS. Minute particles of silica derived from plant cells. These particles are important to **archaeological** research because each plant species produces distinct phytoliths, and they survive in the archaeological record long after the original plant has decomposed. Analysis of phytoliths in archaeological soils can reveal the presence of cultivated plants and help reconstruct prior environments and human **subsistence** practices.

PICKERING CULTURE. **Archaeological culture** found in southern Ontario during the period from 1050 to 650 B.P. (A.D. 900–1300). The Pickering peoples were village **agriculturalists** who cultivated

maize, **beans**, and **squash** and supplemented their diets with **foraging** and **fishing**. Most Pickering villages were heavily **fortified**, with substantial **palisades** surrounding villages placed on defensible hills. The predominant domestic structure at Pickering sites were the **longhouse**, suggesting that, like later **Iroquoian** peoples, several individual families shared a dwelling. By 650 B.P. (A.D.1300), Pickering peoples moved to the southwest and occupied areas in both Ontario and New York state. Most scholars believe that the historic Erie, **Huron**, Neutral, and Petun developed out of the Pickering culture.

PICTOGRAPH. Designs painted onto natural rock surfaces that express artistic or **religious** meanings. Native American pictographs commonly depict **anthropomorphic** and **zoomorphic** figures as well as abstract, geometric symbols. **Ocher** and other natural pigments were used to produce pictographic art by Native American artisans.

PIMA INDIANS. Uto-Aztecan–speaking Native American groups of the desert region of southern Arizona. Closely related culturally and linguistically to the **Papago**, both groups are thought to be the historic descendants of the **Hohokam**. The Pima were semisedentary **agriculturalists** who occupied a series of villages along the Gila and Salt Rivers. They practiced extensive **irrigation** agriculture, **cultivating maize**, **beans**, cotton, and the giant saguaro cactus. Given their larger, more populous villages, the Pima maintained a greater sense of group identity than did the geographically dispersed Papago. The Pima have a history of animosity with the **Apache**, who are said to have raided their settlements during the 16th and 17th centuries. The discovery of gold in California in 1849 brought increasing numbers of American settlers and prospectors onto Pima lands, eventually pushing them away from their most fertile territories and water sources. The Pima were eventually granted three small reservations in southern Arizona, where at present more than 10,000 Pima reside.

PIÑON SEEDS. Edible seeds produced by the Piñon tree (*Pinus edulis*). Piñon seeds were a staple food for many Native American peoples of the **Great Basin** and **California** culture areas. These seeds are high in riboflavin, niacin, and protein, and were harvested in large numbers. Piñon seeds were roasted or ground into meal.

PIPE. A device for smoking **tobacco** or other grasses, consisting of a long stem attached to a bowl in which the material to be smoked is placed. Native American pipes were commonly stone or **ceramic**, with many pipes having elaborate **anthropomorphic** and **zoomorphic** designs. Pipe smoking for Native Americans was not simply a form of recreation, but was a ceremonial and **religious** activity. *See also* CALUMET.

PIPESTONE. *See* CATLINITE.

PIT HOUSE. Semisubterranean domestic structures primarily linked to the **Basketmaker** culture of the **Southwest** during the period from approximately 1650 to 950 B.P. (A.D. 300–1000). Pit houses usually consisted of an earth-covered log roof over a circular or rectangular semisubterranean excavation. Entry was made through either a door in the sidewall or a hole in the roof. Most pit houses have a central hearth used for cooking and heating. The semisubterranean nature of these structures allowed them to remain cool in the summer and warm in the winter. Later pit houses were larger than those constructed during earlier periods, with more substantial roofs and interior support posts. Many scholars believe that pit houses were the predecessors of **kivas**, with **religious** ceremonies remaining hidden in underground chambers while domestic structures began to be constructed above ground.

PLAINS CULTURE AREA. *See* GREAT PLAINS CULTURE AREA.

PLAINS WOODLAND TRADITION. **Cultural** period of the central and eastern **Great Plains** between 1700 and 1000 B.P. (250 B.C.–A.D. 950), characterized by the presence of similarities in **ceramic** styles, earthen architecture, and **subsistence** practices. These similarities are thought to have developed as a result of cultural influences from groups in the **Eastern Woodlands**. The most prominent manifestation of the Plains Woodland tradition is the Kansas City **Hopewell**. The Kansas City Hopewell **exhibit** many of the cultural characteristics of Eastern **Hopewell** groups, including large, densely populated villages, and possessed very similar **artifact assemblages**.

PLANO CULTURE. Late **Paleoindian** and early **Archaic cultural tradition** of the Rocky Mountains and Great Lakes regions during the period from 9000 to 5000 B.P. (7000–3000 B.C.). Plano material culture is defined by the presence of characteristic **projectile points** and the lanceolate **Cody** knife, as well as an increased presence of **manos**, **metates**, milling stones, and other **tools** used to process plant foods. Plano peoples are thought to represent a transition from the big-game **hunting** tradition to that of a more balanced **subsistence** regime.

PLANTS. Native American groups **subsisted** upon a wide variety of plants, with local diets shaped by cultural food preferences and locally available resources. **Foraging** groups took advantage of nuts, weeds, grasses, fruits, and roots, while **agricultural** groups continued to collect local subsistence resources while fulfilling the majority of their food needs through the **cultivation** of **domesticated** plants. *See also* ACORNS; AGAVE; BEANS; *CHENOPODIUM BERLANDIERI*; GOURDS; KNOTWEED; MAIZE; MARSHELDER; MAYGRASS; PIÑON SEEDS; PRIMARY FOREST EFFICIENCY; QUID; SCREWBEAN; SEAL; SQUASH; SUMPWEED; TEOSINTE.

PLATEAU CULTURE AREA. Geographic area composed of the Columbia Plateau between the Rocky and Cascade mountain ranges, including portions of present-day eastern Washington, northern Idaho, western Montana, northeastern and central Oregon, northeastern California, and southeastern British Columbia, Canada. The earliest evidence of human occupation of the Plateau region dates to the **Paleoindian** period, approximately 13,000 B.P. (11,000 B.C.). Inhabitants of this region largely remained **foragers** throughout their history, with transitions from highly mobile groups to more semisedentary, resource-specific foraging activities. By about 6000 B.P. (4000 B.C.), pit houses appear in the region, indicating more sedentary populations. By 1450 B.P. (A.D. 500), Plateau cultures demonstrate a series of cultural adaptations related to salmon **fishing**, including **fish weirs** and nets. These patterns largely continued well into the **historic period**, with precontact Plateau cultures developing into the historic Coeur d'Alene, Flathead, Klamath, Kutenai, Modoc, **Nez Percé**, **Salish** Spokane, Thompson, Umatilla, and others.

PLATFORM MOUNDS. Earthen structures primarily associated with the **Mississippian** peoples of the **Eastern Woodlands**, typically consisting of rectangular mounds with flat surfaces on their tops. **Archaeological** and **ethnohistoric** data suggest that platform mounds were used as supportive bases for a range of important structures, including **chiefly** residences, temples, and **charnel houses**. One of the best-known Mississippian platform mounds is **Monks Mound** at **Cahokia**.

PLEISTOCENE. Sixth epoch of the Cenozonic era, also referred to as the Quaternary. This geologic period is commonly associated with the major glacial periods during the period between 1.8 million years ago until about 11,000 B.P. (9000 B.C.). The Pleistocene ended with the advent of warmer global climates during the present **Holocene** epoch.

POCHTECA. Long-distance **traders** from the Aztec empire of **Mesoamerica** who are believed to have engaged in trade with some groups of the **Southwest**. Some scholars have identified the southwestern traveler image of **Kokopelli** with the *pochteca*.

POINT OF PINES SITE. Major **archaeological** site located on the San Carlos **Apache** Reservation in east-central Arizona with evidence of human presence from 4000 to 450 B.P. (2000 B.C.–A.D. 1500). Excavations at this site by **Emil Haury** helped to define the Mimbres component of **Mogollon** culture. Haury's research revealed a large, 70-room pueblo at the site. Based on **ceramic** evidence, he proposed that a group of **Anasazi** (Kayeta) peoples migrated to the area from the north around 680 B.P. (A.D. 1270). He believed that these people merged with the local Mogollon after relocating to the region. Haury's research also indicated that a large fire consumed most of the pueblo in the early 14th century.

POINTS. *See* PROJECTILE POINTS.

POMPEII EFFECT. Term used to describe **archaeological** contexts in which normally perishable **artifacts** have been preserved due to chance environmental conditions. Derived from the superb preservation of artifacts at the Italian village of Pompeii, the most common situations that promote high levels of preservation are anaerobic environments like mudslides, volcanic ash, ice, or bogs. The **Ozette** site is considered the best example of the Pompeii Effect in North American archaeology.

PONCE DE LEÓN, JUAN (1460–1521). Spanish explorer of noble birth who sailed with **Christopher Columbus** to Hispaniola in 1493 on his second voyage to the Americas. He led an expedition to Puerto Rico in 1508 and was later appointed governor of the province. Inspired by contemporary tales of the "fountain of youth," Ponce de León sailed for Bimini Island in 1513, but missed his intended target, landing instead on the coast of Florida, just north of present-day St. Augustine. He claimed Florida for the Spanish crown and returned to Puerto Rico. In 1521 he led a colonization force to coastal Florida, but was repelled by local Native Americas. He later died in Cuba of wounds received during this ill-fated expedition.

PORT AUX CHOIX SITE. Archaeological site on the Northern Peninsula of Newfoundland, Canada, related to peoples of the **Maritime Archaic Tradition** approximately 7000 B.P. (5000 B.C.). Excavations at Port aux Choix, the site of a Maritime Archaic cemetery indicate that these individuals were covered with red **ocher** at the time of **burial**, with exotic **trade** goods placed in the burials.

POSTPROCESSUAL ARCHAEOLOGY. Theoretical approach to **archaeology** developed by Ian Hodder and others in the 1980s and 1990s. Postprocessual archaeology is a reaction to the explicit positivism and materialism of **processual archaeology**. Although there are numerous individual theoretical programs that find inspiration in the postprocessual critique, most share a concern with **religion**, ideology, gender, art, and other aspects of **culture** that do not leave unambiguous traces in the archaeological record. Postprocessualists see archaeology as a political discipline involving the interpretations of individual archaeologists in the present as much as the story of past peoples.

POTAWATOMI INDIANS. Algonquian-speaking Native American groups of the Great Lakes region, including portions of the present states of Michigan, Wisconsin, Illinois, and Indiana. Closely related **culturally** and linguistically to the **Ojibwa** and **Ottawa**, the Potawatomi were semisedentary **agriculturalists** who supplemented their diets with **foraging, fishing**, and collecting maple sugar. They were a matrilineal society composed of 15 matri**clans**. The arrival of Europeans displaced many **Northeastern** Native American groups, who in turn migrated into the Potawatomi homeland. The **Iroquois**, in particular, placed pressure on the Potawatomi, forcing them to migrate westward. In the early 19th century, the Potawatomi were removed from their lands east of the Mississippi River by the U.S government with most presently residing on reservations in Kansas, Oklahoma, and Ontario, Canada.

POT-HUNTER. Nonprofessional looters who vandalize **archaeological** sites in search of **artifacts** for their private collections or for monetary gain. Pot-hunting activities negatively impact North American archaeological sites, with professional archaeologists engaged in a rage of educational efforts designed to dissuade such actions. The U.S. government has made pot hunting on federal and tribal lands illegal in an effort to preserve archaeological sites from the negative impacts of pot hunting.

POTLATCH. Ceremonial feast practiced by many Native American groups of the **Northwest Coast culture area**. These feasts were sponsored by individual matrilineages or **clans**, and normally involved the distribution of gifts to those in attendance based on their social status. During the **historic period**, the potlatch became a source of social competition between rival social groups, with extravagant gift giving and the destruction of prestige items by the hosts in an effort to display their superior social positions and wealth.

POTTERY. *See* CERAMICS.

POVERTY POINT CULTURE. Archaeological culture composed of a number of sites in the lower Mississippi Valley of Louisiana, Mississippi, and Arkansas between around 4000 and 1250 B.P. (2000–700 B.C.). The **Poverty Point site** is the type site for this **culture**, with diagnostic **artifacts** characteristic of this culture consisting of nonlocal **lithics** (**chert**, galena, hematite, magnetite, slate, and **steatite**), hand-molded clay cooking objects (**Poverty Point objects**), as well as a range of chipped and ground stone **tools** (**adzes**, **beads**, **celts**, drills, **figurines**, **gorgets**, hoes, pendants, perforators, and plummets). In addition, **copper** and other items related to a long-distance **trade** network in the **Eastern Woodlands** are also present. Poverty Point peoples practiced broad-spectrum **foraging**, but the biotic diversity of the lower Mississippi Valley was rich enough to permit them to become semisedentary foragers. Poverty Point peoples also constructed some of the earliest and large **earthworks** in North America. Given the large size of settlements and the presence of such extensive trade networks, some scholars contend that Poverty Point represents one of the earliest sociopolitically complex societies in North America. Archaeologists are uncertain about the factors leading to the decline of this culture around 1150 B.P. (800 B.C.)

POVERTY POINT OBJECTS. Class of unique **artifacts** found at sites related to the **Poverty Point culture**, consisting of small, clay balls used for cooking. These objects were produced out of local clays that were molded into geometric shapes and then fired. Poverty Point objects were then used to cook food in large, subterranean oven pits. These small cooking balls helped control the cooking temperature of meats within these earth ovens without the need for direct heating over open fires.

POVERTY POINT SITE. Large **archaeological** site located on Bayou Maçon in northeastern Louisiana, with evidence of occupation from approximately 4000 to 1250 B.P. (2000–700 B.C). The Poverty Point site is the **type** site for the culture of the same name, and was a major ceremonial and **trade** center for the lower Mississippi River valley. Poverty Point contains some of the earliest **earthworks** in North America, with one large mound, four smaller mounds, and six concentric earthen ridges in the shape of an incomplete octagon. The largest mound at Poverty Point, Mound A, is believed to be an effigy mound, forming a bird with outstretched wings. Archaeological research at Poverty Point indicates that the site was the center of trade for a variety of nonlocal materials, including **cherts** from present-day Alabama, Arkansas, Illinois, Indiana, Kentucky, Mississippi, Ohio, and Tennessee; **copper** from the Great Lakes; galena from Missouri; hematite and magnetite from Arkansas; and **steatite** from the Appalachian regions of Alabama and Georgia. The immediate areas around Poverty Point are **lithic** poor, making the importation of lithic materials important to the livelihood of local peoples. The rich biotic communities surrounding Bayou Maçon are thought to have allowed the occupants of Poverty Point to practice semisedentary **foraging**. Around 1250 B.P. (700 B.C.), Poverty Point was abandoned for reasons yet to be completely understood.

POWELL, JOHN WESLEY (1834–1902). Pioneering American geologist and ethnologist. Powell attended Wheaton and Oberlin Colleges, later enlisting as a captain in the U.S. Army during the Civil War. He lost his right arm at the elbow during the Battle of Shiloh, but continued his military service and was later promoted to the rank of major. Following the war, he served as a professor of geology at Illinois Wesleyan University and was later made a curator at the museum of Illinois Normal University. During the 1860s he led expeditions along the Green and Colorado Rivers, becoming the first person to successfully navigate through the Grand Canyon. Powell became director of the U.S. Geological Survey, and helped found the Smithsonian Institutions **Bureau of American Ethnology** (BAE). Powell served as an advocate for American **archaeology** and was responsible for many of the BAE's earliest archaeological and ethnographic investigations.

POWHATAN INDIANS. Confederacy of more than 30 individual **Algonquian**-speaking Native American groups occupying the Virginia tidewater and eastern Chesapeake Bay. Named for chief Powhatan, to whom each group gave tribute and military support, the Powhatan occupied more than 100 heavily **fortified** villages. The Powhatan were sedentary **agriculturalists** who cultivated **maize**, **beans**, and **squash**. During the **historic period**, the Powhatan experienced both friendly and hostile relations with English settlers, with the marriage of Powhatan's daughter, Pocahontas, to Englishman John Rolfe in 1614 bringing about a short period of peace between the two groups. With the death of Powhatan in 1618, hostilities began again, with the Powhatan attacking English settlements in Virginia in 1622. For more than a decade, conflicts between the Powhatan and English led to the devastation of Powhatan villages. By the late 17th century, Powhatan lands had been reduced considerably, and by the early 18th century many of the individual groups united in the confederacy had become extinct. At present, more than 3,000 Powhatan reside in Virginia.

PRE-CLOVIS CULTURE. Term applied to peoples proposed to have occupied portions of the Americas prior to the development of the **Clovis culture**. The pre-Clovis hypothesis, as it is sometimes referred to, proposes that there were humans in North America long before Clovis peoples, with these humans leaving small collections of unifacial and bifacial **tools** without the presence of formal **projectile points**. Although the presently available evidence is sparse, advocates of a pre-Clovis occupation of North America point to a series of **archaeological** sites with lithic remains suggestive of human manipulation prior to 13,000 B.P. (11,000 B.C.), and possibly as early as 30,000 B.P. (28,000 B.C.).

PRESTATION. *See* TRIBUTE.

PRESTIGE GOODS ECONOMIES. Economic system in which political power is associated with control over, and ready access to, high-status prestige goods. Prestige goods are items that are normally restricted to elite control because of the great expense involved in their production or procurement. Prestige goods can be either raw materials or finished goods, but they are generally thought to be exotic items associated with long-distance **trade** networks and esoteric knowledge. A prestige goods economy is one in which local political leaders can monopolize access to material objects necessary for public claims of heightened social status. The control of prestige goods in public arenas demonstrates an elite's preeminent position in extralocal trade networks. Archaeologists propose that the basis of sociopolitical power in many Native American societies was derived from the control of local prestige-goods economies. Examples of Native American prestige goods economies include **Mississippian** societies and **Chaco Canyon**.

PRIMARY FOREST EFFICIENCY. Theoretical view proposed by **Joseph R. Caldwell** that contends that **Archaic** period peoples of the

Eastern Woodlands became increasingly well adapted to local environmental conditions, with new technologies and regional **cultural traditions** arising in response to local **subsistence** opportunities. Caldwell viewed this adaptive process as the means through which groups developed increasingly efficient subsistence strategies for exploiting the plant and animal resources available to them.

PROCESSUAL ARCHAEOLOGY. Theoretical approach to **archaeology** developed by **Lewis Binford** and others in the 1960s. Advocates of processual archaeology, also called new archaeology, promote an explicitly scientific perspective in both archaeological methodology and theory. Adherents to the program of new archaeology contrasted their attempts at rigorous science and hypotheses testing to the **culture historical** approach of the "old archaeology." From the perspective of new archaeology, the goal of archaeology is cultural explanation rather than merely cultural description. *See also* POSTPROCESSUAL ARCHAEOLOGY.

PROJECTILE POINT. Inclusive term applied to arrow, spear, and dart points. Characterized by a symmetrical tip, a relatively thin cross-section, and an element to allow the point to be **hafted** to a shaft, these objects are projectile weapons used in **hunting** and **warfare**. Native Americans produced a wide variety of projectile points, with archaeologists using these **artifacts** to understand the temporal and spatial aspects of their **cultures**.

PRONGHORN. Small, hoofed, **deer**like mammal indigenous to the Americas from Saskatchewan, Canada, to the desert of northern Mexico, also known as the *American antelope (Antilocapra americana)*, pronghorned antelope, and prongbuck. The natural habitat of the pronghorn consists of grasslands and sagebrush areas of North American plains and deserts. The pronghorn has branched horns, weighs between 40 and 57 kilograms (90–125 pounds), stands about 1 meter (3.3 feet) tall, and has a white or buff tail. The pronghorn is the fastest animal indigenous to the Western Hemisphere, capable of running at speeds of about 100 kilometers (60 miles) per hour. The pronghorn was a source of food for many groups in western North America.

PSEUDOARCHAEOLOGY. Term for the selective use of **archaeological** data to promulgate nonscientific, fictional accounts of the North American past. Common forms of pseudoarchaeology are found in claims of extraterrestrial contacts and undocumented cultural contacts between Native Americans and peoples from other world regions. Examples of pseudoarchaeology include the **mound builder controversy**, the **Cardiff Giant**, the **Kensington Rune Stone**, and other non-evidence-based and antiscientific explanations for archaeological phenomena.

PUEBLO. Term applied to both a group of Native American peoples in the **Southwest** (including the **Hopi, Zuñi**, and others) and the multi-storied **adobe** structures in which they live. Puebloan peoples are considered to be descendants of **Anasazi** peoples, and their use of adobe pueblo structures provides a direct cultural link to the ancient Anasazi.

PUEBLO BONITO. The largest **pueblo** ruin in **Chaco Canyon**. Pueblo Bonito is a semicircular group of room blocks constructed between 1030 and 800 B.P. (A.D. 920–1150), containing more than 600 rooms and rising to a height of five stories. At its peak, it is thought that as many as 1,200 people resided at Pueblo Bonito. The main living quarters at Pueblo Bonito are larger than those at other **Anasazi** sites, with interior rooms connected by rooms with unique T-shaped doorways. The central courtyard at Pueblo Bonito contains two great **kivas**, with an additional 37 smaller kivas scattered throughout the site. Pueblo Bonito, like the other settlements in Chaco Canyon, was abandoned in the late 12th century as a response to a major drought in the region.

– Q –

QUEQERTASUSSUK SITE. Archaeological site located in the eastern **Arctic** on an island in Disko Bay, Greenland, with evidence of human occupation from approximately 4400 to 3150 B.P. (2400–1150 B.C.). Considered part of the **Saqqaq complex**, the Queqertasussuk site contained well-preserved organic materials, including numerous wooden **artifacts**, as well as others of bone and antler. This site also contains the oldest recorded human remains in the Arctic. Queqerta-sussuk remains are related to the **Arctic small-tool tradition**, with the site interpreted as a summer camp used for **seal hunting**.

QUID. Desiccated fibrous plant remains resulting from the human chewing of plants in an effort to extract carbohydrates and other nutrients. Quids are commonly found in caves and other **archaeological** contexts supporting the preservation of perishable materials. Analysis of quids from **archaeological** sites in the **Southwest** and **Great Basin** regions has revealed a great deal of direct information on natural environments, human **subsistence** practices, and the seasonality of site occupations.

QUIVARA. Spanish term for a Native American province on the **Great Plains** purported to have a large population and fabulous riches. First sought by the Spanish explorer **Francisco Coronado** in 1541, Quivara turned out to be a small **agricultural** village somewhere along the Arkansas River in central Kansas or the Canadian River in the Texas Panhandle. Archaeologists and ethnohistorians traditionally have interpreted Quivara as having been a **Wichita** village. *See also* CIBOLA.

– R –

RADIOCARBON DATING. Chronometric **dating** method used to determine the age of organic **archaeological** materials. Also known as *carbon-14 dating*, radiocarbon dating was developed by physicist Willard F. Libby, who received the 1960 Nobel Prize in Chemistry for the technique. Radiocarbon dating is based on the principle that all living organisms absorb various carbon isotopes during their lifetime, with some of these isotopes (particularly C14) being unstable, radioactive forms. Once an organism dies, the radioactive C14 begins to decay, converting into nonradioactive C12. Libby's team discovered that C14 was converted to C12 at a stable rate, approximately 5,730 ± 40 years (referred to as the Cambridge half-life). Thus, the ratio of C14 to C12 in an organic material could be used to calculate the age of that material. Radiocarbon dating is effective at dating organic remains no older than approximately 50,000 years. The recent development of **Accelerator mass spectrometry** (AMS) radiocarbon dating has improved both the accuracy and age estimates capable from C14 samples. Archaeologists rely upon radiocarbon dating as a principle means for dating **artifacts** because it is highly accurate, requires small sample sizes, and is relatively inexpensive.

RANKED SOCIETIES. Societies in which an unequal access to prestige and sociopolitical power exists, usually based upon the status of one's lineage or **clan** affiliation. These societies are also defined as those in which the number of valued social positions is lower than the number of people desirous of filling these positions. Tribes are generally defined as ranked societies, with **big men** filling the most important sociopolitical positions based on their social rank and prestige.

RECIPROCITY. Mode of **exchange** in which economic interactions between individuals take place on equal terms, with neither party holding a dominant position. Reciprocity was a central component of many Native American economic exchanges, especially those among peoples organized into **bands** and **tribes**.

REDISTRIBUTION. Mode of exchange in which a centralized authority receives goods for subsequent distribution to the members of society. Redistribution traditionally has been considered a hallmark of **chiefdoms**, where sociopolitical power is thought to be cultivated through the control of surplus foodstuffs and other resources by local political leaders. Most interpretations of complex Native American societies (e.g., **Cahokia**, **Chaco Canyon**, and **Northwest Coast**) stress the importance of redistribution to local economies and the rise of sociopolitical complexity.

RED PAINT PEOPLE. Nineteenth-century term used to describe **archaeological** remains in Maine and the Maritime Provinces of Canada where the remains of deceased individuals had been covered with red **ocher** at the time of **burial**. Archaeological investigations by Charles Willougby and **Warren K. Moorehead** brought tremendous publicity to these peoples, leading to public controversy concerning their age and ethnic affiliation. Recent archaeological investigation has revealed those responsible for these remains to be the **Maritime Archaic** peoples of approximately 9000–3000 B.P. (7000 B.C. to 1000 B.C.).

REFITTING. Attempts to reconstruct **lithic artifacts** by combined formal **tools** and lithic **debitage** to reveal information about the various stages involved in the production of a stone **tool**. Sometimes referred to as conjoining, refitting is thought to provide a critical insight into the decision-making process of the individual who made the stone tool, and reveal similarities and differences between stone tool makers of distinct **cultural traditions**.

RELIGION. The beliefs and ritual practices concerning supernatural spiritual forces and the afterlife. There was tremendous diversity among Native American peoples concerning the nature of their religious beliefs and practices. However, many Native American groups recognized the heightened supernatural powers of the **shaman**. These individuals frequently supervised religious rituals and served as healers to the sick. Shamans were also required to entered altered states of consciousness by ingesting hallucinogenic substances such as mushrooms, peyote, and tobacco. During these altered states, they were thought to be able to communicate with supernatural forces and intercede on behalf of their communities.

Native American groups practiced a wide variety of religious rituals, with the **black drink** ceremony, **Sun Dance**, and World Renewal Ceremony among them. **Artifacts** such as those related to the **Southeastern Ceremonial Complex**, as well as **medicine wheels, petroglyphs**, sacred **bundles**, and other highly stylized objects are thought to have played major roles in the religious practices of Native American peoples. Although there was no uniform Native American belief system, most Native American religions involved the recognition that there were powerful spiritual forces in the world that were responsible for both good and bad fortune. One was thus forced to entreat these spirits for help and assistance. At the same time, many groups held to forms of ancestor veneration and strong beliefs in **witchcraft**.

Following contacts with **colonial** Europeans, the apocalyptic visions of the Shawnee prophet **Tenskwataw**, and later the **Ghost**

Dance promoted by the **Pauite** prophet Wovoka, led to new forms of religious experience for many Native American peoples. These manifestations of Native American religious beliefs were brutally repressed by the United States, with major efforts undertaken to convert native peoples to Christianity. Although the effort to convert indigenous peoples began as early as first contacts, during the late 19th and early 20th centuries, these efforts culminated in the development of a boarding school system designed to destroy Native American **languages** and religious practices and to assimilate Native Americans to "civilized" white society. At present, Native American religious practices are experiencing a resurgence, with many nonnative peoples turning to these practices as a form of religious devotion.

REMOTE SENSING. General term applied to **archaeological** investigative techniques designed to reveal the presence of subsurface archaeological remains without the need for digging. The most common remote-sensing techniques used by North American archaeologists include ground penetrating radar (GPR), magnetometers, soil resistivity, and aerial photography. Remote sensing is advantageous because it is more cost effective than traditional excavation techniques, and because it allows archaeologists to target their investigations to only those areas believed to have a high probability of containing the cultural materials for which they are searching.

REMOVAL. The forced relocation of Native American groups from their **traditional** territories to reservations. The most famous case of removal involved the **Trail of Tears**, where Native Americans from the **Southeast** were forcibly relocated to lands in Oklahoma.

REVITALIZATION MOVEMENTS. Religious practices designed to return stability to society and purge it from some perceived ill. The most prominent Native American revitalization movement was the **Ghost Dance**.

RITES OF PASSAGE. Ritual acts that mark an individual's transition from one form of social standing to another. These ceremonies normally accompany the transition to adulthood, marriage, death, and other socially defined changes in status. One of the most important

Native American rites of passage was the **Sun Dance** ritual practiced by groups of the northern **Great Plains**.

RIVER BASIN SURVEYS. Series of **archaeological** projects supported by the Smithsonian Institution beginning in 1945 under the **Bureau of American Ethnology** and lasting into the 1960s. The River Basin Surveys were designed to recover archaeological information in the major river drainages of North America, many of which were threatened by impending dam construction. These surveys were conducted primarily in the **Great Plains**, Midwest, and **Southeast** and were successful in providing unprecedented amounts of archaeological data and training numerous professional archaeologists.

RIVERTON CULTURE. Terminal **Woodland culture** primarily found in southern Indiana along the White, Wabash, and Ohio River valleys during the period from 3500 to 1250 B.P. (1500–700 B.C.). Riverton culture is interpreted as a local riverine-adapted culture and its material culture consists of micro**tools** and **projectile points**. Riverton houses were small, circular structures, with subterranean storage features beneath their floors. The presence of extensive **middens** and **storage pits** at Riverton sites, together with reconstructions of Riverton site distributions, suggest that these peoples were becoming less mobile, with a greater focus on a few key **subsistence** resources.

ROANOKE COLONY. English **colonial** settlement founded by Sir Walter Raleigh in 1585 on Roanoke Island, near the coast of present-day North Carolina at the southern entrance to Albemarle Sound. The Roanoke colony was the first English settlement in North America, but its first inhabitants remained for only 10 months. A second group of colonists arrived in 1587, with the birth of Virginia Dare at Roanoke heralded as the first English birth in North America. A supply ship from England arrived at Roanoke Island in 1590 to find the colony deserted. The abandonment of Roanoke and the fate of the colonists remain an enduring mystery.

ROCKSHELTER. Shallow cave or rock overhang large enough to have permitted occupancy by humans. **Archaeological** deposits are commonly found within North American rockshelters, as they provided ready shelter from the environment. Most North America rockshelter sites were occupied by **Paleoindian** and **Archaic** peoples, and are thought to have provided expedient shelter for highly mobile **foragers**. **Modoc Rockshelter**, **Rodgers Shelter**, and the Stanfield-Worley Bluff Shelter are examples of archaeologically significant North American rockshelter sites.

RODGERS SHELTER SITE. **Archaeological** site located along the Pomme de Terre River in the Missouri Ozarks that possesses evidence of occupation by **Paleoindian** peoples of the **Dalton tradition** from 10,500 to 9900 B.P. (8500 to 7900 B.C.). Remains at Rodgers Shelter include a series of **hearths** containing the remains of **bison**, **deer**, elk, fish, rabbit, squirrel, turkey, turtle, and a variety of nuts. Archaeologists have used the **subsistence** remains recovered from Rodgers Shelter to reconstruct the diets of late Paleoindian peoples and the early **Holocene** environment of the region. The site also contains a sizeable Middle **Archaic** occupation.

RUBY SITE. **Archaeological** site located along a dry gulch near the Powder River in Wyoming with evidence of use by Late **Archaic** period peoples circa 3000–1450 B.P. (1000 B.C.–A.D. 500). This site is a corral, where Native American peoples stampeded **bison** into an enclosure where they could be killed with minimal threat to the hunters. Archaeologist George Frison also identified a small structure related to **shamanic** activity at the Ruby Site, which he believes was used by shaman for **religious** rituals designed to ensure the procurement of bison.

RUSSELL CAVE SITE. **Archaeological** site located in a small cave in northeastern Alabama with evidence of periodic human occupations from approximately 10,000 B.P. (8000 B.C.) until the **historic period**. Archaeological excavations within the cave by the Smithsonian Institution in the 1950s revealed almost 10 meters (32 feet) of cultural debris. Archaeological evidence indicates that **Paleoindian** and **Archaic** peoples used Russell Cave as a base camp during the fall and winter months when local **subsistence** resources matured.

– S –

SACAGAWEA. Shoshone woman who was captured by the **Hidatsa** while only a young girl and eventually traded to a Canadian **trader**, Toussaint Charbonneau. In 1805 the **Lewis and Clark expedition** met Charbonneau and Sacagawea at Fort Mandan on the Missouri River and hired them as guides and interpreters. Although her role as an expedition guide has been questioned, Sacagawea is thought to have aided the expedition on its journey to the Pacific Ocean. Following the expedition, Sacagawea and Charbonneau moved to St. Louis, but at this point tribal histories and European accounts differ as to her fate. Historical documents indicate that she died of fever in 1812, but tribal histories suggest that she lived until the mid-1880s. She remains one of the best-known Native American women and was even honored by the United States with the minting of the Sacagawea dollar coin.

SACHEM. Title conferred upon members of the ruling council of the **Iroquois Confederacy**. *Sachem* were considered to be the most prominent members of their matrilineage, and were responsible for representing their communities and social groups at council meetings.

SALADO CULTURE. Cultural tradition of southeastern Arizona and southwestern New Mexico that represents a mixture of **Mogollon**, **Hohokam**, and **Anasazi** traits. Although most scholars believe that the Hohokam and Mogollon had a long history of interaction prior to the Salado culture, a group of Anasazi migrated into the area at approximately 850 B.P. (A.D. 1100). The interaction of peoples from these three distinct cultural traditions resulted in a unique **cultural tradition**, primarily defined by the appearance of black-on-white and, later, polychrome **ceramics**. In addition to these distinctive ceramics, Salado peoples had unique **burial** practices, **basketry**, blankets, fine shell work, and houses.

SALISHAN LANGUAGE FAMILY. Family of more than 20 individual **languages** spoken by Native American groups of the **Northwest Coast** and **Plateau**, including groups occupying portions of present-day British Columbia, Idaho, Montana, and Washington. Salishan languages include **Bella Coola**, Colville, Coeur d'Alene, Squamish, Tillamook, Twana, and others. Salishan languages are considered to be highly complex, with a large number of consonants and a small number of vowels. In addition, these languages lack distinct formal boundaries between nouns and verbs, making translation into other languages extremely difficult.

SALISH INDIANS. Salishan-speaking Native American groups of the **Algonquian**-Washakan language family located in the **Northwest Coast** and **Plateau** culture areas. Also referred to as the Flathead, the Salish occupied both coastal and interior regions of present-day British Columbia, Montana, and Washington. There were considerable variations in **subsistence** practices and other aspects of **culture** between the Coastal and Interior Salish, with coastal groups resembling other Northwest Coast groups and interior peoples more similar to the mobile Plateau peoples. The Salish were first recorded by Europeans during the **Lewis and Clark expedition**, and figure prominently in accounts of the journey through the region. The term Flathead was first applied to the Salish by indigenous groups of the Northwest Coast that practiced extreme forms of **artificial cranial deformation**, making their heads pointed in comparison with the unaltered crania of the Salish. The introduction of the **horse** by Europeans radically transformed the practices of interior groups, with these peoples adopting a more **Great Plains** lifestyle, including mobile **bison hunting**. Coastal Salish peoples were centered around Puget Sound, with the name of one of their important chiefs providing the name for modern Seattle. The Coastal Salish were village-based **foragers** who primarily depended upon **salmon**, shellfish, and other coastal subsistence resources. At present there are more than 7,000 interior Salish on reservation lands in western Montana, and more than 10,000 Coastal Salish in British Columbia and Washington.

SALMON. Common term for a variety of large fishes of the genera *Salmo* and *Oncorhynchus* of the northern Pacific and Atlantic oceans. Salmon have characteristic pink flesh and were a staple food for Native American peoples of both the **Northwest Coast** and **Northeast** culture areas. Salmon migrate from the ocean to fresh water to spawn, and were captured and eaten by groups along the coasts as well as interior groups located along the rivers in which they spawn.

SALT PAN. Shallow, nearly flat **ceramic** container used to collect salt from salinated water. Salt pans were normally filled with salt water that was allowed to evaporate, leaving a salt residue behind. The salt was then collected from these pans and used as a cooking spice. Native American salt pans are found in a variety of locations, with the salt produced from these sites frequently used as an important **trade** item.

SALVAGE ARCHAEOLOGY. *See* CULTURAL RESOURCE MANAGEMENT.

SAN DIEGUITO COMPLEX. Distinct **Paleoindian tradition** found in present-day southern California and Arizona, thought to be contemporary with late **Clovis** and dated to approximately 11,000 B.P. (9000 B.C.). Although a limited number of sites from this complex have been identified, most appear to cluster around marshes and lakes, indicating a unique **subsistence** strategy for these Paleoindian peoples. San Dieguito material **culture** is characterized by rudimentary scraping and chopping **tools**, with little evidence of formal **projectile points**, suggestive of a shift in **subsistence** practices toward increased **foraging**.

SANTA ROSA–SWIFT CREEK CULTURE. *See* SWIFT CREEK CULTURE.

SAQQAQ COMPLEX. Group of **archaeological** sites located in the eastern **Arctic** dated from approximately 4400 to 3150 B.P. (2400–1150 B.C.). Sites belonging to the Saqqaq complex are suggested to have been bases for whale-**hunting** expeditions. However, some scholars suggest that these sites represent scavenging activities of stranded whales rather than whale hunting. Evidence from the **Queqertasussuk site** supports the contention that the Saqqaq complex peoples did engage in whale-hunting activities.

SAUK INDIANS. Algonquian-speaking Native American group who occupied portions of Michigan prior to European contacts. Closely related **culturally** and linguistically to the **Fox**, the Sauk were forced to abandon their traditional homeland in the early 17th century due to increased aggression by the **Ottawa** and other eastern groups. The Sauk, together with the Fox, migrated north across the Straits of Mackinac, eventually settling in present-day Wisconsin. The Sauk and Fox combined to form a potent military force and engaged in near-constant **warfare** with the **Ojibwa** and other groups. They also banded together for mutual defense, fighting wars against the **Illinois**, **Sioux**, and the French. Military incursions by the French dramatically reduced the Sauk population further. During the mid-18th century, the Sauk and Fox moved into the Illinois territory. They were forcibly removed to lands west of the Mississippi in the 1830s, but returned to reclaim their Illinois lands during the Black Hawk War. After the end of hostilities, the Sauk and Fox moved west, settling on reservations in Iowa, Kansas, and Oklahoma. At present, there are approximately 5,000 Sauk in the United States.

SCREWBEAN. Mesquite shrub (*Prosopis pubescens*) of the desert **Southwest** belonging to the legume family (*Fabaceae*). Like other mesquites of the Southwest, the screwbean has characteristic pods containing small beans that were a food source for Native American peoples of the region. The screwbean was used to make tea, syrup, and a ground meal, while the rest of the plant was used to produce **basketry**, fabrics, and medicine, and as firewood.

SEAL. General term applied to any of the various aquatic carnivorous mammals of the families Phocidae and Otariidae, found throughout coastal areas of the Northern Hemisphere. Seals were a staple source of food for many Native American groups, especially the **Eskimo** and **Inuit**. Not only are seals a good source of food, but also their hides could be processed into clothing, and their fat used for oil.

SECOTAN. Algonquian-speaking Native American peoples who lived near the modern Outer Banks of North Carolina. The Secotan were semisedentary village **agriculturalists** who cultivated **maize**, **beans**, **squash**, **sunflowers**, and **tobacco**, and supplemented their diets through **foraging**. Given their coastal location, the Secotan were heavily impacted by early European contacts. A drawing of the main village of Secotan produced by John White in the 1580s (later elaborated upon and published by Theodor de Bry in 1619) provides contemporary researchers a great deal of information concerning the spatial organization of Native American villages of the region.

SENECA INDIANS. Iroquoian-speaking Native American peoples who resided in western New York and eastern Ohio, and formed the largest single **culture** group within the **Iroquois Confederacy**. Like other Iroquois groups, the Seneca were village **agriculturalists** who resided in large **fortified** villages with individual matrilineages occupying large domestic **longhouses**. Individual Seneca settlements were governed by **councils** of adult males and a male village **chief**, but women within each matrilineage retained a great deal of power over sociopolitical decisions within the family and longhouse. Seneca women were agriculturalists and **foragers**, while men engaged in **hunting** and **warfare**. Warfare with surrounding Native American groups was frequent, particularly given the Seneca's location on the western edge of the Iroquoian Confederacy. The Seneca supported the English during the Revolutionary War, with many of their villages destroyed by American troops in 1779. The Seneca were later relocated to reservations in western New York, where more than 5,000 Seneca continue to reside.

SEQUOYAH (1766–1843). Political and social leader among the **Cherokee** who created a syllabary for the Cherokee **language**. Also known as *George Guess* and *Sogwali*, Sequoyah was a trained silversmith and a trader who resided in northern Georgia. Believing that his people needed a way to write their language, he created a system for recording the Cherokee language. Although the exact date for his formulation of the syllabary is debated, by 1822 Sequoyah was teaching this system to other Cherokee. His efforts led to basic literacy among the majority of Cherokees, and the publication of books, bibles, and a Cherokee-language weekly newspaper.

SERIATION. Relative **dating** technique based on the construction of a presumed temporal order for a group of **artifacts** or **assemblages** by measuring shared elements of similarity. *See also* DATING.

SERPENT MOUND. A large **zoomorphic** effigy mound located atop a plateau overlooking Brush Creek in Adams County, Ohio. More than 400 meters (1,300 feet) in length, Serpent Mound represents an uncoiling serpent, with several possible **archaeoastronomical** alignments. Although the date of its construction is debated, evidence from surrounding **archaeological** sites suggest that it was constructed by **Adena** peoples between 1150 and 850 B.P. (circa 800 B.C.–A.D. 100). Serpent Mound is interpreted as a major Adena **religious** and ceremonial center.

SHAMAN. Part-time **religious** practitioner thought to possess the esoteric knowledge necessary to control supernatural powers. Shamans act as ritual healers who direct communal religious rituals. They are also commonly believed to be capable of taking on nonhuman form and leaving their bodies during trances. **Shamanism** was originally defined for several Arctic and Asian peoples, but has been expanded to include the religious practices of groups throughout the world. Many Native Americans recognized the important religious and medical powers of shaman.

SHAMANISM. System of **religious** belief in which powerful, unseen supernatural forces permeate the world, and can only be controlled through the efforts of **shamans**, specialized religious practitioners.

SHELL MIDDEN. **Archaeological** site formed through the accumulation of discarded shellfish remains by humans. Shell middens are common along North American rivers and coastal regions, and frequently contain a wide variety of **artifacts** and features.

SHELL MOUND. **Mound** formed through the massive accumulation of discarded shellfish remains by humans. Shell mounds are common along North American rivers and coastal regions, particularly those of the **Eastern Woodlands** of the United States. *See also* SHELL MOUND ARCHAIC.

SHELL MOUND ARCHAIC. Widespread cultural phenomena found in the Midwest and **Southeast**, characterized by an increased exploitation of freshwater and saltwater shellfish during the late **Ar-**

chaic period (6000–3000 B.P. [4000–1000 B.C.]). Shell Mound Archaic sites frequently contain large **mounds** of shell that are interpreted as indications of increased seasonal exploitation of shellfish and other marine resources, and greater sedentism. These mounds contain not only large amounts of shell, but large numbers of human **burials** are also frequently recovered from these mounds.

SHIELD ARCHAIC. Cultural tradition of the northern boreal forest of the northern Great Lakes and subarctic regions of Canada, including portions of the Northwest Territory, Saskatchewan, Manitoba, and Ontario during the period from 6500 to 2000 B.P. (4500–50 B.C.). Shield Archaic peoples were broad-spectrum **foragers** who relied upon **caribou**, moose, and fish, as well as a wide variety of plant resources. Shield Archaic **artifact assemblages** are characterized by **adzes**, **knives**, scrapers, and side-notched **projectile points**. Available evidence suggests that Shield Archaic peoples were seasonally mobile, taking advantage of resources on ecotonal boundaries. The largest Shield Archaic sites cluster near locations where migrating **caribou** could be killed.

SHOOP SITE. Archaeological site in south-central Pennsylvania considered one of the largest and earliest presently known **Paleoindian** period sites in eastern North America, with evidence of occupation as early as 11,000 B.P. (9000 B.C.). The Shoop site is located on a small hill, and is thought to represent an occupation by a group **hunting** migrating **caribou**.

SHOSHONE INDIANS. Uto-Aztecan–speaking groups of the Great Basin, including portions of present-day Idaho, Nevada, Oregon, Utah, and Wyoming. The Shoshone are divided into Northern and Southern (also referred to as Western Shoshone) divisions, with these **cultural** divisions exacerbated by the introduction of the **horse** by Europeans. Although both groups were **foragers**, the Northern Shoshone became highly mobile **bison hunters** and adopted cultural practices of many **Great Plains** groups after the introduction of the horse. The Southern Shoshone, however, remained small groups of mobile foragers well into the historic period. At present there are more than 10,000 Shoshone in Nevada, Utah, and Wyoming.

SIDE-NOTCHED TRADITION. A distinctive style of **projectile point** common throughout most regions of North America from the **Archaic** period, approximately 8000 B.P. (6000 B.C.) until the **historic period**. These **artifacts** have characteristic side notches, where **lithic** materials were removed from the sides of the point near the base to allow for **hafting**. Earlier side-notched projectile points have been identified along the lower Atlantic coast, including those from the **Hardaway site**. Some scholars contend that these **artifacts** represent a distinct **Paeloindian** culture that may predate **Clovis culture**. However, additional research is needed to sufficiently evaluate these claims.

SINODONTY. Series of morphological similarities between the teeth of Native American and Siberian peoples that are thought to provide genetic evidence for the migration of early peoples from Asia into the Americas. Classic features of sinodonty include shovel-shaped incisors, upper first premolars with a single root, and lower first molars with three roots. These dental features only occur in northern Asian and Native American groups. Estimates of genetic differentiation suggest that northern Asian and Native American dental characteristics have existed in separate populations for approximately 14,000 years, further supporting the Beringial model for the initial presence of humans in the Americas.

SIOUX INDIANS. Confederation of Hokan–Siouan-speaking Native American groups who occupied the northern **Great Plains** when first recorded by Europeans. Also referred to as the Dakota, these peoples are thought to have migrated westward as a response to territorial pressure from the **Ojibwa** and other eastern groups armed with European firearms. The Sioux eventually displaced the **Cheyenne** and **Kiowa** from the Black Hills, staking claim to territory in present-day Iowa, Manitoba, Minnesota, North and South Dakota, Saskatchewan, and Wisconsin. The Sioux are composed of seven distinct tribal groups, with three general divisions: the Santee (composed of the Wahpekute, Mdewakantonwan, Wahpetonwan, and Sisitonwan), the Nakota (consisting of the Ihanktonwan and Ihanktowana), and the Lakota (primarily the Titonwan or Teton). The Sioux were primarily mobile **foragers** who specialized in **bison hunting**.

The United States forced the Sioux to give up lands in the eastern portion of their territory, with the Sioux eventually confined to a reservation in the Dakotas in 1876. Although reserved for the Sioux in treaties, the discovery of gold in the Black Hills brought increasing numbers of white settlers onto Sioux lands. These territorial invasions and miserable conditions on the reservation led many Sioux to leave the reservation and return to migratory life on the Plains. This revolt led to armed conflict with the U.S. Cavalry, including the defeat of U.S. forces under the command of George Armstrong Custer at the Battle of Little Bighorn. This uprising culminated in the massacre of more than 200 men, women, and children by U.S. forces at Wounded Knee on December 29, 1890. At present there are more than 115,000 Sioux in the United States and Canada, with a large number residing on the Pine Ridge reservation in South Dakota.

SITTING BULL (1831–1890). Lakota (Teton) chief who led the **Sioux** peoples in resistance to confinement on reservation lands in the Dakotas. Sitting Bull (Tatanka-Iyotanka) led a series of military skirmishes with the U.S. Cavalry between 1863 and 1868, culminating in the establishment of a Sioux reservation in southwestern South Dakota. The discovery of gold in the Black Hills in the 1870s brought American settlers into renewed conflict with the Sioux. Sitting Bull led Sioux forces in resistance to these encroachments on Sioux lands, eventually leaving the reservation and engaging in a series of battles with the U.S. Cavalry. These engagements included the Battle of Little Bighorn, where forces under the command of George Armstrong Custer were defeated. Sitting Bull led his followers into Canada, but declining **bison** populations forced the Sioux to near starvation. They eventually surrendered and returned to their reservation. Sitting Bull's exploits earned him immense fame, leading to his participation in Buffalo Bill's Wild West Show for a short time. During the **Ghost Dance** revitalization movement, Sitting Bull was thought to be a potential agitative influence, and during a raid by Lakota tribal police he was shot and killed.

SKRAELING. Norse (Viking) name for the Indian peoples they encountered during their colonization attempts in Vinland (North America). Eric the Red's saga records battles with *Skraelings*, and they are cited as one of the primary reasons these new colonies were abandoned. Modern scholars believe that the native peoples the Norse encountered were probably the **Beothuk** and **Micmac** peoples. *See also* L'ANSE AUX MEADOWS.

SKULL DEFORMATION. *See* ARTIFICIAL CRANIAL DEFORMATION.

SLAVERY. State of bound servitude where an individual is treated as the property of a slaveholder or household. The predominant form of North American slavery involved the importation of Africans by **colonial** British and Americans for forced labor in the **agricultural** fields of the **Southeast**. However, this was not the only form of slavery practiced in North America. The British and Americans also impressed Native Americans into slavery as well, with slave raids on indigenous communities resulting in decreased population densities and the movement of many Native American groups away from colonial settlements. In addition to these forms of slavery, there are **ethnohistoric** documentation and **archaeological** evidence for the practice of slavery prior to the arrival of Europeans in the Americas. The most highly developed form of Native American slavery was that of the **Northwest Coast**, where large numbers of slaves were taken during raids on neighboring groups.

SLOAN SITE. Archaeological site in northeastern Arkansas with evidence of a **Paleoindian** cemetery related to the **Dalton tradition** dated to approximately 10,500 B.P. (8500 B.C.). The Sloan site is the oldest presently known cemetery in the Americas. Containing the remains of at least 12 individuals, Sloan site **burials** contained a variety of chipped stone **artifacts**, with most in complete, unused condition. The condition of these burial inclusions, and comparisons with Dalton materials from other contexts, suggest that these artifacts were specialized **grave goods**.

SNAKETOWN SITE. Archaeological site located on the Gila River near modern-day Phoenix, Arizona, occupied by **Hohokam** peoples from 2,100 to 450 B.P. (A.D. 50–1500). Research at the site, considered one of the most significant Hohokam sites, by **Emil Haury** and others provided the basic definition of Hohokam material **culture** and **culture history**. Snaketown is also notable for the presence of several **ball courts** similar to those found in **Mesoamerica**.

SOAPSTONE. *See* STEATITE.

SOCIAL STRATIFICATION. The ranking of social groups (and individuals) according to possessed wealth, power, and prestige. Stratified societies are those in which there is unequal access to resources by individuals, with this inequality not based on gender, age, or other similar factors. Instead, access to resources in stratified societies is usually based on what might be considered class distinctions. Although the majority of Native American societies were **ranked societies**, stratified societies were not unknown to indigenous societies. Select precontact groups in the **Southwest, Northwest Coast**, and **Southeast** were socially stratified, including those at **Chaco Canyon, Paquime, Cahokia**, and **Moundville**, and others.

SOCIETY FOR AMERICAN ARCHAEOLOGY (SAA). Organization dedicated to the study of **archaeological** sites in the Americas. Founded in 1934, the SAA works to encourage research in American archaeology, including public education and the conservation of archaeological resources. The SAA presently has more than 6,000 members and publishes the preeminent archaeological journal in the United States, *American Antiquity*.

SOUTHEAST CULTURE AREA. Large geographical region encompassing the area from the Atlantic Ocean west to the Trinity River in Texas, and from the Gulf of Mexico north to the lower Ohio River valley. Given the size and environmental variation of the Southeast culture area, there are three major subareas: the Piedmont, Coastal Plain, and Southern Appalachian Mountains. Occupied by a large number of distinct Native American peoples, the largest indigenous groups of the Southeast included the **Caddo, Catawba, Cherokee, Chickasaw, Choctaw, Creek, Natchez**, and Seminole. A variety of **languages** were spoken in the Southeast, with Caddoan, **Iroquoian, Muskogean**, and Siouan comprising the most widely spoken language families.

The earliest occupation of the Southeast was by **Paleoindian** peoples (circa 11,000 B.P. [9000 B.C.]). These peoples engaged in **subsistence** activities similar to those of Paleoindians in other regions, including the **hunting** of **megafauna**, including the **mastodon**, giant ground sloth, American capybara, and giant armadillo. During the **Archaic** period, between 10,000 and 5000 B.P. (8000–3000 B.C.), southeastern peoples diversified their subsistence practices, becoming increasingly specialized at taking advantage of local plant and animal resources, including **deer**, turkey, and other land mammals; fish and shellfish; nuts; and an array of plant species. Subsequent occupation of the Southeast during the **Woodland** period (circa 3000–1000 B.P. [1000 B.C.–A.D. 950]) shows additional **cultural** adaptations, including larger populations and increased sedentism, the production of **ceramics**, plant **cultivation**, the construction of large earthen funerary **mounds**, and the strengthening of long-distance **trade** networks. By about 1000 B.P., a series of sociopolitically complex societies developed along the Mississippi River and other major rivers in the region. These **Mississippian** period peoples (circa 1000–400 B.P. [A.D. 950–1550]) lived in large **fortified** villages, practiced an intensified form of **maize agriculture**, participated in regularized long-distance trade networks, produced distinctive shell-tempered ceramics, built massive earthen **platform mounds**, and were organized into **socially stratified chiefdoms** (*see* **Cahokia**, **Moundville**, and **Etowah**).

Following European contacts, the indigenous societies of the Southeast experienced a reduction in population and a concomitant decline in sociopolitical complexity. During the **historic period**, the indigenous peoples of the Southeast engaged in a series of relationships with the Spanish, French, English, and colonial Americans. Many of these interactions resulted in the reduction of Native American lands and increased tensions among native peoples. In the 1830s, the U.S. government passed the Indian Removal Act and began the process of moving native peoples from the region to Indian Territory (the present-day state of Oklahoma). This forced **removal** of indigenous peoples has come to be known as the *Trail of Tears*, as more than 45,000 Native Americans were removed from their lands east of the Mississippi River.

SOUTHEASTERN CEREMONIAL COMPLEX. Term applied to a series of **archaeological** materials sharing distinctive **anthropomorphic** and **zoomorphic** motifs found throughout the **Southeast** during the period from approximately 700 to 250 B.P. (A.D. 1250–1700). Formerly referred to as the "Southern Cult," most Southeastern Ceremonial Complex items, including **ceramics** and carved shell **gorgets**, were recovered from **burial** contexts, suggesting that they represent a pan-regional **religious** ideology and iconographic system. Recent research has challenged this idea, proposing that there are significant subregional and temporal variations in Southeastern Ceremonial Complex materials. Given these stylistic and temporal differences, it is suggested that the underlying meanings of these items were highly variable as well.

SOUTHERN CULT. *See* SOUTHEASTERN CEREMONIAL COMPLEX.

SOUTHWEST CULTURE AREA. Geographical region extending from southern Utah and Colorado south to the Sonoran Desert of Chihuahua, Mexico, and from western Texas to the Gulf of California. The environment of the Southwest is generally similar to that of the **Great Basin**, but the Southwest possesses more dependable water supplies and a warmer climate. The Southwest was home to a number of distinct Native American groups in both the prehistoric and **historic periods**. The earliest human occupation of the Southwest was by **Paleoindian** peoples, from approximately 12,500 to 9500 B.P. (10,500 B.C.–7500 B.C.). The majority of Paeloindian sites in the Southwest, like the **Clovis** site, suggest that the first inhabitants of this region were nomadic **foragers** who specialized in **hunting megafauna**. The **Southwestern Archaic** period that followed, from 9500 to 1750 B.P. (7500 B.C.–A.D. 200), was a time of gradual **cultural** change, with indigenous peoples becoming increasingly sedentary and broadening their **subsistence** practices. The Archaic was followed by several centuries of increasing reliance on **cultivated** plants (*see* **Lower Sonoran Agricultural Complex**) and adaptations to life in permanent villages.

By 1750 B.P. (circa A.D. 300), the three major prehistoric cultural traditions of the Southwest, **Anasazi, Hohokam**, and **Mogollon**, began to coalesce. These cultural traditions are thought to have exerted tremendous influence on cultural practices throughout the Southwest, with large, permanent river valley villages; ceremonial centers; **kivas**; and other cultural features common to many groups during this period. Even at the height of this regional population nucleation in river valleys and dependence upon **agriculture**, other Southwestern groups continued to be nomadic **foragers**, occupying the desert environments of the region. These desert cultures were the cultural antecedents of the historic **Mojave**, **Yuma**, **Pima**, **Papago**, and others. By around 750 B.P. (A.D. 1200), environmental conditions are thought to have become hotter and drier in the Southwest, with agricultural production compromised by an extended, regionwide drought. Following this environmental shift, many groups continued to practice village agriculture, becoming the historic Puebloan groups of the historic period, including the **Hopi**, **Zuñi**, **Tewa**, and others. During the period between 1150 and 950 B.P. (A.D. 800 to 1000), **Athabaskan** groups migrated into the Southwest from the north. These groups were nomadic foragers whose descendants include the historic **Apache** and **Navajo**.

The first contacts between Native American groups of the Southwest and Europeans came in the form of early Spanish exploration of the region, and the eventual establishment of Catholic missions by the Spanish throughout the region. As with other areas of North America, the indigenous peoples of the region experienced the devastating impacts of European-introduced **diseases** and the expansionistic **colonial** policies of Mexico and the United States.

SOUTHWESTERN ARCHAIC PERIOD. Cultural tradition found in the **Southwest culture area** during the period from 9500 to 1750 B.P. (7500 B.C.–A.D. 200). This was a period of culture change that included responses to warmer and drier environmental conditions in the region. Southwestern Archaic peoples were organized as small **bands** of mobile **foragers** with defined regional territories. These peoples primarily **subsisted** upon a wide variety of wild plants and animals, and were engaged in **trade** and **exchange** with other groups, resulting in a sharing of stone **tools** styles. Toward the end of this period, circa 2200–1800 B.P. (250 B.C.–A.D. 150), Southwestern Archaic peoples became more sedentary, with evidence of **ceramic** production and limited **agriculture**.

SPANISH BORDERLANDS. Geographic region stretching across the southern half of the continental United States. This region includes all of the present states from California to the Carolinas, and represents the area of maximum Spanish exploration, colonization, and settlement in the Americas. This region played an important role in the colonial history of North America, and research by **ethnohistorians** and **archaeologists** in the Spanish Borderlands has revealed much about the impacts of the cultural contacts on Native American cultures.

SPAULDING, ALBERT CLANTON (1914–1990). American **archaeologist** who received his archaeological training at the University of Michigan and Columbia University. He worked for the **Works Progress Administration** (WPA) supervising archeological research, and later held a series of academic appointments at the University of Kansas, the University of Michigan, the University of Oregon, and the University of California, Santa Barbara. In addition, Spaulding served as the director of anthropology for the National Science Foundation, helping to shape archaeology and **anthropology** as scientific disciplines. Spaulding's primary field research focused on the prehistory of the Aleutian Islands, but he is best known for his advocacy of quantitative methods in the analysis of archaeological materials. Spaulding is also remembered for his participation in a vigorous professional debate with **James A. Ford** (termed the Ford–Spaulding debate) in which they disagreed concerning the nature of archaeological typologies.

SPIER, LESLIE (1893–1961). Pioneering American **anthropologist** who studied under **Franz Boas** at Columbia University, receiving his Ph.D. in 1920. Spier conducted fieldwork in **archaeology** and cultural anthropology, with his research ranging from the Northern **Great Plains** to the **Northwest Coast** and the **Southwest**. Spier is best remembered for his research at several **Zuñi** sites, where he pioneered the use of **stratigraphic seriation**. Later in his career, Spier focused more on ethnographic research than archaeology, but he remained an eminent figure in American archaeology. He held positions at the American Museum of Natural History, the University of Washington, and the University of New Mexico, as well as short-term positions at several other American universities. Spier helped found the *Southwestern Journal of Anthropology* and the *University of New Mexico Publications in Anthropology*, and edited both journals until his death.

SPIRO SITE. Archaeological site located on the Arkansas River in eastern Oklahoma with evidence of human occupation between approximately 1100 and 500 B.P. (A.D. 850–1450). The Spiro site began as a small village, but grew to become a major population and **trade** center on the eastern edge of the **Great Plains**. Spiro has 12 earthen **mounds**, and a large central plaza, with both the spatial design of the village and the local **artifact assemblage** suggestive of occupation by **Mississippian** peoples. Excavations at the Craig Mound, a large burial mound at the site, revealed a number of elaborate **copper** and carved shell items bearing **Southeastern Ceremonial Complex** designs. The extent of nonlocal materials and exotic finished goods at Spiro make it a unique Mississippian site, with some archaeologists speculating that it was a center for trade and **exchange** between peoples of the **Eastern Woodlands** and Great Plains.

SQUASH. Any of the various tendril-bearing plants of the genus *Cucurbita* in the gourd family. The principal North American species is *Cucurbita pepo*, which is a quick-growing, small-fruited squash that was widely cultivated by Native Americans as a food source.

SQUIRE, EPHRAIM GEORGE (1821–1888). Civil engineer, educator, lawyer, and journalist who moved from the East Coast to Ohio in 1844. He became editor of the *Scioto Gazette*, a newspaper based in Chillicothe, Ohio. In addition to his editorial duties, Squire became increasingly interested in the **mound** sites of the Scioto River valley. Together with **Edwin Davis**, he undertook the mapping and excavation of Native American **archaeological** sites in the Ohio and Scioto River valleys. Their efforts led to the publication of *Ancient Monuments of the Mississippi Valley*, in which they presented not only maps of the major archaeological sites of the region but also their theories as to the **culture** responsible for their construction. Much of our knowledge of the archaeological sites of the Ohio River valley is due to their careful recording. Many of the sites documented by Squire and Davis have since been destroyed, with their record serving as the only evidence of their nature and extent.

STATE. Term used to describe the sociopolitical organization of large-scale societies. States are usually defined by the presence of sedentary populations numbering in the tens of thousands, with territorial integrity, and with a strong political infrastructure that controls the operation of legal sanctions and the legitimate use of force. Although no Native American societies north of Mexico are thought to have functioned as true states, some **archaeologists** contend that the complex Native American polities, like that of **Cahokia**, functioned with some elements consistent with a state level of sociopolitical organization.

STEATITE. Variety of soft, grayish-brown or green talc that occurs in natural strata in the Appalachians and other areas of North America. Commonly referred to as soapstone, steatite was quarried by Native Americans and used to produce stone vessels, cooking platforms, and other common **tools**.

STORAGE PIT. Circular depressions of various sizes and depths intentionally excavated by humans to facilitate the storage of food and other resources. These facilities functioned as simple storage cellars where resources could be protected from predation or public display for household use. Storage pits are common at **archaeological** sites in all regions and temporal periods in North America.

STRATIGRAPHY. The study of strata in both compositional and spatial dimensions to reveal information on site usage, cultural activities, and environmental change. Stratigraphy is commonly used as a form of relative **dating** in archaeology, allowing archaeologists to determine changing sequences in **artifact** production and use.

SUBARCTIC CULTURE AREA. Large geographic area stretching across the entire North American continent, from the Bering Sea to the Labrador Sea, covering the Alaskan interior and most of Canada. The northern boundary between the **Subarctic** and **Arctic culture areas** corresponds with the environmental change from **taiga** to **tundra**. The Subarctic region is characterized by short, warm, summers and limited precipitation, while the winters are exceptionally long and cold. The earliest human occupation of the region was by **Paleoindian** peoples, with sparse **archaeological** evidence of humans in this region until approximately 7000 B.P. (circa 5000 B.C.). Approximately 6500–4500 B.P. (4500–2500 B.C.), Subarctic groups exhibit characteristics of the **Northern Archaic tradition**, associated with **subsistence** practices centering on **caribou**. By 4200 B.P., the **Arctic small-tool tradition** appears in the region. The **Archaic**-period lifestyle predominates in the region until about 450 B.P. (A.D. 1500). These peoples were highly nomadic **foragers** who hunted **deer**, **caribou**, **elk**, and moose, with evidence from the earliest period of European contact in the 16th century suggesting that Subarctic peoples were exclusively **Athabaskan** and **Algonquian** speakers.

Initial contacts between Europeans and Subarctic peoples related to the **fur trade**, with these exchanges stimulating tremendous cultural change for these indigenous peoples. Over**hunting** quickly reduced local caribou and moose populations, leading to increased competition between native hunters and the starvation of many Subarctic peoples. European-introduced **diseases** also vastly reduced Subarctic populations. In addition, many coastal groups abandoned their **traditional cultural** practices and adopted European lifestyles and economic practices. Long-standing social and political traditions began to disappear. Although western Subarctic groups were insulated from the early impacts of European contacts, by the late 19th century the discovery of gold in British Columbia and Alaska led to increased contacts with Europeans and a similar decline in traditional indigenous cultural practices.

SUBSISTENCE. The specific manner in which a group of people procures the food resources they require for survival. Subsistence practices are highly varied based on both local environmental and cultural factors, but most human groups procure their food resources through one or more of the following: **agriculture**, **fishing**, **foraging**, and **hunting**. Native American peoples developed specific subsistence practices in response to local resources and environments and, in some cases, modified their environments through the introduction of nonindigenous domesticated plant species.

SUDDEN SHELTER SITE. Archaeological site located along Ivie Creek on the Wasatch Plateau of Utah, with evidence of occupation during the **Archaic** period, approximately 8400–3300 B.P. (6400–5300 B.C.). The Sudden Shelter site contains more than 20 cultural strata, providing one of the most complete records of human occupation in this region. Sudden Shelter is interpreted as a summer base camp, with materials from this site providing substantial evidence of environmental change in the region during its occupation.

SUMPWEED. A plant species (*Iva annua*), native to North America, commonly referred to as *marsh elder*. Sumpweed was an important component of **Woodland** subsistence practices in eastern North America, and may have been consumed by indigenous peoples as early as the **Archaic** period.

SUN DANCE. Important **religious** ceremony for many groups of the **Great Plains**. Normally held at the time of the summer solstice, the Sun Dance was intimately related to the cycle of life and seasonal change. The **Arapaho, Arikara, Assiniboine, Blackfoot, Cheyenne, Crow, Hidatsa, Kiowa, Ojibwa**, Omaha, **Shoshone, Sioux, Ute**, and other groups practiced the Sun Dance, with the specific rituals practiced as part of the Sun Dance varying by group. Participants in the Sun Dance were forced to endure extreme conditions and harsh torture, with their bodily sacrifices seen as symbolic of the spiritual rebirth of all life on earth. The U.S. government outlawed the Sun Dance in 1904, although the ceremony continued to be practiced in secret by many Plains peoples. At present, legal restrictions on the practice have been lifted, with many Plains peoples reviving the Sun Dance ritual.

SUNFLOWERS. Term applied to more than 60 species of plants in the genus *Helianthus*, native to North and South America. The sunflower has a rough, hairy stem that grows to between 1 and 4.5 meters (3–15 feet) in height, with broad rough leaves and large, brown, yellow, or purple compound flowers. The common sunflower (*Helianthus annuus*) was **domesticated** by Native Americans and served as a major food source for many indigenous peoples. Prior **archaeological** research suggested that this plant was first domesticated in the **Southeast**

during the **Woodland** period (circa 3000 B.P. [1000 B.C.]), but recent archaeological evidence suggests that it was domesticated in **Mesoamerican** at approximately 4500 B.P. (2500 B.C.).

SURVEY. The systematic attempt to identify the location of **archaeological** sites through the use of written and oral evidence, as well as the presence of surface and subsurface **artifacts** and features. In North America, archaeological surveys are commonly conducted as pedestrian surveys, where field personnel visually inspect exposed ground surface and/or excavate small test units to evaluate the presence or absence of subsurface archaeological remains. *See also* CULTURAL RESOURCE MANAGEMENT.

SWANTON, JOHN REED (1873–1958). Pioneering American **anthropologist** and **ethnohistorian** who worked with **Franz Boas** at Columbia University and received his Ph.D. from Harvard University in 1900. Swanton conducted fieldwork in the **Northwest Coast** and **Southeast**, and worked primarily for the **Bureau of American Ethnology** (BAE) at the Smithsonian Institution. Swanton was a prolific scholar whose principal contribution to American anthropology included expansive compendia of **culture histories** for Native American groups of the Southeast.

SWIFT CREEK CULTURE. **Archaeological culture** of southern Alabama, Georgia, and northwestern Florida that dates to the Middle **Woodland** period (1800–1200 B.P. [A.D. 150–650]). Swift Creek culture is thought to have developed out of the earlier **Deptford culture**. Available evidence indicates that Swift Creek peoples practiced horticulture and lived in small villages located along rivers, bayous, and marshes where they obtained additional **subsistence** resources. Mortuary data indicate the use of exotic, nonlocal materials in **burial** contexts, including items of galena, hematite, and mica, as well as **copper** panpipes, ear ornaments, and other **artifacts**. Some scholars believe that these exotic items indicate the presence of cultural influence from the **Hopewellian interaction sphere** in the Gulf region. Swift Creek material culture is primarily identified by unique complicated stamped, incised, shell-stamped, punctated, cord-marked, and burnished **ceramics**.

SWEATLODGE. A small structure constructed by many Native American groups of the **Great Plains** and **Eastern Woodlands**, consisting of a wooden framework covered by animal skins, and used for ritual purification. Rocks were heated in a fire and then doused with water to produce heat and steam within the lodge encouraging participants to sweat profusely. It was believed that the sweatlodge ritual purified both the body and spirit.

– T –

TAIGA. Subarctic evergreen coniferous forest biome of northern North America lying to the south of the **tundra** biome. The taiga zone is rich in fur-bearing animals, including **bears**, **elk**, fox, and wolves.

TATHAM MOUND SITE. Archaeological site located north of modern Tampa, Florida, with evidence of early contact between local Native American peoples and Europeans. The Tatham Mound contained several hundred human **burials** with **grave goods** consisting of early European **trade** items in direct association with Native American **artifacts**. A large number of iron objects within the Tatham Mound are thought to have been **trade** goods brought to the **Southeast** during the expedition of **Hernando de Soto**. Analysis of the human remains from Tatham Mound indicates the presence of sword wounds on two individuals and a possible mass inhumation of almost 80 people, suggesting that conflict and **disease** accompanied the earliest encounters between Native Americans and Europeans in the region.

TATTOOED SERPENT. Name of the preeminent social leader among the **Natchez Indians** of the **Southeast** during the early 19th century. Tattooed Serpent was the **Great Sun**, serving as both **chief** and priest of the Natchez people. He was considered divine, receiving extreme social deference from commoners in both life and death. He was carried on a litter, resided in a secluded structure atop a **mound**, and possessed the power of life and death over his subjects. Descriptions of Tattooed Serpent's **burial** ritual indicate that his funerary rite included sacrificial retainers to serve him in the next life. Descriptions of Tattooed Serpent's power over Natchez social, political, economic, and religious affairs are frequently used as a source of analogies for the prerogatives of social elites during the **Mississippian** period.

TATTOOING. Permanent marks or designs made on the body through the introduction of pigment beneath the skin. Tattooing was common among Native American peoples, and is thought to have contained both communal, cultural meanings (social status or group membership) and individual meanings.

TAXONOMY. The classification of **archaeological artifacts** into groupings that reflect distinct morphological features. Archaeologists have long debated the nature of their typologies, with some scholars insistent that they represent classifications that held meaning for the producers of these objects, while other researchers contend that these classifications are primarily a product of archaeological analysis that would hold little meaning for past peoples. The most famous North American exchange regarding taxonomic classification in archaeology was the debate between **James A. Ford** and **Albert Spaulding** in the 1950s, termed the Ford–Spaulding debate.

TAYLOR, WALTER WILLARD (1913–1997). American **archaeologist** who worked in the **Southwest** and northern Mexico. Although his contributions to field archaeology are considerable, Taylor's major contribution to American archaeology came in the area of theory. Taylor's dissertation was published in 1948 as *A Study of Archaeology*, in which he argued that American archaeology needed a stronger integration between the analysis of **artifacts** and the **cultural** contexts in which they were produced and used, termed the **conjunctive approach**. Taylor also criticized the **culture historical** orientation of then-contemporary archaeology, arguing for many of the shifts in method and theory that would later be taken up by **Lewis Binford** in the formulation of **processual archaeology**.

TECUMSEH (1768–1813). Shawnee political and military leader who worked to unify the Native Americans of the **Eastern Woodlands** against encroachments by **colonial** Americans. Together with his brother, the **Shawnee** prophet **Tenskwatawa**, Tecumseh urged Native Americans to give up all the practices and material goods of the

Europeans and return to their traditional ways of life. He raised a large army of Native American warriors to counter the Americans, but his forces were defeated in the Battle of Tippecanoe, and Tecumseh and his movement were effectively broken. Tecumseh and his followers supported the English during the War of 1812, in hopes that they would allow Native Americans to return to their previous ways of life. Tecumseh was killed by American forces in the Battle of the Thames in 1813.

TEEPEE. *See* TIPI.

TEMPER. Materials added to clay during the manufacture of **ceramics** to prevent their cracking during the firing process. Tempering agents include vegetal fibers, feathers, rock fragments, sand, shell, pulverized sherds, and other materials. Items selected as tempering agents change frequently with a ceramic **tradition**, and together with stylistic elements, are used to trace both temporal and **cultural** changes.

TENNESSEE VALLEY AUTHORITY (TVA). Government agency established during the Great Depression (1933) to bring electricity to and develop the resources of the Tennessee River valley. During the construction of dams along the river to generate electricity, the TVA sponsored a series of **archaeological** investigations at sites that were to be impacted by dam construction. Between 1934 and 1942, 10 reservoirs were constructed on the Tennessee River and its tributaries, with archaeological research conducted in nine of them, including the Norris, Wheeler, Pickwick, Guntersville, Chickamauga, Watts Bar, Fort Loudoun, Douglas, Cherokee, and Kentucky reservoirs. These efforts recorded hundreds of previously unreported archaeological sites, with many of the major sites excavated before their inundation.

TENSKWATAWA (1775–1837). Shawnee religious leader and brother of **Techumseh**. Known as the *Prophet*, Tenskwataw led a religious and political movement designed to promote unity among the Native American peoples of the Ohio River valley (circa 1805–1812). Antagonized by the continual erosion of Native American territories at the hands of the colonial Americans, Tenskwatawa traveled throughout the

Eastern Woodlands preaching resistance to assimilation and additional land concessions. His efforts led to armed conflict with American forces in 1811, but his movement was crushed at Tippecanoe by forces under the direction of William Henry Harrison.

TEOSINTE. A tall annual plant (*Euchlaena mexicana*) that is indigenous to Mexico and is thought to be the wild progenitor of domesticated **maize**. Teosinte is a wild grass that grows throughout central Mexico, and it is believed that human modification of the plant and its local environment eventually led to the hybridization of the plant and its eventual **domestication** as maize.

TEWA INDIANS. Tanoan-speaking Native American groups of the Rio Grande Valley of northern New Mexico. The Tewa are a **Puebloan** people consisting of two main branches, the Northern Tewa and the Southern Tewa (also called the Tano). The Tewa are village **agriculturalists** who were first recorded by Europeans during the expedition of **Francisco Coronado** (1540). The Southern Tewa were dispersed during the Pueblo revolts of the 1680s and 1690s, eventually moving to Arizona to live with the **Hopi**. The Tewa were also heavily impacted by European **diseases** (particularly smallpox) during the 19th century. The Northern Tewa were less impacted by European contacts. At present, there are more than 3,000 Tewa in New Mexico and Arizona.

THERMOLUMINESCENCE DATING (TL). Chronometric **dating** technique based on the principle that some clay-bearing materials, including **ceramics**, give off radiant light when heated. The intensity of the light these items emit is proportional to the amount of radiation to which the sample has been exposed and the time that has elapsed since the sample was first fired. This measure is then calculated for the object, and an age can then be calculated for the object.

THOMAS, CYRUS (1825–1910). Pioneering American **archaeologist** who helped found the Illinois Natural History Society and the Natural History Museum at Southern Illinois Normal College (now Southern Illinois University). Thomas later worked for the **Bureau of**

American Ethnology at the Smithsonian Institution (1881–1910), where he was selected to lead the Smithsonian's famous Mound Explorations. His efforts, and the subsequent report of his investigations, provided a conclusive solution to the **mound builder controversy** by demonstrating that Native Americans had built the earthen **mounds** of North America.

THREE SISTERS. Term commonly used by **Iroquoian** groups to describe the three principal agricultural crops of the Eastern Woodlands, **maize**, **beans**, and **squash**.

THULE TRADITION. **Archaeological tradition** found at sites in Alaska from 2000 to 400 B.P. (50 B.C.–A.D. 1550) thought to have developed out of the earlier **Norton tradition**. The Thule tradition represents adaptations to the **Arctic** environment that include the **hunting** of sea mammals in open water with the aid of drag floats. Large, seagoing skin **boats** were also a Thule innovation. Winters were spent in large communities with semisubterranean domestic structures, with food supplied from stored meat supplies gathered in the summer and fall. Summers were spent in smaller, dispersed social groupings, engaged in a range of both maritime and terrestrial **subsistence** activities.

THUNDERBIRD SITE. **Archaeological** site located in the Shenandoah Valley of Virginia, with evidence of **Paleoindian** occupation dated to approximately 11,000 B.P. (9000 B.C.). The Thunderbird site was a **chert** quarry, with evidence of specific activity areas related to the primary stage of bifacial **lithic tool** production. The site also contains **fluted projectile points**, making it one of the earliest Paleoindian sites in the **Eastern Woodlands**.

TIMUCUA INDIANS. Confederacy of Timucuan-speaking Native American peoples of Florida. The Timucua were village **agriculturalists** who lived in large, **fortified** villages. Social organization was highly structured, with powerful **chiefs** exercising considerable power within Timucuan communities. The Timucua were heavily impacted by early French and Spanish exploration and colonization in Florida, and were eventually forced into missions by the Spanish.

During the late 17th and early 18th centuries, Native American groups from the English colonies in Georgia and South Carolina armed the **Creeks** and other groups and led a series of devastating **slave** raids on the Spanish missions. Between 1702 and 1706, the English and their Native American allies vastly reduced the Timucua, and by the 19th century the Timucua were completely annihilated.

TIPI. Portable shelter used as a primary domestic structure for Native Americans of the **Great Plains** consisting of a conical-shaped tent supported by long, slender support poles. Tipis were developed as an adaptation to the highly mobile **subsistence** practices of Plains groups following the migratory **bison** herds, and their use expanded with the introduction of the **horse** and the expansion of bison **hunting** by Native American groups of the region.

TLINGIT INDIANS. Tlingit-speaking Native American groups of the **Northwest Coast culture area** who inhabit the islands and coastal mainland of southern Alaska. Largely **subsisting** upon **salmon fishing**, the **hunting** of marine mammals, and coastal fishing, the Tlingit are considered the northernmost Northwest Coast group. Social organization is based on matri**clans**, with social ranking based on the material and social prominence of each matrilineage and clan. Individual lineages also control access to certain subsistence resources and lands. Wood is the primary medium of artistic expression, with large carved house posts and **totem poles** expressing social membership and unique **clan** designs. The Tlingit also historically practiced the **potlatch**. At present, there are approximately 15,000 Tlingit in Alaska and British Columbia.

TOBACCO. Any of several species of plants in the genus *Nicotiana* used in various ways (smoking, snuffing, and chewing) to release the nicotine contained in the plant's leaves. Native to the Americas, Indian tobacco (*Nicotina rustica*) was grow and smoked by a variety of Native American groups. This plant grows to a height of 1–2 meters (4–6 feet) and bears flowers and huge leaves. Tobacco was used by Native Americans in a variety of **religious** and social ceremonies, and was thought to possess medicinal properties. *See also* CALUMET; PIPE.

TOOL. A device designed to perform, or assist in the performance of, some type of work. Native American tools consisted of a wide range of objects manufactured of bone, **lithic**, and other naturally available materials. The tools, including items such as the **bow and arrow**, **celts**, grinding stones, **knives**, **projectile points**, and many others, were used by indigenous peoples to provide their **subsistence** needs, construct their houses and communities, and provide protection.

TOPANGA CULTURE. **Archaeological culture** of southern California thought to be descended from the **San Dieguito** culture, and dated to approximately 8000–3000 B.P. (6000–1000 B.C.). The Topanga culture is representative of the Millingstone **cultural tradition**, with **artifacts** consisting of **core tools** and ground stone implements, including **manos** and **metates**. Topanga peoples **hunted** small animals, and their toolkits are thought to have included **atlatls**.

TOTEMISM. Complex **religious** and social ideologies and related ritual practices associated with the symbolic use of plants or animals to represent a specific social group, normally a **clan**. Totems are believed to hold special significance for its members, with mythic histories frequently used to tie groups to their totem and a series of taboos associated with the totemic species. The majority of Native American societies practiced some form of totemism.

TOTEM POLE. Carved and painted wooden log, displayed vertically, and produced by many Native American groups of the **Northwest Coast culture area**. Totem poles are related to **totemic** belief systems and commonly display mythological images, usually animal spirits, whose significance is their association with lineages and **clans**. Totem poles depict family legends and connect social groups to their mythological totems, and were frequently erected to identify property ownership and mark gravesites.

TRADE. Patterns of human interaction that involve the transfer of material goods or services between individuals or societies. Trade occurs within local communities, between communities, over long distances, and between members of the same culture and those from different cultures. Unlike other types of **exchange**, trade is thought of as consisting of transactions carried out for economic reasons. Trade networks existed in prehistoric and historic times in North America, linking populations through commercial and social contacts. *See also* FUR TRADE.

TRADE BEADS. Variety of small glass **beads** produced in Europe and **traded** to Native Americans in exchange for commodities desired by the Europeans. These beads were produced in the millions and occur commonly in **historic period** Native American **archaeological** sites.

TRADITION. Term used to denote a continuity of design features in material **culture** over time. These continuities in material culture are frequently interpreted as representing stability in other areas of cultural behavior and a distinct, long-standing way of life.

TRAIL OF TEARS. Term applied to the forced **removal** of Native Americans from the **Southeast** to Indian Territory (Oklahoma) during the 1830s. The **Cherokee**, **Creek**, and **Choctaw** were the principal participants in the Trail of Tears, and their removal by the U.S. military took place in direct conflict with a U.S. Supreme Court order preventing their removal. However, President Andrew Jackson continued with the confiscation of Native American lands east of the Mississippi River. The forced march of thousands of Native Americans to Oklahoma was poorly conceived, with too little food supplied for the journey and freezing temperatures, leading to the deaths of thousands of Native Americans.

TRAVOIS. A wooden framework placed on the back of a dog or **horse** by peoples of the **Great Plains** as a means of expeditiously moving material items. The travois enabled Plains peoples to move heavy loads over long distances and permitted them to follow migrating **bison** herds with greater speed.

TREE-RING ANALYSIS. *See* DENDROCHRONOLOGY.

TRIBE. Term used to describe the sociopolitical organization of intermediate societies where social and political power is largely based upon **kinship**. Tribes are most commonly village **agriculturalists**, and are characterized by the presence of highly fluid social-**ranking** systems. In tribes, each kinship group is commonly linked to other groups through clan affiliations, to provide a basis for communal labor projects and for common defense. Although the term commonly has been applied to all Native American groups, many indigenous groups actually were organized sociopolitically as **bands** and **chiefdoms**.

TRIBUTE. Gifts of food or other resources provided as a material recognition of social and/or political superiority on the part of those receiving such payments. Native American societies of the **Mississippian** period are thought to have paid tribute to larger, more powerful polities in order to ensure peaceful relations.

TROYVILLE–COLES CREEK CULTURE. Archaeological culture of the lower Mississippi River valley of Louisiana, dated between approximately 1550 and 840 B.P. (A.D. 400–1110). Thought to have developed out of earlier **Marksville culture**, Troyville–Coles Creek demonstrates the presence of new styles of **ceramics**; increased numbers of earthen **mounds**, with most of larger size than those of Marskville; and new sociopolitical ritual activities. Troyville mounds were not primarily mortuary facilities, but were instead used as bases for **religious** and civic structures. Troyville–Coles Creek peoples produced distinctive, clay tempered **ceramics**, including rounded jars and shallow bowls. They practiced a mixed **subsistence** strategy of **foraging** and horticulture, with evidence that they cultivated **squash**, **sunflowers**, and other indigenous **domesticates**.

TSIMSHIAN INDIANS. Penutian-speaking Native American groups of the **Northwest Coast** who occupied lands along the Skeena and Nass Rivers of British Columbia and Alaska. The Tsimshian were primarily maritime **fishers**, but they also relied upon terrestrial **hunting** and **foraging** activities throughout much of the year. They resided in large, wooden houses, occupied by several nuclear families belonging to the same matrilineage and/or **clan**. Social organization was based on matrilineal descent, with social **ranking** of individual lineages and clans. Like other groups of the Northwest Coast, the Tsimshian practiced the **potlatch** ritual. At present, there are approximately 10,000 Tsimshian in British Columbia and Alaska.

TULAROSA CAVE SITE. The largest in a series of **archaeological** cave sites in the Tularosa Canyon region of New Mexico with evidence of human occupation from approximately 2300 to 850 B.P. (300 B.C.–A.D. 1100). Tularosa Cave is remarkable for the density of **artifacts** and for unusual preservation of normally perishable materials. Excavated by **Paul S. Martin** in 1950, Tularosa Cave revealed a great deal of information on **Mogollon cultural** change. Excavations at Tularosa Cave revealed the presence of a large number of **maize** cob fragments (more than 30,000), and well-preserved netting, **basketry**, and wooden materials.

TUNDRA. Treeless, level, or rolling landscapes lying about the **taiga** biome of the extreme northern **Arctic** of North America. This biome is characterized by bare, frozen ground with vegetation normally consisting of mosses, lichens, and small shrubs. Based on the limits of local **subsistence** resources, few animal species exist in the tundra biome, with those that do reside in this region including lemmings, the Arctic fox, the Arctic wolf, **caribou**, and reindeer. These limited resources also discouraged human occupation of this region, with few, small human groups living in the tundra zone.

TURKEY. Common name for one of two large bird species of the genus *Meleagris* indigenous to the Americas. The common North American turkey (*Meleagris gallopavo*) was a source of food for Native American peoples and was domesticated by groups in **Mesoamerica** and the **Southwest**. Adult turkeys grow as large as 1.3 meters (4 feet) in length, and can weigh more than 10 kilograms (20 pounds). Wild turkeys inhabit woodland settings, and primarily subsist on seeds and insects.

TURQUOISE. A blue to blue-green mineral of aluminum and **copper** found in the **Southwest** and prized by Native Americans as a decorative stone. Turquoise was **traded** throughout the Southwest, and may have been a major item in trade relations with groups in **Mesoamerica**.

TYPE. A distinctive formal **artifact** classification based on the presence of one or more consistent artifact attributes that have occurred in a restricted space and during a defined temporal interval. **Artifact** typologies are one of the basic units of artifact analysis, and their identification relies upon well-defined taxonomies of artifact traits.

– U –

ULU. Large, semilunate side-mounted "woman's knife" of slate or bone used by the **Eskimo** and other groups of the **Arctic**.

UMIAKS. Large, open **boats** made of animal skins stretched over an interior wooden frame, and propelled by paddles. Umiaks are larger and deeper than **kayaks**, and were used by the **Inuit** to move heavy loads and **hunt** whales.

UPPER SONORAN AGRICULTURAL COMPLEX. Term applied to the earliest appearance of domesticated plants in the **Southwest**. Consisting of **maize, beans, squash**, and the bottle gourd, the date of first appearance for these cultigens in the region has been intensely debated, but the earliest reliable date for their appearance is approximately 3200 B.P. (1200 B.C.). The immediate impact of these plants on local peoples is thought to have been negligible, but they eventually became the most important local **subsistence** resources.

USE-WEAR. *See* MICROWEAR ANALYSIS.

UTE INDIANS. Shoshonean-speaking Native American groups of western Colorado and eastern Utah. Prior to European contacts, the Ute were highly mobile **foragers** who lived in small **bands** and shared many **cultural** practices with the **Paiute**. The introduction of the **horse** revolutionized Ute social organization and **subsistence** practices, with the Ute became predatory **hunters** of the eastern **Great Basin**. They also attacked livestock and Europeans traveling through their territory. After engaging in a series of wars with the U.S. Cavalry (1864–1879), the Ute were settled on reservations in Utah in 1881. At present, there are more than 5,000 Utes in southeastern Utah and southwestern Colorado.

UTO-AZTECAN LANGUAGE FAMILY. Family of more than 30 individual Native American **languages** spoken by groups in the **Great Basin, Southwest,** and **Mesoamerica**. Uto-Aztecan languages in North America include **Ute, Hopi, Shoshone,** Nahuatl, and others. Uto-Aztecan is traditionally divided into northern and southern branches. The northern branch was spoken from present-day Idaho and Oregon to southern California and Arizona, and includes **Comanche, Hopi,** Northern and Southern **Paiute,** Ute, and Northern and Eastern Shoshone. The southern branch was spoken in present-day Arizona and New Mexico, into northern and central Mexico, and includes **Pima, Papago,** Tarahumara, Yaqui, Cora, Huichol, and Nahuatl.

– V –

VACA, ALVA NUÑEZ CABEZA DE (1490–1557). *See* CABEZA DE VACA, ALVA NUÑEZ.

VAIL SITE. Archaeological site located on the shore of Aziscohos Lake in a high mountain river valley in Oxford County, Maine, with evidence of **Paleoindian** period occupation dated to more than 10,500 B.P. (8500 B.C.). Archaeological materials from the Vail site indicate the presence of a Paleoindian encampment and two nearby **caribou kill sites**. The Vail site is the earliest presently known site in Maine, and the material **culture** found at the site is closely linked with that of the **Debert site** in Nova Scotia.

VERRAZANO, GIOVANNI DA (1480–1527). Italian navigator who explored the Atlantic Coast of North America for the French. In 1524 Verrazano explored the Atlantic Coast in search of a westward passage to Asia. He explored the coastal region from Cape Fear northward, becoming the first European to explore New York Harbor and Narragansett Bay. He continued northward to Newfoundland before returning to France. He later led expeditions to Brazil (1527) and to the West Indies (1529), where he was killed by indigenous peoples. Detailed information from his explorations was incorporated into maps of the New World, providing an improved understanding of the North American continent.

VINLAND. Land in North America explored and settled by Norse (Viking) settlers led by **Leif Eriksson** at approximately 950 B.P. (A.D. 1000). Located along the Atlantic coast of northeastern Canada, this land of wild grapes, or **Vinland**, is mentioned in ancient Norse sagas. A colonizing expedition of 130 Vikings settled in Vinland around 946 B.P. (A.D. 1004), but abandoned their settlements in 937 B.P. (A.D. 1013) due to incessant **warfare** with the indigenous peoples of the region, whom they referred to as *Skraelings*. **Archaeological** research along the Newfoundland coast suggests that the remains at **L'Anse aux Meadows** represent the Norse settlement of Vinland.

– W –

WAMPUM. Small cylindrical **beads** made from polished shells and fashioned into long strings or belts by Native Americans of the **Northeast culture area**. Also called *peag*, wampum was used by certain Northeastern peoples as a type of currency, and formed an important component of ceremonial **exchanges** between cultural groups.

WARFARE. Armed conflict waged against an enemy. Although the nature of warfare among Native American peoples changed dramatically with the introduction of firearms by Europeans, there is ample evidence of warfare between Native Americans prior to the arrival of Europeans. The primary evidence for warfare consists of blunt-force trauma in skeletal materials and the intensive **fortification** of sites with **palisades** and other forms of military architecture. **Ethnohistorical** evidence of indigenous warfare is also helpful in reconstructing the nature of pre-Columbian warfare among Native American groups.

WARING, ANTONIO J., JR. (1915–1964). Physician and avocational **archaeologist** educated at Yale University. Waring was trained as a pediatrician and practiced medicine in Savannah, Georgia, until his retirement in 1962. Waring's interest in archaeology was primarily influenced by **Joseph R. Caldwell**, William Sears, and other archaeologists working for the **Works Progress Administration** (WPA) in Georgia during the late 1930s. Waring assisted with excavations at

Irene, **Kolomoki**, and other **Southeastern** archaeological sites. His major contributions to American archaeology include his interpretations of **Southeastern Ceremonial Complex** art using ethnographic analogies from historic Southeastern peoples.

WASHITA FOCUS. Group of sedentary horticultural villages located on the southern **Great Plains** in present-day Oklahoma during the period from approximately 1150 to 575 B.P. (A.D. 800–1375). The Washita Focus is thought to have developed with influence from **Woodland** groups to the east, and featured a flexible **subsistence** base that allowed for the inclusion of horticulture, **bison hunting**, and **foraging** depending upon resource availability and prevailing environmental conditions. The Washita Focus declined at approximately 575 B.P. (A.D. 1375) as a response to prolonged drought in the region and increased **warfare** with nomadic groups of the southern Plains.

WATSON, PATTY JO (1932–). American **archaeologist** who received her Ph.D. from the University of Chicago in 1959, studying under Robert J. Braidwood. Watson began her career focusing on the archaeology of the Near East, conducting field research in Iraq, Iran, and Turkey. In the 1960s her research shifted to North America, with a series of projects in the **Southeast** and Midwest directed at the origins of **agriculture** in North America. Watson is considered one of the pioneers in the field of **ethnoarchaeology**, and was one of the first archaeologists to advocate for the explicitly scientific perspective of **processual archaeology**.

WEBB, WILLIAM S. (1882–1964). Physicist turned **archaeologist** who played a major role in the development of **Southeastern** archaeology during the Great Depression. Webb was professor of physics at the University of Kentucky, but he had long-standing interests in Native Americans and archaeology. During the Great Depression, he helped found the Department of Anthropology at the University of Kentucky. He led excavations throughout the region with the support of the National Research Council and the Smithsonian Institution. Webb also founded a museum at the University of Kentucky that now bears his name.

WEDEL, WALDO RUDOLPH (1908–1996). Pioneering American **archaeologist** who received his Ph.D. from the University of California, Berkeley, in 1936, studying under **Alfred L. Kroeber** and Carl Saur. Wedel's archaeological career was spent investigating the prehistory of the **Great Plains**, particularly the states of Nebraska and Kansas. Wedel served as the chief archaeologist for the Smithsonian Institution and as field director for the Smithsonian's **River Basin Survey** of the Missouri River. Wedel's research helped shape the nature of archaeological inquiry on the Plains.

WEEDEN ISLAND CULTURE. Archaeological culture indigenous to the western Gulf Coast of Florida during the period from 1650 to 950 B.P. (A.D. 300–1000). Believed to have developed out of the preceding **Swift Creek culture**, Weeden Island culture is characterized by the construction of earthen **burial mounds** containing nonlocal goods with Middle **Woodland** motifs and Gulf tradition **ceramics** that are distinct from the earlier Swift Creek wares. Weeden Island peoples were initially horticulturalists, **foragers**, and **fishers**, but at around 1150 B.P. (A.D. 800) **maize** began to be **cultivated** in the interior coastal plain of Florida, becoming an increasingly important component of Weeden Island diets. Weeden Island peoples also constructed **platform mounds** that served as supports for elite **charnel houses**. Weeden Island culture is thought to have exerted influence throughout the lower **Southeast**, with evidence of **trade** and Weeden Island–style ceramics appearing in late Woodland contexts in present-day Alabama, Georgia, Mississippi, and Tennessee.

WEIR. *See* FISH WEIR.

WICHITA INDIANS. Confederacy of **Caddoan**-speaking Native American groups that inhabited the region between the Arkansas River in Kansas and the Brazos River in Texas. The Wichita were village **agriculturalists**, cultivating **maize, beans, squash**, and **tobacco**, and also participated in seasonal **bison** hunts. Wichita domestic structures were circular, grass-covered, dome-shaped buildings with an interior diameter of roughly 10 meters (33 feet). The Wichita commonly **tattooed** their faces, arms, and chests, and were referred to as "tattooed people" by other Native American groups of the southern **Great Plains**. The Wichita first encountered Europeans in 1541 as members of the expedition of **Francisco de Coronado** searched for **Quivara**. They were later forced to migrate to the south due to incursions in their territory by the **Osage** and **Chickasaw**. The Wichita were eventually forced onto a reservation on the Washita River in Oklahoma. Approximately 500 Wichita continue to reside in Oklahoma.

WICKIUP. Common domestic structure for groups of the **Great Basin** and northern **Southwest** culture areas, including the **Apache** and southern **Shoshone**, consisting of a small, dome-shaped lodge constructed of an interior framework of wooden poles and covered with brush, grass, or reed mats. Wickiups were generally expedient shelter, and could be erected very quickly by highly mobile **foraging** groups.

WILLEY, GORDON R. (1913–2002). Pioneering American **archaeologist**, who received his Ph.D. from Columbia University in 1942. Willey worked throughout the Americas and is perhaps best known for his research on Mayan sites in Belize, Guatemala, and Honduras, as well as his pioneering settlement pattern research in the Viru Valley of Peru. Before shifting his research focus to **Mesoamerica** and South America, Willey worked in the **Southeast**, refining cultural chronologies and **ceramic** analyses in Georgia and Louisiana. Willey was employed by the Smithsonian Institution, and was later named the first Charles P. Bowditch Professor of Central American and Mexican Archaeology and Ethnology at Harvard University. Willey's *Archaeology of the Florida Gulf Coast* (1949) was immensely influential, and remains an important resource for Southeastern archaeologists.

WILLIAMSON SITE. **Archaeological** site located near the Nottoway River in Dinwiddie County, Virginia, with evidence of occupation by **Paleoindian** period peoples at approximately 10,000 B.P. (8000 B.C.). The Williamson site is considered one of the largest **Clovis** sites in eastern North America, with evidence that the site was a Paleoindian **lithic** quarry and base camp.

WINDOVER SITE. **Archaeological** site located near Titusville, Florida, with extensive evidence of occupation by **Archaic** period peoples approximately 8000 B.P. (6000 B.C.). Windover is one of the largest and earliest presently known Native American cemeteries, with more than 160 human **burials** identified during archaeological excavation. The burials at the Windover site were remarkably well preserved, having been underwater since their initial burial. This moist context enabled many perishable materials to be preserved, with individual burial cloths, wooden **artifacts**, and plant remains surviving. In addition, the brains of many individuals buried at the Windover site were so well preserved that it was possible to extract DNA from them and compare it to that of modern Native American populations.

WISCONSIN GLACIATION. Name given to the last major episode of glaciation in North America, coinciding with the terminal **Pleistocene** epoch, from about 70,000 to 10,000 B.P. (68,000–8000 B.C.). **Paleoindian** peoples encountered the last stages of the Wisconsin Glaciation when they entered the continent from northern Asia. These expansive glaciers retreated with the development of the warmer climates accompanying the **Holocene**.

WITCHCRAFT. The belief that magic can manipulate supernatural forces and bend them to an individual's will. Most traditional Native American **religious** beliefs viewed witchcraft as a distinct form of supernatural power from **shamanism**, with witchcraft generally seen as a source of malevolent occurrences. Accusations of witchcraft were prevalent in many Native American communities, with almost all negative impacts, from losing in a gambling game to severe illness, explained as the results of witchcraft.

WOMEN. *See* GENDER ROLES.

WOODLAND. **Cultural** period of the **Eastern Woodlands** that dates from approximately 3000 to 1000 B.P (1000 B.C.–A.D. 950). Traditionally defined as the time period when **ceramics** were first widely produced and Native American peoples became increasingly sedentary, the Woodland period witnessed increasing regional populations and a diversification of cultural **traditions** and **subsistence** practices. Punctuated by the development of the **Adena** and **Hopewell** cultures,

archaeological sites dated to the Woodland period possess evidence of the first cultivation of **maize** in eastern North America. This period also witnessed the widespread construction of earthen **burial mounds** and specialized mortuary facilities, as well as the establishment of long-distance **trade** networks and **interaction spheres**.

WORKS PROGRESS ADMINISTRATION (WPA). A governmental relief program founded in 1935 to provide employment for many who were unemployed during the Great Depression. Although WPA initiatives included highway and building construction, they also included large-scale archaeological excavations in the **Southeast**. These projects were focused on some of the largest archaeological sites in the Southeast (**Moundville**, **Etowah**, and so on) and provided much of the critical data needed to produce regional **culture histories**.

– X –

X-RAY DIFFRACTION ANALYSIS. Scientific technique used to identify the constituent minerals in the raw materials from which **artifacts** were made. This technique can also be used to identify particular clay minerals in **archaeological** sediments, and assist in the interpretation of landform changes over time.

– Y –

YAQUI INDIANS. Uto-Aztecan–speaking Native American groups of the **Southwest** who occupied territory stretching from the Sonoran Desert to the Pacific Coast of Mexico, including extreme southern Arizona. The Yaqui were village **agriculturalists** who actively resisted Spanish colonization during the 16th and 17th centuries. During the 19th century, they fought against Mexican encroachments on their lands, with most of their land seized by Mexicans in the 1880s. After this confiscation, many Yaqui migrated across the border into Arizona, creating new settlements near Tucson and Phoenix, Arizona. In the 1930s many returned to Mexico when much of their land was returned, while others remained on the Pascua Yaqui reservation south of Tucson. At present, there are approximately 40,000 Yaqui in Arizona and Sonora, Mexico.

YOUNGER DRYAS. The most significant climatic event to occur during the last period of deglaciation in North America. At approximately 12,500 B.P. (10,500 B.C.), the North American climate suddenly reverted to previous **Pleistocene**-like bitterly cold conditions. Analysis of ice cores indicate that temperatures in North America dropped an average of 7 degrees in less than a decade, a considerable climatic change for such a relatively short temporal period. During the Younger Dryas, glaciers began to expand and the sea levels dropped, while forests and grasslands constricted, conditions thought to have led to the ultimate extinction of **mammoths** and other species of **megafauna**. This sudden climatic change would have adversely impacted human groups as well. Ice core analysis indicates that the Younger Dryas ended at approximately 11,000 B.P. (9000 B.C.).

YUMA INDIANS. Hokan-speaking Native American groups of the lower Colorado River valley and adjacent areas in present-day Arizona, California, and northern Mexico, including the Yuma proper, Mojave, Maricopa, Hualapai, and Havasupai. The Yuma are thought to be the historic descendants of the **Hohokam**, and were primarily small-scale **agriculturalists** who supplemented their diets with **foraging** activities. The Yuma also acted as **traders** between groups in the **Southwest** and the **California** coast, specializing in the **exchange** of shells for **baskets** and **ceramics**. At present, there are more than 4,000 Yuma in Arizona and California.

YUROK INDIANS. Yurok-speaking Native American groups of the **Northwest Coast** who occupied territory between the Klamath and Trinity Rivers in southern Oregon and northern California. The Yurok are considered the southernmost of the **Northwest Coast** cultures, but they also exhibited cultural practices of the **California** groups to their south. The Yurok subsisted on **salmon** and **acorns**, and used **dentalia shells** as currency. In 1855 a reservation was established for the Yurok in northern California. At present, there are more than 4,500 Yurok in the United States.

– Z –

ZOOARCHAEOLOGY. Analysis of **faunal remains** from **archaeological** contexts. Commonly referred to as faunal analysis, zooarchaeology involves the identification and analysis of distinct animal species from archaeological sites. Zooarchaeological studies examine the nature of human **subsistence** practices and the relationships between people, animals, and the environment.

ZOOMORPHIC. The use of animal motifs to decorate an object. Native Americans used a variety of animal representations, with these motifs appearing in **ceramics, earthworks, figurines, pipes, petroglyphs**, and other media.

ZUÑI INDIANS. Zuñian-speaking Native American groups of present-day western New Mexico. Considered the historic **Puebloan** descendants of earlier **Anasazi** peoples, the Zuñi occupied a series of villages along the Zuñi River in western New Mexico when first recorded by Europeans, with these villages eventually coalescing into a single community, that of Zuñi pueblo (*Halona*). Some scholars believe that it was these Zuñi communities that helped produce the Spanish myth of the Seven Cities of **Cibola**. Like other **Southwestern** groups, the Zuñi are primarily **maize agriculturalists**, but unlike other Puebloan groups, the Zuñi language is distinctive, with strong ties to the **languages** of several **California** groups. At present, there are more than 6,000 Zuñi residing in New Mexico and Arizona.

Appendix A
Museums with North American Collections

UNITED STATES

Alabama

Alabama Department of Archives
and History
624 Washington Avenue
Montgomery, Alabama 36130
(334) 242-4435
www.archives.state.al.us

Alabama Museum of Natural
History
University of Alabama
Smith Hall
Tuscaloosa, AL 35487
(205) 348-7550
http://amnh.ua.edu

Moundville Archaeological Park
Highway 69
Moundville, AL 35474
(205) 371-2234
http://moundville.ua.edu/home
.html

Alaska

University of Alaska Museum
P.O. Box 756960

907 Yukon Drive
Fairbanks, AK 99775-6960
(907) 474-7505
www.uaf.edu/museum

Arizona

Amerind Foundation
2100 N. Amerind Road
P.O. Box 400
Dragoon, AZ 85609
(520) 586-3666
www.amerind.org

Arizona State Museum
University of Arizona
1013 E. University Blvd.
Tucson, Arizona 85721
(520) 621-6302
www.statemuseum.arizona.edu

Museum of Northern Arizona
3101 N. Fort Valley Road
Flagstaff, AZ 86001
(928) 774-5213
www.musnaz.org

Pueblo Grande Museum and
Archaeological Park

4619 E. Washington Street
Phoenix, AZ 85034
(602) 495-0901
www.ci.phoenix.az.us/PARKS/
pueblo.html

California

California Academy of Sciences
875 Howard Street
San Francisco, CA 94118
(415) 750-7145
www.calacademy.org

Cantor Arts Center at Stanford
University
328 Lomita Drive and Museum
Way
Stanford, CA 94305
(650) 723-4177
www.stanford.edu/dept/SUMA

Fowler Museum of Cultural
History
University of California, Los
Angeles
P.O. Box 951549
Los Angeles, CA 90095-1549
(310) 825-4361
www.fmch.ucla.edu

Museum of Anthropology
California State University,
Chico
Chico, CA 95929
(530) 898-5397
www.csuchico.edu/anth/
Museum

Natural History Museum of
Los Angeles County
900 Exposition Boulevard
Los Angeles, CA 90007
(213) 763-3466
www.nhm.org

Page Museum at the La Brea
Tar Pits
5801 Wilshire Blvd.
Los Angeles, CA 90036
(323) 934-7243
www.tarpits.org

Phoebe Hurst Museum of
Anthropology
103 Kroeber Hall
University of California,
Berkeley
Berkeley, CA 94720
(510) 643-7648
http://hearstmuseum.berkeley
.edu/visitor/main.html

San Diego Museum of Man
1350 El Prado
Balboa Park
San Diego, CA 92101
(619) 239-2001
www.museumofman.org/html/
contact.html

Santa Barbara Museum of
Natural History
2559 Puesta del Sol
Santa Barbara, CA 93105
(805) 682-4711
www.sbnature.org

Southwest Museum
234 Museum Drive
Los Angeles, CA 90065
(323) 221-2164
www.southwestmuseum.org

Colorado

Denver Art Museum
100 West 14th Avenue Parkway
Denver, CO 80204
(720) 865-5000
www.denverartmuseum.org

Denver Museum of Nature and
Science
2001 Colorado Blvd.
Denver, CO 80205
(303) 322-7009
www.dmns.org

University of Colorado Museum
of Natural History
218 UCB
Boulder, CO 80309
(303) 492-6892
http://cumuseum.colorado.edu

Connecticut

Connecticut State Museum of
Natural History
University of Connecticut
2019 Hillside Rd., Unit 1023
Storrs, CT 06269-1023
(860) 486-4460
www.mnh.uconn.edu

Mashantucket Pequot Museum
and Research Center
110 Pequot Trail
P.O. Box 3180
Mashantucket, CT 06339
(800) 411-9671
www.pequotmuseum.org

Peabody Museum of Natural
History
Yale University
P.O. Box 208118
170 Whitney Avenue
New Haven, CT 06520-8118
(203) 432-5050
www.peabody.yale.edu

Florida

Florida Museum of Natural
History
University of Florida—Powell
Hall
SW 34th Street and Hull Road
P.O. Box 112710
Gainesville, FL 32611-2710
(352) 846-2000
www.flmnh.ufl.edu

Indian Temple Mound Museum
139 Miracle Strip Parkway SE
Fort Walton Beach, FL 32548
(904) 243-6521
www.sunnyfl.com/attractions/ind.
htm

St. Petersburg Museum of
History

335 Second Avenue NE
St. Petersburg, FL 33701
(727) 894-1052
www.stpetemuseumofhistory.org/

Georgia

The Columbus Museum
1251 Wynnton Road
Columbus, GA 31906
(706) 649-0713
www.columbusmuseum.com/

Georgia Museum of Natural
  History
University of Georgia
Riverbend Research Road
Athens, GA 30602
(706) 542-1663
http://naturalhistory.uga.edu

Idaho

Idaho Museum of Natural History
Idaho State University
5th Avenue and Dillon Street
Pocatello, ID 83209
(208) 282-3317
http://imnh.isu.edu

Illinois

Anthropology Museum
Northern Illinois University
DeKalb, IL 60115
www.niu.edu/anthro_museum

Dickson Mounds Museum
Lewistown, IL 61542

(309) 547-3189
www.museum.state.il.us/ismsites/
  dickson/

Field Museum
Roosevelt Road and Lake Shore
  Drive
Chicago, IL 60605
(312) 922-9410
www.fmnh.org

Illinois State Museum
Springs and Edwards
Springfield, IL 62706
(217) 782-7387
www.museum.state.il.us

Indiana

William Hammond Mathers
  Museum
601 East 8th Street
Indiana University
Bloomington, IN 47405
(812) 855-6873
www.indiana.edu/~mathers

Iowa

Museum of Natural History
10 Macbride Hall
Iowa City, IA 52242
(319) 355-0480
www.uiowa.edu/~nathist

Kansas

Kansas History Center
6425 SW Sixth Avenue
Topeka, KS 66615

www.kshs.org/places/khc/index
.htm

Museum of Anthropology
University of Kansas
Lawrence, KS 66045
www.ukans.edu/~kuma

Native American Heritage
    Museum
1727 Elgin Road
Highland, KS 66035-9801
(785) 442-3304
www.kshs.org/places/native
    american

Pawnee Indian Village State
    Historic Site
480 Pawnee Trail
Republic, KS 66964
(785) 272-8681
www.kshs.org/places/pawneeindi
    an/index.htm

Kentucky

William S. Webb Museum of
    Anthropology
University of Kentucky
1020A Export Street
Lexington, KY 40506-9854
(859) 257-8208
www.uky.edu/AS/Anthropology/
    Museum/museum.htm

Louisiana

Lafayette Natural History Museum
637 Girard Park Drive

Lafayette, LA 70503
(337) 291-5544
www.lnhm.org

Museum of Natural Science
119 Foster Hall
Louisiana State University
Baton Rouge, LA 70803
(225) 578-3080
www.museum.lsu.edu/MNS/
    index.html

Maine

Abbe Museum
26 Mount Desert Street
Bar Harbor, ME 04609
(207) 288-3519
www.abbemuseum.org

Hudson Museum of
    Anthropology
University of Maine
5746 Maine Center for the Arts
Orono, ME 04469
(207) 581-1901
www.umaine.edu/hudsonmuseum

Maryland

Baltimore Museum of Art
10 Art Museum Drive
Baltimore, Maryland 21218
(410) 396-6317
http://artbma.org/home.html

National Museum of the
    American Indian
Smithsonian Institution

4220 Silver Hill Road
Suitland, MD 20746
(301) 238-6624
www.nmai.si.edu

Massachusetts

Peabody Essex Museum
East India Square
Salem, MA 01970
(978) 745-9500
www.pem.org/homepage

Peabody Museum
Harvard University
11 Divinity Avenue
Cambridge, MA 02138
(617) 496-1027
www.peabody.harvard.edu/
default.html

Robert S. Peabody Museum of
Anthropology
Phillips Academy
Andover, MA 01810
(978) 749-4490
www.andover.edu/rspeabody/
home.htm

Michigan

Detroit Historical Museum
5401 Woodward Avenue
Detroit, MI 48202
(313) 833-9721
www.detroithistorical.org

Michigan State University
Museum

East Lansing, MI 48824
(517) 355-7474
www.museum.msu.edu

Museum of Anthropology
University of Michigan
Ruthven Museum Building
1109 Geddes Avenue
Ann Arbor, MI 48019
(734) 764-0485
www.umma.lsa.umich.edu

Museum of Ojibwa Culture
500-566 N. State
St. Ignace, MI 49781
(906) 643-9161
www.stignace.com/attractions/
ojibwa/rates.html

Minnesota

Minnesota Historical Society
345 W. Kellogg Boulevard
St. Paul, MN 55102-1906
(651) 296-6126
www.mnhs.org

The Science Museum of
Minnesota
120 W. Kellogg Street
St. Paul, MN 55192
(651) 221-9444
www.smm.org

Mississippi

The University Museums
University of Mississippi
5th and University Avenue

Oxford, MS 38655
(662) 915-7073
www.olemiss.edu/depts/
u_museum/index.htm

Missouri

Museum of Anthropology
University of Missouri, Columbia
104 Swallow Hall
Columbia, MO 65211
(573) 882-3573
http://coas.missouri.edu/
anthromuseum

Montana

Museum of the Rockies
Montana State University
600 West Kagy Boulevard
Bozeman, MT 59717
(404) 994-2251
www.montana.edu/wwwmor

Nebraska

Museum of the Fur Trade
6321 Highway 20
Chadron, NE 69337
(308) 432-3843
www.furtrade.org

University of Nebraska State
  Museum
307 Morrill Hall
University of Nebraska—Lincoln
Lincoln, Nebraska 68588
(402) 472-2642
www.museum.unl.edu

Nevada

Nevada State Museum
600 N. Carson Street
Carson City, NV 89710
(702) 486-5172
dmla.clan.lib.nv.us/docs/museums
/cc/carson.htm

Nevada State Museum and
  Historical Society
700 Twin Lakes Drive
Las Vegas, Nevada 89107
(702) 486-5205
dmla.clan.lib.nv.us/docs/museums
/cc/carson.htm

New Jersey

New Jersey State Museum
Calhoun and West State Street
Trenton, NJ 08625
(609) 292-6464
www.state.nj.us/state/
museum

New Mexico

Indian Pueblo Cultural Center
2401 12th Street NW
Albuquerque, NM 87104
(505) 843-7270
www.indianpueblo.org

Maxwell Museum of
  Anthropology
University of New Mexico
Albuquerque, NM 87131-1201
(505) 277-4405
www.unm.edu/~maxwell

Museum of New Mexico
Museum of Indian Arts and
  Culture
710 Camino Lejo
Santa Fe, NM 87504-2087
(505) 827-6463
www.miaclab.org/indexfl.html

New York

American Museum of Natural
  History
Central Park West at 79th Street
New York, New York 10024
(212) 769-5100
www.amnh.org

New York State Museum
Room 3122
Cultural Education Center
Empire State Plaza
Albany, NY 12230
(518) 474-5877
www.nysm.nysed.gov

Rochester Museum and Science
  Center
657 East Avenue
Rochester, NY 14607
(585) 271-4320
www.rmsc.org/msindex.htm

North Carolina

Museum of Anthropology
Wake Forest University
P.O. Box 7267
Winston-Salem, NC 27109

(336) 758-5282
www.wfu.edu/MOA

Rankin Museum of American and
  Natural History
131 W. Church Street
Ellerbe, NC 28338
(910) 652-6378
www.rankinmuseum.com

Schiele Museum of Natural
  History
1500 East Garrison Boulevard
Gastonia, NC 28054
(704) 866-6900
www.schielemuseum.org

North Dakota

North Dakota Heritage Center
State Historical Society of North
  Dakota
612 East Boulevard
Bismarck, ND, 58505
(701) 328-2666
www.state.nd.us/hist

Ohio

Cincinnati Museum Center
1301 Western Avenue
Cincinnati, OH 45203
(513) 287-7000
www.cincymuseum.org

Cleveland Museum of Natural
  History
1 Wade Oval

University Circle
Cleveland, OH 44106
(216) 231-4600
www.cmnh.org

Ohio Historical Society
1982 Velma Avenue
Columbus, OH 43211
(614) 297-2300
www.ohiohistory.org

Oklahoma

Five Civilized Tribes Museum
Agency Hill on Honor Heights
Drive
Muskogee, OK 74401
(918) 683-1701
www.fivetribes.org

Gilcrease Museum
1400 North Gilcrease Museum
Road
Tulsa, OK 74127
(918) 596-2700
www.gilcrease.org

Sam Noble Oklahoma Museum
of Natural History
University of Oklahoma
2401 Chautauqua Avenue
Norman, OK 73072
(405) 325-4712
www.snomnh.ou.edu/homepage/
index.shtml

Oregon

The High Desert Museum
59800 South Highway 97
Bend, OR 97702-7963
(541) 382-4754
www.highdesert.org

Oregon State Museum of
Anthropology
1680 East 15th Avenue
1224 University of Oregon
Eugene, Oregon 97403-1224
(541) 346-3031
http://oregon.uoregon.edu/~osma/
sma.html

Pennsylvania

Carnegie Museum of Natural
History
4400 Forbes Avenue
Pittsburgh, PA 15206
(412) 622-3131
www.carnegiemuseums.org/cmnh

Matson Museum of Anthropology
Department of Anthropology
Pennsylvania State University
409 Carpenter Building
University Park, PA 16802
(814) 865-3853
www.anthro.psu.edu/mat_mus/
index1.html

Pocono Indian Museum
Route 209
P.O. Box 261
Bushkill, PA 18324

(570) 588-9338
www.poconoindianmuseum.
com

State Museum of Pennsylvania
300 North Street
Harrisburg, PA 17120
(717) 787-4980
www.statemuseumpa.org

University of Pennsylvania
Museum
33rd and Spruce Streets
Philadelphia, PA 19104-6324
(215) 898-4000
www.museum.upenn.edu

Rhode Island

Haffenreffer Museum of
Anthropology
300 Tower Street
Bristol, RI 02809
(401) 253-8388
www.brown.edu/Facilities/
Haffenreffer

Museum of Natural History and
Planetarium
Roger Williams Park
Providence, RI 02905
(401) 785-9450
www.osfn.org/museum

South Carolina

South Carolina State Museum
301 Gervais Street

Columbia, SC 29211
(803) 898-4921
www.museum.state.sc.us

South Dakota

W. H. Over Museum
1110 Ratingen St.
Vermillion, SD 57069
(605) 677-5277
www.usd.edu/whover

Tennessee

C. H. Nash Archaeological
Museum
1987 Indian Village Drive
Memphis, TN 38109
(901) 785-3160
http://cas.memphis.edu/
chucalissa

Frank H. McClung Museum
University of Tennessee
1327 Circle Park Drive
Knoxville, TN 37996-3200
(865) 974-2144
http://mcclungmuseum.utk.edu

Texas

Centennial Museum
University of Texas at El Paso
El Paso, TX 79968
(915) 747-5411
www.utep.edu/museum/home
.html

Dallas Museum of Art
1717 North Harwood
Dallas, TX 75201
(214) 922-1200
www.dm-art.org

Institute of Texan Cultures
801 S. Bowie Street
San Antonio, TX 78205
(210) 458-2300
www.texancultures.utsa.edu/
public/index.htm

Museum of Texas Tech
University
Fourth Street and Indiana Avenue
Box 43191
Lubbock, TX 79409
(806) 742-2490
www.depts.ttu.edu/museumttu/
about.html

Panhandle-Plains Historical
Museum
2503 4th Avenue
Canyon, Texas 79015
(806) 651-2244
www.panhandleplains.org

Utah

Utah Museum of Natural History
University of Utah
Presidents Circle
Salt Lake City, UT 84112
(801) 581-6927
www.umnh.utah.edu

Vermont

Chimney Point State Historic Site
Vermont Division for Historic
Preservation
7305 VT Route 125
Vergennes, VT 05491
(802) 759-2412
www.dhca.state.vt.us/Historic
Sites/html/chimneypoint.html

Virginia

Alexandria Archaeology Museum
The Torpedo Factory Art Center
105 N. Union Street, #327
Alexandria, Virginia 22314
(703) 838-4399
http://oha.ci.alexandria.va.us/
archaeology

The Virginia Museum of Natural
History
1001 Douglas Avenue
Martinsville, Virginia 24112
(434) 982-4605
www.virginia.edu/vmnh-uva

Washington

Burke Museum of Natural
History and Culture
University of Washington
17th Avenue NE
Seattle, WA 98195
(206) 534-5590

www.washington.edu/
   burkemuseum

Museum of Anthropology
Washington State University
Pullman, WA 99164
(509) 335-3936
http://libarts.wsu.edu/anthro/
   museum

Washington, D.C.

Dumbarton Oaks
1703 32nd Street NW
Washington, DC 20007
(202) 339-6401
www.doaks.org

Smithsonian Institution
National Museum of Natural
   History
10th Street and Constitution
   Avenue
Washington, DC 20560
(202) 357-2700
www.mnh.si.edu

West Virginia

West Virginia State Museum
The Cultural Center
Capitol Complex
1900 Kanawha Boulevard
   East
Charleston, WV 25305
(304) 558-0220
www.wvculture.org/
   museum

Wisconsin

Logan Museum of Anthropology
Beloit College
Beloit, WI 53511
(608) 363-3677
www.beloit.edu/~museum/
   logan

Milwaukee Public Museum
800 Wells Street
Milwaukee, WI 53233
(414) 278-2702
www.mpm.edu

Wyoming

Wyoming State Museum
Barrett Building
2301 Central Avenue
Cheyenne, WY 82002
(307) 777-7022
http://wyomuseum.state.wy.us

CANADA

Alberta

Provincial Museum of Alberta
12845 102 Avenue
Edmonton, Alberta T5N 0M6
(780) 454-6629
www.pma.edmonton.ab.ca

British Columbia

Museum of Anthropology
University of British Columbia

6393 Northwest Marine Drive
Vancouver, BC V6T 1Z2
(604) 822-5087
www.moa.ubc.ca

Royal British Columbia Museum
657 Belleville Street
Victoria, BC V8W 9W2
(250) 356-7226
http://rbcm1.rbcm.gov.bc.ca

Ontario

London Museum of Archaeology
Lawson-Jury Building
1600 Attawandaron Road
London, ON N6G 3M6
(519) 473-1360
www.uwo.ca/museum

Royal Ontario Museum
100 Queen's Park
Toronto, ON M5S 2C6
(416) 586-5549
www.rom.on.ca

Québec

Canadian Museum of
  Civilization
100 Laurier Street
P.O. Box 3100
Station B, Hull

Québec J8X 4H2
(819) 776-7000
http://cyberboutique
.civilisations.ca

McCord Museum of Canadian
  History
690 Sherbrooke Street West
Montreal, Quebec
H3A 1E9
(514) 398-7100
http://museum.gov.ns.ca/mikmaq/
  mccord.htm

Montreal Museum of
  Archaeology and History
350 Place Royale (Corner of De
  la Commune)
Old Montréal, Québec
Canada
H2Y 3Y5
(514) 872-9150
www.pacmuscum.qc.ca/indexan
.html

UNITED KINGDOM

British Museum
Great Russell Street
London, England WC1B 3DG
0207-323-8299
www.thebritishmuseum.ac.uk

Appendix B

Major North American Archaeological Sites Available for Public Tours

UNITED STATES

Alabama

Moundville Archaeological Park
Highway 69
Moundville, AL 35474
(205) 371-2234
http://moundville.ua.edu/home
.html

Russell Cave National Monument
729 County Road 98
Bridgeport, AL 35740
(256) 495-2672
www.nps.gov/ruca

Arizona

Pueblo Grande Museum and
Archaeological Park
4619 E. Washington Street
Phoenix, AZ 85034
(602) 495-0901
www.ci.phoenix.az.us/PARKS/
pueblo.html

Arkansas

Parkin Archaeological State Park
Highway 64

Parkin, AR 72373
(870) 755-2500
www.uark.edu/campus-
resources/archinfo/parkin.html

Toltec Mounds Archaeological
State Park
490 Toltec Mounds Road
Scott, AR 72142
(501) 961-9442
www.cast.uark.edu/parkin/
toltecvisitpg.html

California

Calico Early Man Site
Interstate 15
Barstow, CA 92311
(760) 252-6000
www.ca.blm.gov/barstow/calico
.html

Indian Grinding Rock State
Historic Park
14881 Pine Grove-Volcano Road
Pine Grove, CA 95665
(209) 296-7488
www.parks.ca.gov/default.asp?
page_id=553

Page Museum at the La Brea
 Tar Pits
5801 Wilshire Blvd.
Los Angeles, CA 90036
(323) 934-7243
www.tarpits.org

Colorado

Anasazi Heritage Center
27501 Highway 184
Dolores, CO 81323
(970) 882-5600
www.co.blm.gov/ahc/index.
 htm

Hovenweep National Monument
McElmo Route
Cortez, CO 81321
(970) 562-4282
www.nps.gov/hove/

Mesa Verde National Park
P.O. Box 8
Mesa Verde, CO 81330
(970) 529-4465
www.nps.gov/meve/home.htm

Connecticut

Mashantucket Pequot Museum
 and Research Center
110 Pequot Trail
P.O. Box 3180
Mashantucket, CT 06339-3180
(800) 411-9671
www.pequotmuseum.org

Florida

Crystal River Archaeological
 State Park
3400 N. Museum Point
Crystal River, FL 34428
(352) 795-3817
http://citruscounty-fl.com/
 CrysRiv.html

Florida Underwater
 Archaeological Preserves
Office of Cultural and Historic
 Programs
500 S. Bronough Street
Tallahassee, FL 32399-0250
(850) 245-6300
http://dhr.dos.state.fl.us

Indian Temple Mound Museum
139 Miracle Strip Parkway
Fort Walton Beach, FL 32548
(904) 234-6521
www.sunnyfl.com/attractions/
 ind.htm

Lake Jackson Mounds State
 Archaeological Site
1022 De Soto Park Drive
Tallahassee, Florida 32301
(850) 922-6007
www.abfla.com/parks/
 LakeJacksonMounds/
 lakejackson.html

Mission San Luis de Apalachee
2020 West Mission Road

Tallahassee, Florida
(850) 487-3711
http://dhr.dos.state.fl.us/bar/
san_luis

Georgia

Etowah Indian Mounds State Park
813 Indian Mounds Road
Cartersville, GA 30120
(770) 387-3747
www.gastateparks.org/info/etowah/

Kolomoki Mounds Historic Park
205 Indian Mounds Road
Blakely, GA 39823
(229) 724-2150
www.georgiaplanning.com/
history/kolomoki/

Ocmulgee National Monument
207 Emery Highway
Macon, GA 31217
(478) 752-8257
www.nps.gov/ocmu/

Idaho

Nez Perce National Historical Park
39063 U.S. Highway 95
Spalding, ID 83540
(208) 843-2261
www.nps.gov/nepe/

Illinois

Cahokia Mounds State Historic
Site
30 Ramey Street

Collinsville, IL 62234
(618) 346-5160
http://medicine.wustl.edu/
~mckinney/cahokia/cahokia.
html

Dickson Mounds Museum
Lewistown, IL 61542
(309) 547-3189
www.museum.state.il.us/ismsites/
dickson/

Indiana

Angel Mounds State Historic Site
8215 Pollack Avenue
Evansville, IN 47715
(812) 852-3956
www.angelmounds.org/

Mounds State Park
4306 Mounds Road
Anderson, IN 46017
(756) 642-6627
www.state.in.us/dnr/parklake/
parks/mounds.html

Iowa

Effigy Mounds National
Monument
151 Highway 76
Harpers Ferry, IA 52146
(563) 873-3491
www.nps.gov/efmo/

Toolesboro Indian Mounds
Highway 99

Toolesboro, IA 52653
(319) 523-8381
www.iowahistory.org/sites/tools
boro/toolesboro_mounds.html

Kansas

Pawnee Indian Village State
Historic Site
480 Pawnee Trail
Republic, KS 66964
(785) 272-8681
www.kshs.org/places/pawnee
indian/index.htm

Kentucky

Mammoth Cave National Park
P.O. Box 7
Mammoth Cave, KY 42259
(270) 758-2180
www.nps.gov/maca/home.htm

Wickliffe Mounds Research
Center
94 Green Street, Highway
51/60/62W
Wickliffe, KY 42087
(270) 335-3681
http://campus.murraystate.edu/
org/WMRC/WMRC.htm

Louisiana

Marksville State Historic Site
837 Martin Luther King Dr.
Marksville, LA 71351
(888) 253-8954

www.crt.state.la.us/crt/parks/
marksvil/marksvle.htm

Poverty Point State Historic Site
LA Route 577
Epps, Louisiana 71237
(888) 926-5492
www.crt.state.la.us/crt/parks/
poverty/pvertypt.htm

Michigan

Mackinac State Historic Park
P.O. Box 873
Mackinaw City, MI 49757
(906) 847-3328
www.mackinacparks.com/

Minnesota

Grand Portage National
Monument
P.O. Box 426, 211 Mile Creek
Road
Grand Portage, MN 55605
(218) 387-2788
www.nps.gov/grpo/

Jeffers Petroglyphs Historic Site
27160 County Road 2
Comfrey, MN 56019
(507) 628-5591
www.mnhs.org/places/sites/jp/
index.html

Lower Sioux Agency Historic
Site
32469 Redwood County Hwy. 2

Morton, MN 56270
(507) 697-6321
www.mnhs.org/places/sites/lsa/
index.html

Pipestone National Monument
36 Reservation Ave.
Pipestone, MN 56164
(507) 825-5464
www.nps.gov/pipe

Mississippi

Emerald Mound
RR 1, NT-143
Tupelo, MS 38801
www.cr.nps.gov/aad/feature/
emerald.htm

Grand Village of the Natchez
Indians
400 Jefferson Davis Boulevard
Natchez, MS 39120
(601) 446-6502
www.mdah.state.ms.us/hprop/
gvni.html

Winterville Mounds
2415 Highway 1 North
Greenville, MS
(662) 334-4684
http://mdah.state.ms.us/hprop/
winterville.html

Missouri

Graham Cave State Park
217 Hwy. TT

Montgomery City, MO 63361
(573) 564-3476
www.mostateparks.com/
grahamcave.htm

Mastodon State Historic Site
1050 Museum Drive
Imperial, MO 63052
(636) 464-2976
www.mostateparks.com/
mastodon.htm

Osage Village State Historic
Site
1009 Truman
Lamar, MO 64759
(417) 682-2279
www.mostateparks.com/
osagevillage/geninfo.htm

Towosahgy State Historic Site
13640 South Hwy. 102
East Prairie, MO 63845
(573) 649-3149
www.mostateparks.com/
towosahgy/geninfo.htm

Trail of Tears State Park
429 Moccasin Springs
Jackson, MO 63755
(573) 334-1711
www.rosecity.net/tears/tears1
.html

Van Meter State Park
Route 1, Box 47
Miami, MO 65344
(660) 886-7537

www.mostateparks.com/vanmeter
.htm

Washington State Park
Route 2, Box 450
De Soto, MO 63020
(636) 586-5768
www.mostateparks.com/
washington.htm

Montana

Little Bighorn National
Monument
Highway 212
Crow Agency, MT 59022
(406) 638-3204
www.nps.gov/libi/

Pictograph Cave State Park
2300 Lake Elmo Drive
Billings, MT 59105
(406) 247-2940
www.pictographcave.org/

New Mexico

Aztec Ruins National Monument
84 County Road 2900
Aztec, NM 87410
(505) 334-6174
www.nps.gov/azru/

Bandelier National Monument
HCR 1, Box 1, Suite 15
Los Alamos, NM 87544
(505) 672-3861, ext. 517
www.nps.gov/band/

Blackwater Draw Museum and
Archaeological Site
508A New Mexico Route 467
Portales, NM 88130
(505) 562-2910
www.nmculture.org/cgi-bin/
instview.cgi?_recordnum=
BWDM

Chaco Culture National
Historical Park
P.O. Box 220
Nageezi, NM 87037
(505) 786-7014
www.nps.gov/chcu/

Coronado State Monument
State Highway 44
Bernalillo, NM 87004
(505) 867-5351
http://museumofnewmexico.org/
inst.cgi?_fn=Inst&_instid=
CORO

El Morro National Monument
HC 61, Box 43
Ramah, NM 87321
(505) 783-4226
www.nps.gov/elmo/

Gila Cliff Dwellings National
Monument
HC 68, Box 100
Silver City, NM 88061
(505) 536-9461
www.nps.gov/gicl/

Pecos National Historical Park
P.O. Box 418

Pecos, NM 87552
(505) 757-6414, ext. 1
www.nps.gov/peco/

Petroglyph National Monument
6602 Unser Blvd., NW
Albuquerque, NM 87120
(505) 899-0205
www.nps.gov/petr/

Pueblo of Acoma
P.O. Box 309
Acoma Pueblo, NM 87034
(505) 552-6604
www.puebloofacoma.org/index2
.htm

Salinas Pueblo Missions National
Monument
P.O. Box 517
Mountainair, NM 87036
(505) 847-2585
www.nps.gov/sapu/

New York

Ganondagan State Historic Site
1488 State Route 444
Victor, NY 14564
(585) 742-1690
www.ganondagan.org/index.html

North Carolina

Town Creek Indian Mound
509 Town Creek Mound Road
Mt. Gilead, NC 27306
(910) 439-6802

www.ah.dcr.state.nc.us/sections/
hs/town/town.htm

North Dakota

Knife River Indian Villages
National Historic Site
564 County Road 37
Stanton, ND 58571
(701) 745-3300
www.nps.gov/knri/

Ohio

Flint Ridge State Memorial
7091 Brownsville Road, SE
Glenford, OH 43739
(740) 787-2476
www.ohiohistory.org/places/flint/

Fort Ancient State Memorial
6123 State Route 350
Oregonia, OH 45054
(513) 932-4421
www.ohiohistory.org/places/
ftancien/

Fort Hill
13614 Fort Hill Road
Hillsboro, OH 45133
(937) 588-3221
www.ohiohistory.org/places/
fthill/

Hopewell Culture National
Historical Park
16062 State Route 104
Chillicothe, OH 45601

(740) 774-1125
www.nps.gov/hocu/

Inscription Rock
Lake Erie Islands State Park
4049 East Moores Dock Road
Port Clinton, OH 43452
(419) 797-4530
www.ohiohistory.org/places/
inscript/

Miamisburg Mound
State Route 725
Miamisburg, OH 45342
(937) 866-4532
www.ohiohistory.org/places/
miamisbg/

Newark Earthworks State
Memorial
99 Cooper Avenue
Newark, OH 43055
(740) 344-1920
www.ohiohistory.org/places/
newarkearthworks

Serpent Mound
3850 State Route 73
Peebles, OH 45660
www.ohiohistory.org/places/
serpent/

Sun Watch Indian Village
2301 West River Road
Dayton, OH 45418
(937) 268-8199
www.sunwatch.org/

Oklahoma

Spiro Mounds Archaeological
Center
Route 2, Box 339AA
Spiro, OK 74959
(918) 962-2062
www.ok-history.mus.ok.us/
enc/spiro_mounds.htm

Oregon

Fort Clatsop National
Memorial
92343 Fort Clatsop Road
Astoria, OR 97103
(503) 861-2471
www.nps.gov/focl

South Carolina

Charles Towne Landing State
Historic Site
1500 Old Towne Road
Charleston, SC 29407
(843) 852-4200
www.discoversouthcarolina.com/
stateparks/Parkdetail.Asp?Pid=
1575

Colonial Dorchester State
Historic Site
300 State Park Road
Summerville, SC 29485
(843) 873-1740
www.discoversouthcarolina.com/
stateparks/Parkdetail.Asp?Pid=
725

Tennessee

Chucalissa Museum
1987 Indian Village Drive
Memphis, TN 38109
(901) 785-3160
http://cas.memphis.edu/
chucalissa/

Old Stone Fort State Park
732 Stone Fort Drive
Manchester, TN 37855
(931) 723-5073
www.state.tn.us/environment/
parks/parks/OldStoneFort/

Pinson Mounds State Park
460 Ozier Road
Pinson, TN 38366
(731) 988-5614
www.state.tn.us/environment/
parks/parks/PinsonMounds/

Texas

Caddoan Mounds State Historic
Site
RR 2, Box 85C
Alto, TX 75925
(936) 858-3218
www.tpwd.state.tx.us/park/
caddoan/caddoan.htm

Hueco Tanks State Historic Site
6900 Hueco Tanks Road, No. 1
El Paso, TX 79938
(915) 857-1135
www.tpwd.state.tx.us/park/hueco/

Seminole Canyon State Park and
Historic Site
P.O. Box 820
Comstock, TX 78837
(432) 292-4464
www.tpwd.state.tx.us/park/
seminole/seminole.htm

Utah

Anasazi State Park Museum
P.O. Box 1429
Boulder, UT 84716
(435) 335-7308
http://parks.state.ut.us/park_
pages/anasazi.htm

Freemont Indian State Park and
Museum
3820 West Clear Creek Canyon
Road
Sevier, UT 84766
(435) 527-4631
http://parks.state.ut.us/park_
pages/fremont.htm

Virginia

Wolf Creek Indian Village
Route 1, Box 1530
Bastian, VA 24314
(276) 688-3438
www.indianvillage.org/

West Virginia

Grave Creek Mound Historic Site
801 Jefferson Avenue

Moundsville, WV 26041
(304) 843-4128
www.wvculture.org/sites/
gravecreek.html

Wisconsin

Aztalan State Park
Jefferson County Highway Q
Lake Mills, WI 53551
(920) 648-8774
www.dnr.state.wi.us/org/land/
parks/specific/aztalan

Wyoming

Medicine Lodge State
Archaeological Site
P.O. Box 62
Hyattville, WY 82428
(307) 469-2234
http://wyoparks.state.wy.us/
mlodge1.htm

CANADA

Alberta

Waterton Lakes National Park
P.O. Box 50
Waterton Park, AB, Canada TOK
2MO
(403) 859-2224
www.pc.gc.ca/pn-np/ab/waterton/
index_E.asp

British Columbia

Gulf Islands National Park
Reserve
2220 Harbour Road
Sidney, BC, Canada V8L 2P6
(250) 654-4000
www.pc.gc.ca/pn-np/bc/
gulf/index_E.asp

Gwaii Haanas National Park
Reserve and Haida Heritage
Site
P.O. Box 37
Queen Charlotte, BC, Canada
V0T 1S0
(250) 559-8818
www.pc.gc.ca/pn-np/bc/
gwaiihaanas/index_E.asp

Newfoundland

Gros Morne National Park
P.O. Box 130
Rocky Harbor, NL, Canada AOK
4NO
(709) 458-2417
www.pc.gc.ca/pn-np/nl/
grosmorne/index_E.asp

Nova Scotia

Ingonish Beach Highlands
National Park
Ingonish Beach, NS, Canada
BOC 1LO
(902) 224-2306

www.pc.gc.ca/pn-np/ns/
cbreton/index_E.asp

Ontario

Georgian Bay Islands National
Park
P.O. Box 9
Midland, ON, Canada L4R 4K6
(705) 526-9804
www.pc.gc.ca/pn-np/on/
georg/index_E.asp

St. Lawrence Islands National
Park
2 County Road 5, RR 3
Mallorytown, Ontario, Canada
KOE 1RO
(613) 923-5261
www.pc.gc.ca/pn-np/on/
lawren/index_E.asp

Prince Edward Island National
Park
2 Palmers Lane
Charlottetown, PE, Canada C1A
5V6
(902) 672-6350
www.pc.gc.ca/pn-np/pe/pei-ipe/
index_E.asp

Saskatchewan

Grasslands National Park
South Saskatchewan Field Unit
P.O. Box 150
Val Marie, SK, Canada SON 2TO
(306) 298-2257
www.pc.gc.ca/pn-np/sk/
grasslands/index_E.asp

Bibliography

The archaeological literature concerning ancient North America, like everything else pertaining to the archaeology of the continent, varies considerably by region. In addition, there are some temporal periods that have abundant published resources while others are almost completing lacking from the present literature. These biases in the literature have been shaped by a preference in previous archaeological research toward regions and temporal periods with evidence of large, complex human occupations. Simultaneously, there has been comparatively little research in regions and temporal periods characterized by smaller indigenous groups with relatively meager architectural and artifactual remains. In addition, as one recent archaeological study indicates, there is even a bias in the literature toward archaeological sites in close proximity to present-day population centers.

Another issue that should be considered in relation to the literature of ancient North America is that of regional publication trends. Within some regions, archaeologists tend to be more predisposed toward insular forms of publication, while researchers in other regions prefer major national and international journals that receive wider distribution. Such trends skew the citation of archaeological information toward regions where archaeologists are more predisposed to wider venues of publication, thus giving the impression that little of larger archaeological value is being derived from research in other less cited regions.

The presence of "gray" literature is also a problem with archaeological references. Many archaeological findings are self-published, with the results of these efforts restricted to technical publications that circulate only within state agencies and among a limited number of professional archaeologists. This has resulted in information from some of the most important archaeological sites in North America being unavailable to the public at large. When these publications are made available to the interested nonprofessional, they are often written in exceptionally dense language, present large amounts of unsummarized primary data, and are often lacking an interpretive synthesis. Such practices have effectively kept these materials from circulating outside the hands of a select group of professional archaeologists.

Recent trends in archaeological publication have favored the wider circulation of research reports and a diversification of research orientation to address specific regions and temporal periods for which our present knowledge is lacking. Additional efforts are also underway to facilitate the publication of archaeological research results to the public at large through traditional publication venues as well as through the use of the Internet and computer programs.

The best source for general information on Native American cultures and their cultural development is Brian Fagan's *Ancient North America*. This text is used in the vast majority of North American archaeology and culture history survey courses and provides an excellent summary of the principal archaeological sites and cultural developments for all areas of the continent. For more advanced readers, or those seeking more detailed information on individual culture areas or groups, the *Handbooks of North American Indians* are the best sources for this information. Although handbooks have not been completed to date for each culture area, those that are presently complete are presented in the bibliography, with each representing the state of art in ethnohistorical and archaeological research on their respective subjects.

Those desiring a more historical overview of North American history can find excellent summaries in Peter Nabokov's edited book, *Native American Testimony: A Chronicle of Indian-White Relations from Prophecy to the Present, 1492–1992*. A classic summary of Native American culture histories can also be found in Angie Debo's *A History of the American Indians*. Additional historical resources dealing with specific culture groups and temporal periods are enumerated in the bibliography. These resources are useful for researchers seeking more detailed information on specific areas of Native American history and cultural development.

Subsequent sections of the bibliography present region-specific resources containing primary data and summaries of each region. As previously stated, the *Handbooks of North American Indians* are the most accessible sources for information on individual Native American groups of each culture area. The *Handbooks* summarize a great deal of information for most general research purposes, but scholars interested in even more detailed, primary data are referred to materials in each regional section.

Bibliographic information is also provided on the most widely read professional journals dealing with North American archaeological and ethnohistorical issues. In addition, summaries of Native American archaeological and culture historical materials available on the World Wide Web are also provided. However, the reader should be cautioned that the rapid pace of change in Internet publication and the impermanence of many Internet links may mean that the URLs and page locations for these sources of information are subject to change after the publication of this volume.

This bibliography is not intended to be an exhaustive compilation of all reference materials related to the archaeology and ethnography of North America and its indigenous peoples. I have chosen instead to include information on references that provide a contemporary perspective on a variety of topics pertinent to ancient North America. The materials enumerated here, taken as a whole, offer the reader a comprehensive overview of Ancient North America while simultaneously supplying detailed information on individual archaeological sites, culture areas, and temporal periods.

CONTENTS

GENERAL WORKS

Champagne, Duane, ed. *The Native North American Almanac: A Reference Work on Native North Americans in the United States and Canada.* Detroit, Mich.: Gale, 1994.

Coe, Michael D., Dean Snow, and Elizabeth Benson. *Atlas of Ancient America.* New York: Facts on File, 1986.

Daniel, Glyn. *Towards a History of Archaeology.* New York: Thames & Hudson, 1981.

Deutch, Yvonne, ed. *Illustrated Encyclopedia of Mankind.* 21 vols. New York: Marshall Cavendish, 1984.

Fagan, Brian M. *Ancient North America: The Archaeology of a Continent.* 3rd ed. New York: Thames & Hudson, 2000.

———. *Kingdoms of Gold, Kingdoms of Jade: The Americas before Columbus.* New York: Thames & Hudson, 1991.

Hays, Terence E., ed. *Encyclopedia of World Cultures.* Boston: G. K. Hall, 1991.

Hirschfelder, Arlene, and Martha Kreipe Montaño. *The Native American Almanac: A Portrait of Native America Today.* New York: Prentice Hall, 1993.

Homberger, Eric. *The Penguin Historical Atlas of Ancient North America.* New York: Viking Press, 1995.

Hoxie, Frederick E., ed. *Encyclopedia of North American Indians.* Boston: Houghton Mifflin, 1996.

Ingold, Timothy, ed. *Companion Encyclopedia of Anthropology: Humanity, Culture, and Social Life.* London: Routledge, 1994.

Jacobson, Daniel. *Indians of North America.* New York: Franklin Watts, 1983.

Jennings, Jessie D. *Prehistory of North America.* Mountain View, Calif.: Mayfield Press, 1989.

———, ed. *Ancient North Americans.* San Francisco: W. H. Freeman, 1983.

Jones, Jayne Clark. *The American Indian in America.* Minneapolis, Minn.: Lerner, 1973.

Lamberg-Karlovsky, C. C. *Archaeological Thought in America.* Cambridge: Cambridge University Press, 1989.

Malinowski, Sharon, ed. *Encyclopedia of Native American Tribes.* Detroit, Mich.: Gale, 1998.

Palka, Joel. *Historical Dictionary of Ancient Mesoamerica.* Lanham, Md.: Scarecrow Press, 2000.

Silberberg, Robert. *The Mound Builders*. Athens: Ohio University Press, 1986.

Snow, Dean R. *The Archaeology of North America*. New York: Chelsea House, 1989.

Sturtevant, William T., ed. *Handbook of North American Indians*. 10 vols. Washington, D.C.: Smithsonian, 1978–current.

Swidler, Nina, Kurt Dongoske, Roger Anyon, and Alan Downer, eds. *Native Americans and Archaeologists*. Lanham, Md.: AltaMira, 1997.

Thomas, David Hurst. *Exploring Ancient Native America: An Archaeology Guide*. New York: Macmillan, 1994.

———. *The Native Americans: An Illustrated History*. Atlanta, Ga.: Turner, 1995.

Trigger, Bruce G. *A History of Archaeological Thought*. Cambridge: Cambridge University Press, 1989.

Trigger, Bruce G., and Wilcomb E. Washburn, eds. *Cambridge History of the Native Peoples of the Americas*. Parts 1 and 2. Cambridge: Cambridge University Press, 1996.

Willey, Gordon R. *An Introduction to American Archaeology, Volume 1: North and Middle America*. Princeton, N.J.: Prentice-Hall, 1966.

Willey, Gordon R., and Phillip Phillips. *Method and Theory in American Archaeology*. Chicago: University of Chicago Press, 1958.

Willey, Gordon R., and Jeremy A. Sabloff. *A History of American Archaeology*. 3rd ed. New York: W. H. Freeman, 1993.

Williams, Stephen. *Fantastic Archaeology: The Wild Side of North American Prehistory*. Philadelphia: University of Pennsylvania Press, 1991.

Bibliographies

Champagne, Duane, ed. *Chronology of Native North American History: From Pre-Columbian Times to the Present*. Detroit, Mich.: Gale, 1994.

Folsom, Franklin, and Mary Elting Folsom. *America's Ancient Treasures: A Guide to Archeological Sites and Museums in the United States and Canada*. 4th ed. Albuquerque: University of New Mexico Press, 1993.

Gibbon, Guy, ed. *Archaeology of Prehistoric Native America: An Encyclopedia*. Detroit, Mich.: Gale, 1998.

Marken, Jack. *The Indians and Eskimos of North America: A Bibliography of Books in Print through 1972*. Vermillion, S.D.: Dakota Press, 1973.

Murdock, George Peter, and Timothy J. O'Leary, eds. *Ethnographic Bibliography of North America*. 4th ed. 5 vols. New Haven, Conn.: Human Relations Area Files, 1975.

Snow, Dean R., ed. *Native American Prehistory: A Critical Bibliography*. Bloomington: Indiana University Press, 1980.

Ullom, Judith C. *A Comprehensive Bibliography for the Study of American Minorities, Vol. 2: Native Americans*, pp. 783–909. New York: New York University Press, 1976.

Wolfson, Evelyn. *From Abenaki to Zuni: A Dictionary of Native American Tribes*. New York: Walker Publishing, 1988.

Yenne, Bill. The *Encyclopedia of North American Indian Tribes: A Comprehensive Study of Tribes from Abitibi to the Zuñi*. Greenwich, Conn.: Bison Books, 1986.

HISTORY

Adovasio, James M., and R. C. Carlisle. "The Meadowcroft Rockshelter." *Science* 239 (1988): 713–714.

Adovasio, James M., and D. R. Pedler. "Monte Verde and the antiquity of humankind in the Americas." *Antiquity* 71 (1997): 573–580.

Ancient Society. Henry Holt, New York, 1977.

Anderson, David G. "The PaleoIndian Colonization of Eastern North America: A View from the Southeastern United States." In *Early PaleoIndian Economies of Eastern North America*, ed. Barry Isaac and Kenneth Tankersley, Greenwich, Conn.: JAI Press, 1990.

Bandelier, Fanny. *The Journey of Alvar Nuñez Cabeza de Vaca and His Companions from Florida to the Pacific 1528–1538*. New York: Allerton Books, 1872.

Bannon, John Francis, *The Spanish Borderlands Frontier 1513–1821*. Albuquerque: University of New Mexico Press, 1974.

Bass, George. *Ships and Shipwrecks of the Americas*. New York: Thames & Hudson, 1988.

Bonnichsen, R., and D. G. Steele, eds. *Method and Theory for Investigating the Peopling of the Americas*. Corvallis: Oregon State University, 1994.

Bonnichsen, R., and K. L. Turnmire, eds. *Clovis: Origins and Adaptations*. Corvallis: Oregon State University, 1991.

———. *Ice Age People of North America: Environments, Origins, and Adaptations*. Corvallis: Oregon State University. 1999.

Braund, Kathryn E. Holland. *Deerskins and Duffels: The Creek Indian Trade with Anglo-America, 1685–1815*. Lincoln: University of Nebraska Press, 1993.

Clayton, Lawrence A., Vernon James Knight, Jr., and Edward C. Moore, eds. *The De Soto Chronicles: The Expedition of Hernando De Soto to North America in 1539–43*. 2 vols. Tuscaloosa: University of Alabama Press, 1993.

Debo, Angie. *A History of the American Indians*. Norman: University of Oklahoma Press, 1983.

Deetz, James. *In Small Things Forgotten: The Archeology of Early American Life*. New York: Doubleday, 1977.

Deloria, Vine, Jr. *Custer Died for Your Sins: An Indian Manifesto*. Norman: University of Oklahoma Press, 1988.

Dillehay, Tom. *First Settlement of the Americas*. New York: Basic Books, 2000.

Dillehay, Tom, and David Meltzer, eds. *The First Americans: Search and Research*. Boca Raton, Fla.: CRC Press, 1991.

Dincauze, Dina F. "An Archaeological Evaluation of the Case for Pre-Clovis Occupations." *Advances in World Archaeology* 3 (1984): 275–323.

Dixson, E. James. *Quest for the Origins of the First Americans*. Albuquerque: University of New Mexico Press, 1993.

Dowd, Gregory E. *A Spirited Resistance: The North American Indian Struggle for Unity, 1745–1815*. Baltimore, Md.: John Hopkins University Press, 1992.

Fagan, Brian M. *The Great Journey: The Peopling of Ancient America*. New York: Thames & Hudson, 1987.

Ferguson, Leland. *Uncommon Ground: Archaeology and Early African America, 1650–1800*. Washington, D.C.: Smithsonian Institution Press, 1992.

Fiedel, Stuart J. *Prehistory of the Americas*. Cambridge: Cambridge University Press, 1987.

———. "Older than We Thought: Implications of Corrected Dates for Paleoindians." *American Antiquity* 64 (1999): 95–115.

Ford, James A. *A Comparison of Formative Cultures in the Americas: Diffusion of the Psychic Unity of Man*. Washington, D.C.: Smithsonian Institute Press, 1969.

Francis, Lee. *Native Time: A Historical Time Line of Native America*. New York: St. Martin's Press, 1996.

Frison, George. *Prehistoric Hunters of the High Plains*. 2nd ed. New York: Academic Press, 1991.

Frison, George, and Dennis J. Stanford. *The Agate Basin Site: A Record of the Paleoindian Occupation of the Northwestern High Plains*. New York: Academic Press, 1982

Gore, Rick. "The Most Ancient American." *National Geographic* 192 (October 1997): 92–99.

Graham, Russell W. "Kimmswick: A Clovis-Mastodon Association in Eastern Missouri." *Science* 312 (1981): 1115–1117.

Grumet, Robert S. *Historic Contact: Indian People and Colonists in Today's Northeastern United States in the Sixteenth through Eighteenth Centuries*. Norman: University of Oklahoma Press, 1995.

Heath, Barbara. *Hidden Lives: The Archaeology of Slave Life at Thomas Jefferson's Poplar Forest*. Charlottesville: University Press of Virginia, 1999.

Hopkins, David M., John V. Matthews, Jr., Charles Schwegger, and Steven B. Young. *Paleoecology of Beringia*. New York: Academic Press, 1982.

Horowitz, David. *The First Frontier: The Indian Wars and America's Origins, 1607–1776*. New York: Simon and Schuster, 1978.

Hudson, Charles. *The Juan Pardo Expeditions: Explorations of the Carolinas and Tennessee, 1566–1568.* Washington, D.C.: Smithsonian Institution Press, 1990.

——. *Knights of Spain, Warriors of the Sun: Hernando de Soto and the South's Ancient Chiefdoms.* Athens: University of Georgia Press, 1997.

Hudson, Charles, and Carmer Chaves Tesser, eds. *The Forgotten Centuries: Indians and Europeans in the American South, 1521–1704.* Athens: University of Georgia Press, 1994.

Hulton, Paul, and David B. Quin. *The American Drawings of John White, 1577–1590.* Chapel Hill: University of North Carolina Press, 1964.

Isaac, Barry, and Kenneth Tankersley, eds. *Early PaleoIndian Economies of Eastern North America.* Greenwich, Conn.: JAI Press, 1990.

Jelks, Edward B. *Historical Dictionary of North American Archeology.* Westport, Conn.: Greenwood Press, 1988.

Jennings, Francis. *The Invasion of America: Indians, Colonialism, and the Cant of Conquest.* Chapel Hill: University of North Carolina Press, 1975.

Justice, Noel D. *Stone Age Spear and Arrow Points of the Midcontinental and Eastern United States.* Bloomington: Indiana University Press, 1988.

Kelly, R. L., and L. Todd. "Coming into the Country: Early Paleoindian Hunting and Mobility." *American Antiquity* 53 (1988): 231–244.

Leone, Mark P., and Parker B. Potter, Jr., eds. *The Recovery of Meaning: Historical Archeology in the Eastern United States.* Washington, D.C.: Smithsonian Institution Press, 1994.

Leone, Mark P., and Neil Silberman. *Invisible America: Unearthing Our Hidden History.* New York: Henry Holt, 1996.

Markowitz, Harvey, ed. *American Indians.* Englewood Cliffs, N.J.: Salem Press, 1995.

Marriott, Alice, and Carol K. Rachlin. *American Epic: The Story of the American Indian.* New York: G. P. Putnam's Sons, 1969.

Martin, P. S., and R. G. Klein, eds. *Quaternary Extinctions: A Prehistoric Revolution.* Tucson: University of Arizona Press. 1984.

McNeish, Richard S. *Early Man in America: Readings from the Scientific American.* New York: W. H. Freeman, 1973.

Mead, Jim I., and David J. Melzer, eds. *Environments and Extinctions: Man in Late Glacial North America.* Orono: University of Maine at Orono, 1985.

Meltzer, David J. "The Antiquity of Man and the Development of American Archaeology." *Advances in Archaeological Method and Theory* 6 (1983): 1–51.

——. "Clocking the First Americans." *Annual Review of Anthropology* 24 (1995): 21–45.

——. *Search for the First Americans.* Washington, D.C.: Smithsonian Institution Press, 1996.

Milanich, Gerald T. *Laboring in the Fields of the Lord: Spanish Missions and Southeastern Indians*. Washington, D.C.: Smithsonian Institution Press, 1999.

Milanich, Gerald T., and Susan Milbrath. *First Encounters, Spanish Explorations in the Caribbean and the United States, 1492–1570*. Gainesville: University of Florida Press, 1989.

Morgan, L. H. *Systems of Consanguinity and Affinity of the Human Family*. Washington, D.C.: Smithsonian Institution, 1878.

Mullins, Paul. *Race and Affluence: An Archaeology of African America and Consumer Culture*. New York: Kluwer, 1999.

Nabokov, Peter, ed. *Native American Testimony: A Chronicle of Indian-White Relations from Prophecy to the Present, 1492–1992*. New York: Viking, 1991.

Noël-Hume, Ivor. *Historical Archaeology*. New York: Alfred A. Knopf, 1975.

——. *A Guide to Artifacts of Colonial America*. New York: Vintage Books, 1991.

——. *Martin's Hundred*. New York: Alfred A. Knopf, 1982.

Orser, Charles E., and Brian M. Fagan. *Historical Archaeology*. New York: Harper Collins, 1995.

Parkman, Francis. *The Jesuits in North America in the Seventeenth Century*. Boston: Little and Brown, 1927.

Rouse, Irving. *The Tainos: Rise and Decline of the People Who Greeted Columbus*. New Haven, Conn.: Yale University Press, 1992.

Russell, Howard S. *Indian New England before the Mayflower*. Hanover, N.H.: University Press of New England, 1980.

Schoolcraft, Henry R. *Information Respecting the History, Condition and Prospects of the Indian Tribes of the United States*. Philadelphia: J. B. Lippencott, 1860.

Schuyler, Robert L., ed. *Historical Archaeology: A Guide to Substantive and Theoretical Contributions*. Amityville, N.Y.: Baywood, 1978.

Singleton, Theresa, ed. *I, Too, Am America: Archaeological Studies of African-American Life*. Charlottesville: University Press of Virginia, 1999.

Squier, E. G. and E. H. Davis. *Ancient Monuments of the Mississippi Valley Comprising the Results of Extensive Original Surveys and Explorations*. New York: AMS Press.

Stanford, D., and J. Day, eds. *Ice-Age Hunters of the Rockies*. Boulder: University Press of Colorado, 1991.

Struever, Stuart, and Felecia Holton. *Koster: Americans in Search of Their Prehistoric Past*. New York: Anchor Press, 1979.

Swanton, John R. *Indians of the Southeastern United States*. Washington, D.C.: Smithsonian Institution, Bureau of American Ethnology Bulletin no. 137, 1946.

Tanner, Helen H., ed. *Atlas of Great Lakes Indian History*. Norman: University of Oklahoma Press, 1990.

Taylor, W. *A Study of Archaeology*, Southern. Washington, D.C.: American Anthropological Association, [1948] 1983.

Thomas, David Hurst. *St. Catherine's: An Island in Time*. Atlanta: Georgia Endowment for the Humanities, 1988.

Thornton, Russell. *American Indian Holocaust and Survival: A Population History since 1492*. Norman: University of Oklahoma Press, 1990.

Thwaites, Rueben G., ed. *The Jesuit Relations and Allied Documents: Travels and Explorations of the Jesuit Missionaries in New France: 1610–1791*. Cleveland, Ohio: Burrows Brothers, 1940.

Villagrá, Gaspar Perez de. *Historia de la Nueva México*. Albuquerque: University of New Mexico, [1610] 1992.

Washburn, Wilcomb E., ed. *Handbook of North American Indians, Vol. 4: History of Indian-White Relations*. Washington, D.C.: Smithsonian Institution, 1988.

Wesson, Cameron B., and Mark A. Rees, eds. *Between Contacts and Colonies: Archaeological Perspectives on the Protohistoric Southeast*. Tuscaloosa: University of Alabama Press, 2002.

West, Frederick H., ed. *American Beginnings*. Chicago: University of Chicago Press, 1996.

———. *The Archeology of Beringia*. New York: Columbia University Press, 1981.

Willey, Gordon R. *Archaeology of the Florida Gulf Coast*. Washington, D.C.: Smithsonian Institution, 1949.

Williams, Walter L., ed. *Southeastern Indians since the Removal Era*. Athens: University of Georgia Press, 1979.

Yentsch, Anne E. *A Chesapeake Family and Their Slaves: A Study in Historical Archaeology*. Cambridge: Cambridge University Press, 1994.

REGIONAL ARCHAEOLOGIES

Arctic and Subarctic

Balikci, Asen. *The Netsilik Eskimo*. Prospect Heights, Ill.: Waveland, 1989.

Bandi, Hans G. *Eskimo Prehistory*. Fairbanks: University of Alaska Press, 1969.

Berg, G., ed. *Circumpolar Problems; Habitat, Economy, and Social Relations in the Arctic*. Oxford: Pergamon Press, 1973.

Binford, Lewis R. *Nunamiut Ethno-Archaeology*. New York: Academic Press, 1978

Birket-Smith, Kaj. *The Eskimos*. London: Methuen, 1936.

Boas, Franz. *The Central Eskimo*. Sixth Annual Report of the Bureau of American Ethnology. Washington, D.C.: Smithsonian Institution, 1914–1915.

Burch, Ernest S., and Werner Forman. *The Eskimos*. Norman: University of Oklahoma Press, 1988.

Chaussonnet, Valérie, ed. *Crossroads Alaska: Native Cultures of Alaska and Siberia*. Washington, D.C.: Arctic Studies Center, National Museum of Natural History, Smithsonian Institution, 1994.

Collins, Henry B. *Outline of Eskimo Prehistory*. Smithsonian Institution Miscellaneous Collections, vol. 100, Washington, D.C.: Smithsonian Institution, 1940.

Collins, Henry R., Frederica De Laguna, Edmund Carpenter, and Peter Stone. *The Far North: 2000 Years of American Eskimo and Indian Art*. Washington, D.C.: National Gallery of Art, 1973.

Crowe, Keith. *A History of the Original Peoples of Northern Canada*. Montreal: McGill University Press, 1974.

Damas, David, ed. *Handbook of North American Indians, Vol. 5: The Arctic*. Washington, D.C.: Smithsonian Institution Press, 1984.

Dekin, Albert A., Jr. *Arctic Archaeology: A Bibliography and History*. Vol. 1. New York: Garland, 1978.

De Laguna, Frederica. *Chugach Prehistory: The Archaeology of Prince William Sound, Alaska*. Seattle: University of Washington Press, 1956.

Dumond, Don E. "Alaska and the Northwest Coast." In *Ancient North Americas*, ed. Jesse D. Jennings. New York: W. H. Freeman, 1983.

———. *The Eskimos and Aleuts*. New York: Thames & Hudson, 1987.

Fitzhugh, William W., ed. *Prehistoric Maritime Adaptations of the Circumpolar Zone*. Paris: Mouton, 1975.

Fitzhugh, William W., and Valérie Chaussonnet, eds. *Anthropology of the North Pacific Rim*. Washington, D.C.: Smithsonian Institution Press, 1994.

Fitzhugh, William W., and Aaron Crowell. *Crossroads of Continents: Cultures of Siberia and Alaska*. Washington, D.C.: Smithsonian Institution Press, 1988.

Fitzhugh, William W., and Jacqueline S. Olin, eds. *Archaeology of the Frobisher Voyages*. Washington, D.C.: Smithsonian Institution Press, 1993.

French, Alice. *The Restless Nomad*. Winnipeg, Manitoba: Pemmican, 1991.

Gad, Finn. *The History of Greenland*. Toronto: University of Toronto Press, 1971.

Giddings, J. Louis. *The Archaeology of Cape Denbigh*. Providence, R.I.: Brown University Press, 1964.

———. *Ancient Men of the Arctic*. New York: Alfred A. Knopf, 1967.

Gubser, N. J. *The Nunamuit: Eskimo Hunters of Caribou*. New Haven, Conn.: Yale University Press, 1965.

Hansen, Jens Peder Hart, Jorgen Meldgaard, and Jorgen Nordqvist, eds. *The Greenland Mummies*. Washington, D.C.: Smithsonian Institution Press, 1991.

Harp, Elmer, Jr. "Pioneer Cultures of the Subarctic and the Arctic." In *Ancient North Americans*, ed. Jesse D. Jennings. New York: W. H. Freeman, 1978.

Helm, June. *The Indians of the Subarctic: A Critical Bibliography*. Indianapolis: Indiana University Press, 1976.

———. ed. *Handbook of North American Indians, Vol. 6: Subarctic*. Washington, D.C.: Smithsonian Institution, 1981.

Hippler, Arthur E. and John R. Wood. *The Sub-Arctic Athabaskans, A Selected Annotated Bibliography*. Anchorage: University of Alaska Institute of Social and Economic Research, 1974.

Howley, James P. *The Beothuks or Red Indians: The Aboriginal Inhabitants of Newfoundland*. Cambridge: Cambridge University Press, 1974.

Innis, Harold. *The Fur Trade in Canada: An Introduction to Canadian Economic History*. Ann Arbor, Mich.: Books on Demand, 1962.

Jenness, Diamond. *The Indians of Canada*. Toronto: University of Toronto Press, 1934.

Krupnik, Igor. *Arctic Adaptations: Native Whalers and Reindeer Hunters*. Hanover, N.H.: University Press, 1994.

Lantis, Margaret, ed. *Ethnohistory in Southwestern Alaska and the Southern Yukon*. Lexington: University of Kentucky Press, 1970.

Lots, R. James. *Yukon Bibliography*. Ottawa: Department of Northern Affairs and National Resources, 1964.

Marshall, Ingeborg. *A History and Ethnography of the Beothuk*. Montreal: McGill-Queen's University Press, 1996.

Maxwell, Moreau S. *Prehistory of the Eastern Arctic*. Orlando, Fla.: Academic Press, 1985.

———. ed. *Eastern Arctic Prehistory: Paleo-Eskimo Problems*. Memoirs of the Society for American Archaeology, no. 31. Washington, D.C.: Society for American Archaeology, 1976.

McCartney, Allen P., ed. *Thule Eskimo Culture: An Archaeological Retrospective*. Ottawa: National Museum of Man, 1978.

McGee, H. F. *The Native Peoples of Atlantic Canada: A History of Indian-European Relations*. Ottawa: Carleton University Press, 1983.

McGhee, Robert. *Copper Eskimo Prehistory*. Ottawa: National Museum of Man, 1972.

———. *Beluga Hunters: An Archeology Reconstruction of the History and Culture of the Mackenzie Delta Kittegaryumiut*. St. John's: Institute of Social and Economic Research, Memorial University of Newfoundland, 1974.

———. *Canadian Arctic Prehistory*. Ottawa: Museum of Man. 1978.

———. *Canada Rediscovered*. Hull, Quebec: Canadian Museum of Civilization, 1991.

———. *Ancient Canada*. Chicago: University of Chicago Press, 1992.

Morrison, David, and Georges-Herbert Germain. *Inuit: Glimpses of an Arctic Past*. Hull, Quebec: Canadian Museum of Civilization, 1995.

Nelson, Richard D. *Hunters of the Northern Ice*. Chicago: University of Chicago Press, 1969.

Oswalt, Wendell. *Bashful No Longer: An Alaskan Eskimo Ethnohistory*. Norman: University of Oklahoma Press, 1990.

Pastore, Ralph T. *Shanawdithit's People: The Archaeology of the Beothuks*. St. John's, Newfoundland: Breakwater Books, 1992.

Purie, Richard A., ed. *Ethnohistory in the Arctic: The Bering Strait Eskimo*. Fairbanks: Limestone Press, University of Alaska, 1983.

Rowe, Frederick W. *Extinction: The Beothuks of Newfoundland*. Toronto: McGraw-Hill, 1977.

Taylor, J. Garth. *Labrador Eskimo Settlements of the Early Contact Period*. Ottawa: National Museum of Man, 1974.

Taylor, William E. *The Arnapik and Tara Sites: An Archaeological Study of Dorset Culture Origins*. Memoirs of the Society for American Archaeology, no. 22. Washington, DC: Society for American Archaeology, 1968.

Tuck, James A. *Newfoundland and Labrador Prehistory*. Ottawa: National Museum of Man, 1976.

Valentine, V. F., and F. G. Valee, eds. *Eskimo of the Canadian Arctic*. Princeton, N.J.: Van Nostrand, 1968.

Van Stone, James W. *Athabaskan Adaptations: Hunters and Fishermen of the Subarctic Forests*. Chicago: Aldine, 1974.

West, C. Eugene, and Richard Stern. *Bibliography and Index of Alaskan Archaeology*. Vol. 3. Anchorage: Alaska Anthropological Association Monograph Series, Aurora, 1987.

West, Fred H. *The Archeology of Beringia*. New York: Columbia University Press, 1981.

Workman, Karen Wood. *Alaskan Archeology: A Bibliography*. Anchorage: Alaska Division of Parks, 1972.

Wright, James. *The Shield Archaic*. Ottawa: National Museum of Man, 1972.

———. *A History of the Native People of Canada: Vol. 1, 10,000–1,000 B.C.* Ottawa: Canadian Museum of Civilization, 1995.

Younkin, Paula. *Indians of the Arctic and Subarctic*. New York: Facts on File, 1991.

California

Bean, Lowell Jordan, and Lisa J. Bourgealt. *The Cahuilla*. New York: Chelsea House, 1989.

Bee, Robert L. *The Yuma*. New York: Chelsea House, 1989.

Bell, Maureen. *Karuk: The Upriver People*. Happy Camp, Calif.: Naturegraph, 1991.

Brusa, Betty War, and Eugenia Bonnot. *Salinan Indians of California.* Heraldsburg, Calif.: Naturegraph, 1975.

Burrill, Richard. *Rivers of Sorrows: Life History of the Maidu-Nisenan Indians.* Happy Camp, Calif.: Naturegraph Publishers, 1988.

Chartkoff, Joseph L., and Kerry Chartkoff. *The Archaeology of California.* Stanford, Calif.: Stanford University Press, 1984.

Downs, James E. *The Two Worlds of the Washo: An Indian Tribe of California and Nevada.* New York: Holt, Rinehart and Winston, 1966.

Emanuels, George. *California Indians: An Illustrated Guide.* Walnut Creek, Calif.: Diablo Books, 1991.

Erlandson, Jon M. *Early Hunter-Gatherers of the California Coast.* New York: Plenum, 1994.

Faulk, Odie B., and Laura E. Faulk *The Modoc.* New York: Chelsea House, 1989.

Gibson, Robert O. *The Chumash.* New York: Chelsea House, 1991.

Heizer, Robert. F. *The Destruction of California Indians: A Collection of Documents from 1847–1865 Describing Some Things That Happened.* Lincoln: University of Nebraska Press, 1993.

———. ed. *Handbook of North American Indians, Vol. 8: California.* Washington, D.C.: Smithsonian Institution, 1978.

Heizer, Robert F., and M. A. Wipple. *The California Indians: A Source Book.* Berkeley: University of California Press, 1971.

Hudson, Travis, and Thomas Blackburn. *The Material Culture of the Chumash Interaction Sphere.* Socorro, Calif.: Ballena Press, 1983.

Hurtado, Albert L. *Indian Survival on the California Frontier.* New Haven, Conn.: Yale University Press, 1988.

King, Chester. *Evolution of the Chumash.* New York: Garland, 1990.

Knudtson, Peter M. *The Wintu Indians of California and Their Neighbors.* Happy Camp, Calif.: Naturegraph Publishers, 1977.

Kroeber, Theodora. *Ishi, Last of His Tribe.* New York: Bantam, 1973.

Lowell, John Bean, and Thomas C. Blackburn, eds. *Native Californians: A Theoretical Retrospective.* Menlo Park, Calif.: Ballena Press, 1976.

Margolin, Malcolm. *Living in a Well-Ordered World: Indian People of Northwestern California.* Berkeley, Calif.: Heyday Books, 1994.

Miller, Virginia. *UKOMNO'M: The Yuki Indians of Northern California.* Socorro, N.M.: Baloney Press, 1979.

Moratto, Michael J. *California Archaeology.* New York: Academic Press, 1984.

Potts, Marie. *The Northern Maidu.* Happy Camp, Calif.: Naturegraph, 1977.

Powers, Stephen. *Tribes of California.* Berkeley: University of California Press, 1976.

Renfro, Elizabeth. *The Shasta Indians of California and Their Neighbors.* Happy Camp, Calif.: Naturegraph, 1992.

Simpson, Richard. *Ooti: A Maidu Legacy.* Millbrae, Calif.: Celestial Arts, 1977.
Van Tiburg, Jo Anne. *Ancient Images on Stone: Rock Art of the Californians.* Los Angeles: Institute of Archaeology, University of California at Los Angeles, 1983.
Wise, Winifred E. *The California Conquest.* New York: Charles Scribner's Sons, 1967.

Great Basin and Plateau

Ashwell, Reg. *Indian Tribes of the Northwest.* Vancouver, B.C.: Hancock House, 1989.
Brown, Mark H. *The Flight of the Nez Perce.* New York: G. P. Putnam, 1967.
Buan, Carolyn M., and Richard Lewis, eds. *The First Oregonians: An Illustrated Collection of Essays on Traditional Lifeways, Federal-Indian Relations, and the State's Native People Today.* Portland: Oregon Council for the Humanities, 1991.
Clark, Ella C. *Indian Legends from the Northern Rockies.* Norman: University of Oklahoma Press, 1966.
Corless, Hank. *The Weiser Indians: Shoshoni Peacemakers.* Salt Lake City: University of Utah Press, 1990.
D'Azevado, W., ed. *Handbook of American Indians, Vol. 11: The Great Basin.* Washington, D.C.: Smithsonian Institution Press, 1986.
Faulk, Odie B., and Laura E. Faulk. *The Modoc.* New York: Chelsea House, 1988.
Forbes, Jack D. *Native Americans of California and Nevada.* Happy Camp, Calif.: Naturegraph Publishers, 1969.
Franklin, Robert J., and Pamela A. Bunte. *The Paiute.* New York: Chelsea House, 1990.
Grayson, Donald K. *A Natural History of the Great Basin.* Washington, D.C.: Smithsonian Institution Press, 1993.
Lesley, Craig. *River Song.* Boston: Houghton Mifflin, 1989.
Madsen, David, and James O'Connell. *Man and Environment in the Great Basin.* Washington, D.C.: Society for American Archaeology, 1986.
Schuster, Helen. *The Yakima.* New York: Chelsea House, 1990.
Sherrow, Victoria. *Indians of the Plateau and Great Basin.* New York: Facts on File, 1992.
Stowell, Cynthia D. *Faces of a Reservation: A Portrait of the Warm Springs Indian Reservation.* West Salem: Oregon Historical Society Press, 1987.
Swanton, John R. *Indian Tribes of Washington, Oregon, and Idaho.* Fairfield, Wash.: Ye Galleon Press, 1968.
Thomas, David Hurst. *The Archaeology of Monitor Valley, Vol. 1: Epistemology.* New York: American Museum of Natural History, Anthropological Papers 58, 1983.

————. *The Archaeology of Hidden Cave, Nevada*. New York: American Museum of Natural History, Anthropological Papers 61, 1985.

Great Plains

Bamforth, Douglas. *Ecology and Human Organization on the Great Plains*. New York: Plenum, 1988.

Bement, Leland C. *Bison Hunting at Cooper Site: Where Lightning Bolts Drew Thundering Herds*. Norman: University of Oklahoma Press, 1999.

Blaine, Martha R. *The Ioway Indians*. Norman: University of Oklahoma Press, 1978.

Bleeker, Sonia. *The Sioux Indians: Hunters and Warriors of the Plains*. New York: William Morrow, 1962.

Brown, Dee. *Bury My Heart at Wounded Knee: An Indian History of the American West*. New York: Holt, 1991.

Ewers, John C. *The Blackfeet: Raiders of the Northwestern Plains*. Norman: University of Oklahoma Press, 1958.

Fowler, Loretta. *The Arapaho*. New York: Chelsea House, 1989.

Frison, George. *Prehistoric Hunters of the High Plains*. 2nd ed. New York: Academic Press, 1992.

Gibson, Arrell M. *The Kickapoo: Lords of the Middle Border*. Norman: University of Oklahoma Press, 1963.

Grinnell, George Bird. *The Fighting Cheyenne*. Norman: University of Oklahoma Press, 1915.

————. *The Cheyenne Indians: History and Society*. Lincoln: University of Nebraska Press, 1923.

Hickenson, Nancy Parrott. *The Jumanos: Hunters and Traders of the South Plains*. Austin: University of Texas Press, 1994.

Hoebel, E. Adamson. *The Cheyennes: Indians of the Great Plains*. Chicago: Holt, Rinehart and Winston, 1978.

Hoig, Stan. *The Cheyenne*. New York: Chelsea House, 1989.

Holder, Preston. *The Hoe and the Horse on the Plains*. Lincoln: University of Nebraska Press, 1970.

Hook, Jason. *The American Plains Indians*. London: Osprey, 1991.

Hoover, Herbert T. *The Yankton Sioux*. New York: Chelsea House, 1988.

Hoxie, Frederick E. *The Crow*. New York: Chelsea House, 1989.

Hyde, George E. *The Pawnee Indians*. Norman: University of Oklahoma Press, 1974.

Hyde, George. *Red Cloud's Folk: A History of the Oglala Sioux Indians*. Norman: University of Oklahoma, 1984.

Kroeber, Alfred L. *The Arapaho*. Lincoln: University of Nebraska Press, 1983.

Mathews, John Joseph. *Wah'kon-tah: The Osage and the White Man's Road*. Norman: University of Oklahoma Press, 1932.

———. *The Osages: Children of the Middle Waters*. Norman: University of Oklahoma Press, 1961.

Meyer, Roy. W. *The Village Indians of the Upper Missouri: The Mandans, Hidatsas, and Arikaras*. Lincoln: University of Nebraska Press, 1977.

Moore, John H. *The Cheyenne*. Cambridge, Mass.: Blackwell Publishers, 1996.

Rollings, Willard H. *The Comanche*. New York: Chelsea House, 1989.

———. *The Osage: An Ethnohistorical Study of Hegemony on the Prairie-Plains*. Columbia: University of Missouri Press, 1992.

Schneider, Mary Jane. *The Hidatsa*. New York: Chelsea House, 1989.

Speth, John. *Bison Kills and Bone Counts*. Chicago: University of Chicago Press, 1983.

Spindler, Will H. *Tragedy Strikes at Wounded Knee and Other Essays on Indian Life in South Dakota and Nebraska*. Vermillion: University of South Dakota Press, 1972.

Trenholm, Virginia Cole. *The Arapahoes, Our People*. Norman: University of Oklahoma Press, 1970.

Trenholm, Virginia Cole, and Maurine Carley. *The Shoshonis: Sentinels of the Plains*. Norman: University of Oklahoma Press, 1964.

Walker, James R. *Lakota Society*. Lincoln: University of Nebraska Press, 1988.

Wedel, Walter. *Prehistoric Man on the Great Plains*. Norman: University of Oklahoma Press, 1961.

———. "The Prehistoric Plains." In *Ancient North Americans*, ed. Jesse D. Jennings. New York: W. H. Freeman, 1983.

———. *Central Plains Prehistory: Holocene Environments and Culture Change in the Republican River Basin*. Lincoln: University of Nebraska Press, 1986.

Wheat, Joe Ben. *The Olsen-Chubbock Site: A Paleo-Indian Kill*. Memoirs of the Society for American Archaeology, no. 26, 1972.

Wilson, Terry P. *The Osage*. New York: Chelsea House, 1988.

Wood, W. Raymond, ed. *Archaeology of the Great Plains*. Lawrence: University Press of Kansas, 1998.

Wood, W. Raymond, and Margot Liberty, eds. *Anthropology on the Great Plains*. Lincoln: University of Nebraska Press, 1980.

Wunder, John R. *The Kiowa*. New York: Chelsea House, 1989.

Northeast

Anson, Bert. *The Miami Indians*. Norman: University of Oklahoma Press, 1970.

Bailey, Alfred E. *The Conflict of European and Eastern Algonkian Cultures, 1504–1700*. Toronto: University of Toronto Press, 1969.

Baird, W. David. *The Quapaw Indians: A History of the Downstream People.* Norman: University of Oklahoma Press, 1980.

Bonvillain, Nancy. *The Huron.* New York: Chelsea House, 1989.

Braun, Esther K., and David P. Braun. *The First Peoples of the Northeast.* Lincoln, Mass.: Lincoln Historical Society, 1994.

Calloway, Colin G. *The Abenaki.* New York: Chelsea House, 1989.

———. *The Western Abenakis of Vermont 1600–1800: War, Migration and the Survival of an Indian People.* Norman: University of Oklahoma Press, 1990.

———. *Indians of the Northeast.* New York: Facts on File, 1991.

Campisi, Jack. *The Mashpee Indians: Tribe on Trial.* Syracuse, N.Y.: Syracuse University Press, 1991.

Chadwick, Edward Marion. *The People of the Longhouse.* Toronto: Church of England Publishing, 1897.

Clifton, James A. *People of the Three Fires: The Ottawa, Potawatomi, and Ojibway of Michigan.* Grand Rapids: Michigan Indian Press, 1986.

———. *The Potawatomi.* New York: Chelsea House, 1989.

Danziger, Edward J. *The Chippewas of Lake Superior.* Norman: University of Oklahoma Press, 1990.

DeForest, John W. *History of the Indians of Connecticut from the Earliest Known Period to 1850.* Hartford, Conn.: Hamersley, 1852.

Doherty, Craig, and Katherine M. Doherty. *The Iroquois.* New York: Franklin Watts, 1991.

Doherty, Katherine M., and Craig A. Doherty. *The Wampanoag.* New York: Franklin Watts. 1995.

Dunn, Shirly W. *The Mohicans and Their Land, 1609–1730.* Fleischmanns, N.Y.: Purple Mountain Press, 1994.

Edmunds, R. David. *The Potawatomis: Keepers of the Fire.* Norman: University of Oklahoma Press, 1978.

Funk, Robert E. "The Northeastern United States." In *Ancient North Americans*, ed. Jesse D. Jennings. New York: W. W. Norton, 1983.

Graymont, Barbara. *The Iroquois.* New York: Chelsea House, 1988.

Grumet, Robert S. *The Lenapes.* New York: Chelsea House, 1989.

Hagen, William T. *The Sac and Fox Indians.* Norman: University of Oklahoma Press, 1958.

Hauptman, Laurence, and James Wherry. *The Pequots in Southern New England: The Fall and Rise of an American Indian Nation.* Norman: University of Oklahoma Press, 1990.

Jennings, Francis, ed. *The History and Culture of Iroquois Diplomacy: An Interdisciplinary Guide to the Treaties of the Six Nations and Their League.* Syracuse, N.Y.: Syracuse University Press, 1985.

Keesing, Felix M. *The Menomini Indians of Wisconsin: A Study of Three Centuries of Cultural Contact and Change.* Madison: University of Wisconsin Press, 1987.

Kinietz, William. *The Indians of the Western Great Lakes, 1615–1760.* Ann Arbor: University of Michigan Press, 1965.

Mason, Ronald J. *Great Lakes Archaeology.* New York: Academic Press, 1981.

Morgan, Lewis Henry. *League of the Ho-Dé-No-Sau-Nee, Iroquois.* Rochester, N.Y.: Sage & Brother, 1851.

Neusius, Sarah W., ed. *Foraging, Collecting, and Harvesting: Archaic Period Subsistence and Settlement in the Eastern Woodlands.* Carbondale, Ill.: Center for Archaeological Investigations, 1986.

Ourada, Patricia K. *The Menominee Indians: A History.* Norman: University of Oklahoma Press, 1979.

———. *The Menominee.* New York: Chelsea House, 1989.

Parker, Arthur C. *The History of the Seneca Indians.* New York: Ira J. Friedman, 1967.

Porter, Frank W. III. *Indians in Maryland and Delaware: A Critical Bibliography.* Bloomington: Indiana University Press, 1979.

———. *Maryland Indians: Yesterday and Today.* Baltimore: Maryland Historical Society, 1983.

Potter, Stephen R. *Commoners, Tribute, and Chiefs: The Development of Algonquian Culture in the Potomac Valley.* Charlottesville: University Press of Virginia, 1993.

Radin, Paul. *The Winnebago Tribe.* Lincoln: University of Nebraska Press, 1990.

Rafert, Stewart. *The Miami Indians of Indiana: A Persistent People 1654–1994.* Indianapolis: Indiana Historical Society, 1996.

Simmons, William S. *The Narragansett.* New York: Chelsea House, 1989.

Snow, Dean. *The Archaeology of New England.* New York: Academic Press, 1980.

———. *The Iroquois.* Cambridge, Mass.: Blackwell, 1996.

Tanner, Helen H. *The Ojibwa.* New York: Chelsea House, 1992.

Tooker, Elisabeth. *An Ethnography of the Huron Indians 1615–1649.* Syracuse, N.Y.: Syracuse University Press, 1992.

Trigger, Bruce. *The Children of Aataensic: A History of the Huron People to 1660.* Montreal: McGill-Queen's University Press, 1972.

———. *Natives and Newcomers.* Montreal: McGill-Queen's University Press, 1985.

———, ed. *Handbook of North American Indians, Vol. 15: Northeast.* Washington, D.C.: Smithsonian Institution, 1978.

Tuck, James A. *Onondaga Iroquois Prehistory.* Syracuse, N.Y.: Syracuse University Press, 1971.

———. *Newfoundland and Labrador Prehistory*. Ottawa: National Museums of Canada, 1976.

———. *Maritime Provinces Prehistory*. Ottawa: National Museums of Canada, 1984.

Wallace, Anthony F. C. *The Death and Rebirth of the Seneca*. New York: Vintage Books, 1972.

Warren, William Whipple. *History of the Ojibway People*. St. Paul: Minnesota Historical Society Press, 1984.

Weinstein-Farson, Laurie. *The Wampanoag*. New York: Chelsea House, 1989.

Weslager, C. A. *The Delaware Indians: A History*. New Brunswick, N.J.: Rutgers University Press, 1972.

Northwest Coast

Aikens, C. Melvin. "The Far West." In *Ancient North Americas*, ed. Jesse D. Jennings. New York: W. H. Freeman, 1983.

———. *Archaeology of Oregon*. Portland: U.S. Department of the Interior, Bureau of Land Management, Oregon State Office, 1986.

Allen, D. *Indians of the Northwest Coast*. Seattle, Wash: Hancock House, 1977.

Ames, Kenneth, and Herbert Maschner. *Peoples of the Northwest Coast*. New York: Thames & Hudson, 1999.

Bancroft-Hunt, Norman. *People of the Totem: The Indians of the Pacific Northwest*. Norman: University of Oklahoma Press 1979.

Beck, Mary Giraudo. *Potlatch: Native Ceremony and Myth on the Northwest Coast*. Anchorage: Alaska Northwest Books, 1993.

Beckham, Stephen Dow. "The Oregon Coast." In *The First Oregonians: An Illustrated Collection of Essays on Traditional Lifeways, Federal-Indian Relations, and the State's Native People Today*, ed. Carolyn M. Buan and Richard Lewis. Portland: Oregon Council for the Humanities, 1991.

Boas, Franz. *Geographical Names of the Kwakiutl Indians*. New York: Columbia University Press, 1934.

———. *The Mythology of the Bella Coola Indians*. New York: AMS Press, 1975.

———. *Kwakiutl Tales, Part I: Translations*. New York: AMS Press, 1969.

———. *The Religion of the Kwakiutl Indians, Part II: Translations*. New York: AMS Press, 1969.

Brown, John A., and Robert Ruby. *A Guide to the Indian Tribes of the Pacific Northwest*. Norman: University of Oklahoma Press, 1986.

Brown, Vinson. *Peoples of the Sea*. New York: Macmillan, 1977.

Carlson, Roy, ed. *Indian Art Traditions of the Northwest Coast*. Burnaby, B.C.: Simon Fraser University, 1983.

Chase-Dunn, Christopher K., and Kelly M. Mann. *The Wintu and Their Neighbors*. Tucson: University of Arizona Press, 1998.

Drucker, Philip. *Indians of the Northwest Coast*. New York: Natural History Press, 1963.

Gibbs, George. *Indian Tribes of the Washington Territory*. Fairfield, Wash.: Ye Galleon Press, 1967.

Haeberlin, Hermann, and Erna Gunther. *The Indians of Puget Sound*. Seattle: University of Washington Press, 1930.

Halpin, Marjorie M. *Totem Poles: An Illustrated Guide*. Vancouver: University of British Columbia Press, 1981.

Jilek, Wolfgang G. *Indian Healing: Shamanic Ceremonialism in the Pacific Northwest Today*. Surrey, B.C.: Hancock House Publishers, 1982.

McConnaughey, Bayard H., and Evelyn McConnaughey. *Pacific Coast*. New York: Alfred A. Knopf, 1985.

Miller, Jay. *Shamanic Odyssey: The Lushootseed Salish Journey to the Land of the Dead*. Menlo Park, Calif.: Ballena Press, 1988.

Muckle, Robert J. *The First Nations*. Vancouver: University of British Columbia Press, 1998.

Porter, Frank W., III. *Coast Salish Peoples*. New York: Chelsea House, 1989.

Press, Petra. *Indians of the Northwest: Traditions, History, Legends, and Life*. Philadelphia: Courage Books, 1997.

Rohner, Ronald P., and Evelyn C. Rohner. *The Kwakiutl: Indians of British Columbia*. New York: Holt, Rinehart, and Winston, 1970.

Schuster, Helen H. *The Yakima*. New York: Chelsea House, 1989.

Trafzer, Clifford E. *The Chinook*. New York: Chelsea House, 1989.

Turner, Dolby Bevan. *When the Rains Came: And Other Legends of the Salish People*. Victoria, B.C.: Orca Book Publishers, 1992.

Walens, Stanley. *The Kwakiutl*. New York: Chelsea House Publishers, 1992.

Southeast

Anderson, David G., and Kenneth E. Sassaman, eds. *The Paleoindian and Early Archaic Southeast*. Tuscaloosa: University of Alabama Press, 1996.

Bareis, Charles L., and James W. Porter. *American Bottom Archaeology*. Urbana: University of Illinois Press, 1984.

Bense, Judith. *Archaeology of the Southeastern United States*. New York: Academic Press, 1994.

Brain, Jeffrey P. *The Tunica-Biloxi*. New York: Chelsea House, 1989.

Brose, David S., and N'omi Greber, eds. *Hopewell Archaeology*. Kent, Ohio: Kent State University Press, 1979.

Brown, Virginia Pounds. *The World of the Southern Indians*. Birmingham, Ala.: Beechwood Books, 1983.

Burt, Jesse, and Robert B. Ferguson. *Indians of the Southeast: Then and Now*. Nashville, Tenn.: Abingdon Press, 1973.

Corkran, David. *The Cherokee Frontier: Conflict and Survival, 1740–1762*. Norman: University of Oklahoma Press, 1966.

Cotterill, Robert S. *The Southern Indians: The Story of the Civilized Tribes before Removal*. Norman: University of Oklahoma Press, 1954.

Cushman, H. B. *History of the Choctaw, Chickasaw and Natchez Indians*. Norman: University of Oklahoma Press, 1999.

Debo, Angie. *The Road to Disappearance: A History of the Creek Indians*. Norman: University of Oklahoma Press, 1941.

Dial, Adolph L. *The Lumbee*. New York: Chelsea House, 1993.

Ehle, John. *Trail of Tears: The Rise and Fall of the Cherokee Nation*. New York: Doubleday, 1988.

Emerson, Thomas E., Dale L. McElrath, and Andrew C. Fortier, eds. *Late Woodland Societies: Tradition and Transformation across the Midcontinent*. Lincoln: University of Nebraska Press, 2000.

Farnsworth, Kenneth B., and Thomas E. Emerson, eds. *Early Woodland Archeology*. Kampsville Seminars in Archeology, vol. 2. Kampsville, Ill.: Center for American Archeology, 1986.

Feest, Christian F. *The Powhattan*. New York: Chelsea House, 1989.

Foreman, Grant. *Indian Removal: The Emigration of the Five Civilized Tribes of Indians*. Norman: University of Oklahoma Press, 1932.

———. *The Five Civilized Tribes*. Norman: University of Oklahoma Press, 1989.

Garbarino, Merwyn S. *The Seminole*. New York: Chelsea House, 1989.

Gibson, Arrell M. *The Chickasaw*. Norman: University of Oklahoma Press, 1971.

Green, Michael D. *The Creek*. New York: Chelsea House, 1989.

Griffin, James B., ed. *Archaeology of Eastern United States*. Chicago: University of Chicago Press, 1952.

———. "Eastern North American Archaeology: A Summary." *Science* 156 (1967): 175–191.

Hale, Duane K., Arrell M. Gibson, and Frank W. Porter. *The Chickasaw*. New York: Chelsea House, 1991.

Hann, John H. *Apalachee: The Land between the Rivers*. Gainesville: University Presses of Florida, 1988.

Hudson, Charles M. *The Catawba Nation*. Athens: University of Georgia Press, 1970.

———. *The Southeastern Indians*. Knoxville: University of Tennessee Press, 1976.

Knight, Vernon James, and Vincas P. Steponaitis, eds. *Archaeology of the Moundville Chiefdom*. Washington, D.C.: Smithsonian Institution Press, 1998.

Mainfort, Robert C., and Lynne P. Sullivan, eds. *Ancient Earthen Enclosures of the Eastern Woodlands*. Gainesville: University Press of Florida, 1998.

McEwan, Bonnie G., ed. *The Spanish Missions of La Florida*. Gainesville: University Press of Florida, 1993.

McReynolds, Edwin C. *The Seminoles*. Norman: University of Oklahoma Press, 1957.

Merrell, James H. *The Catawbas*. New York: Chelsea House, 1989.

———. *The Indians' New World: Catawbas and Their Neighbors from European Contact to the Era of Removal*. New York: W. W. Norton, 1989.

Milanich, Jerald T. *Florida Indians and the Invasion from Europe*. Gainesville: University of Florida Press, 1995.

Milanich, Jerald T., and Susan Milbrath. *First Encounters, Spanish Explorations in the Caribbean and the United States, 1492–1570*. Gainesville: University of Florida Press, 1989.

Milner, George R. *The Cahokia Chiefdom*. Washington, D.C.: Smithsonian Institution Press, 1998.

Muller, Jon. *Archaeology of the Lower Ohio Valley*. New York: Academic Press, 1986.

———. *Mississippian Political Economy*. New York: Plenum Press, 1997.

Nassaney, Michael S., and Eric S. Johnson. *Interpretations of Native American Life*. Gainesville: University Press of Florida, 2000.

O'Brien, Sean M. *In Bitterness and in Tears: Andrew Jackson's Destruction of the Creeks and Seminoles*. Westport, Conn.: Praeger, 2003.

Pauketat, Timothy R. *The Ascent of Chiefs*. Tuscaloosa: University of Alabama Press, 1994.

Pauketat, Timothy R., and Thomas E. Emerson, eds. *Cahokia: Domination and Ideology in the Mississippian World*. Lincoln: University of Nebraska Press, 1997.

Perdue, Theda. *The Cherokee*. New York: Chelsea House, 1989.

Perttula, Timothy K. *The Caddo Nation: Archaeological and Ethnohistoric Perspectives*. Austin: University of Texas Press, 1992.

Phillips, James, and James A. Brown, eds. *Archaic Hunters and Gatherers in the American Midwest*. New York: Academic Press, 1983.

Roundtree, Helen. *The Powhatan Indians of Virginia*. Norman: University of Oklahoma Press, 1989.

———. *Pocahontas's People: The Powhatan Indians of Virginia through Four Centuries*. Norman: University of Oklahoma Press, 1990.

Sassaman, Kenneth E., and David G. Anderson, eds. *Archaeology of the Mid-Holocene Southeast*. Gainesville: University Press of Florida, 1996.

Smith, Bruce D., ed. *Rivers of Change: Essays on Early Agriculture in Eastern North America*. Washington, D.C.: Smithsonian Institution Press, 1992.

Smith, F. Todd. *The Caddo Indians: Tribes at the Convergence of Empires, 1542–1854*. College Station: Texas A&M University Press, 1995.

Steponaitis, Vincas P. *Ceramics, Chronology, and Community Patterns*. New York: Academic Press, 1983.

Swanton, John R. *Indian Tribes of the Lower Mississippi Valley and Adjacent Coast of the Gulf of Mexico*. Bulletin 43. Washington, D.C.: Bureau of American Ethnology, Smithsonian Institution, 1911.

———. *Early History of the Creek Indians and their Neighbors*. Reprint, Gainesville: University of Florida Press, 1998.

Walthall, John. *Prehistoric Indians of the Southeast: Archeology of Alabama and the Middle South*. Tuscaloosa: University of Alabama, 1990.

Wauchope, Robert. *Archaeological Survey of Northern Georgia*. Memoirs of the Society for American Archaeology, no. 21. Washington, D.C.: Society for American Archaeology, 1965.

Widmer, Randolph J. *The Evolution of the Calusa: A Non-Agricultural Chiefdom on the Southwest Florida Coast*. Tuscaloosa: University of Alabama Press, 1988.

Woodward, Grace Steele. *The Cherokees*. Norman: University of Oklahoma Press, 1963.

Wright, J. Leitch, Jr. *The Only Land They Knew: The Tragic Story of the American Indian in the Old South*. New York: The Free Press, 1981.

———. *Creeks and Seminoles: The Destruction and Regeneration of the Muscogulge People*. Lincoln: University of Nebraska Press, 1986.

Southwest

Bahti, Tom. *Southwestern Indian Tribes*. Las Vegas, Nev.: KC Publications, 1975.

Baldwin, Gordon C. *The Apache Indians*. New York: Four Winds Press, 1978.

Bee, Robert L. *The Yuma*. New York: Chelsea House, 1989.

Cordell, Linda. *Archaeology of the Southwest*. 2nd ed. New York: Academic Press, 1997.

Cordell, Linda, and George J. Gumerman, eds. *Dynamics of Southwest Prehistory*. Washington, D.C.: Smithsonian Institution Press, 1989.

Creamer, Winifred. *The Architecture of Arroyo Hondo Pueblo, New Mexico*. Santa Fe, N.M.: School of American Research Press, 1993.

Crown, Patricia L., and James W. Judge, eds. *Chaco and Hohokam*. Santa Fe, N.M.: School of American Research Press, 1991.

Cushing, Frank Hamilton. *Zuñi*. Lincoln: University of Nebraska Press, 1979.

———. *Zuni Folk Tales*. Tucson: University of Arizona Press, 1992.

Dobyns, Henry F. *The Pima-Maricopa*. New York: Chelsea House, 1989.

Dutton, Bertha P. *American Indians of the Southwest*. Albuquerque: University of New Mexico Press, 1983.

Fontana, Bernard L. *Of Earth and Little Rain: The Papago Indians*. Flagstaff: University of Arizona Press, 1990.

Forbes, Jack D. *Apache, Navaho, and Spaniard*. Norman: University of Oklahoma Press, 1960.

Gumerman, George J. *The View from Black Mesa*. Tucson: University of Arizona Press, 1984.

Haury, Emil. *The Hohokam, Desert Farmers and Craftsmen: Excavations at Snaketown, 1964–1965*. Tucson: University of Arizona Press, 1976.

Huckell, Bruce B. "The Archaic Prehistory of the North American Southwest." *Journal of World Prehistory* 10 (1996): 305–374.

Iverson, Peter. *The Navajos, A Critical Bibliography*. New York: Marshall Cavendish University Press, 1976.

Jones, Dewitt, and Linda S. Cordell. *Anasazi World*. Portland, Ore.: Graphic Arts Publishing Company, 1985.

LeBlanc, Steven A. *The Mimbres People: Ancient Pueblo Potters of the American Southwest*. New York: Thames & Hudson, 1983.

Lekson, Stephen. *The Chaco Meridian: Centers of Political Power in the Ancient Southwest*. Walnut Creek, Calif.: AltaMira Press, 1999.

Liptak, Karen. *Indians of the Southwest*. New York: Facts on File, 1991.

Melody, Michael. *The Apache*. New York: Chelsea House, 1989.

Ortiz, Alfonso, ed. *Handbook of North American Indians, Vol. 9: Southwest*. Washington, D.C.: Smithsonian Institution, 1979.

———. *Handbook of North American Indians, Vol. 10: Southwest*. Washington, D.C.: Smithsonian Institution, 1983.

Plog, Fred. *The Study of Ancient Culture Change*. New York: Academic Press, 1974.

Plog, Stephen. *Ancient Peoples of the American Southwest*. New York: Thames & Hudson, 1997.

Reid, Jefferson, and Stephanie Whittlesey. *The Archaeology of Ancient Arizona*. Tucson: University of Arizona Press, 1997.

Sando, Joe S. *Pueblo Nations: Eight Centuries of Pueblo Indian History*. Santa Fe, N.M.: Clear Light, 1992.

Sonnichsen, C. L., *The Mescalero Apaches*. Norman: University of Oklahoma Press, 1958.

Trimble, Stephen. *The People: Indians of the American Southwest*. Santa Fe, N.M.: School of American Research, 1993.

Underhill, Ruth M. *The Navajos*. Norman: University of Oklahoma Press, 1956.

Walker, Steven L. *Indian Cultures of the American Southwest*. Flagstaff: Camelback Publications, 1994.

Warren, Scott. *Cities in the Sand: The Ancient Civilizations of the Southwest.* San Francisco, Calif.: Chronicle Books, 1992.

Whalen, Michael E., and Paul E. Minnis. *Casas Grandes and Its Hinterland: Prehistoric Regional Organization in Northwest Mexico.* Tucson: University of Arizona Press, 2001.

Willis, S. H. *Early Prehistoric Agriculture in the American Southwest.* Santa Fe, N.M.: School of American Research Press, 1989.

Worchester, Donald E. *The Apaches: Eagles of the Southwest.* Norman: University of Oklahoma Press, 1979.

CULTURE

Arts

Anderson, Duane. *Legacy: Southwest Indian Art at the School of American Research.* Santa Fe, N.M.: School of American Research, 1998.

Covarrubias, Miguel. *The Eagle, the Jaguar and the Serpent: Indian Art of the Americas: North America: Alaska, Canada, the United States.* New York: Knopf, 1954.

Culin, Stewart. *Games of the North American Indians.* Lincoln: University of Nebraska Press, 1992.

Dickens, Roy S., ed. *Of Sky and Earth: Art of the Early Southeastern Indians.* Atlanta: Georgia Department of Archives and History, 1982.

Ewers, John C. *Blackfeet Crafts.* Stevens Point, Wisc.: Schneider Books, 1986.

Feder, Norman. *American Indian Art.* New York: Harry N. Abrams, 1971.

Feest, Christian F. *Native Arts of North America.* New York: Thames & Hudson, 1992.

Fichter, George S. *American Indian Music and Musical Instruments.* New York: David McKay, 1978.

Halpin, Marjorie M. *Totem Poles: An Illustrated Guide.* Seattle: University of Washington Press, 1983.

Hill, Richard W., Sr., Nancy Marie Mitchell, and Lloyd New. *Creativity Is Our Tradition: Three Decades of Contemporary Indian Art at the Institute of American Indian Arts.* Santa Fe, N.M.: Institute of American Indian Arts Press, 1992.

Holm, Oscar William (Bill). *Northwest Coast Indian Art: An Analysis of Form.* Seattle: University of Washington Press, 1965.

Koch, Ronald. *Dress Clothing of the Plains Indians.* Norman: University of Oklahoma Press, 1990.

Laubin, Reginald, and Gladys Laubin. *Indian Dances of North America: Their Importance to Indian Life.* Norman: University of Oklahoma Press, 1977.

——. *The Indian Tipi: Its History, Construction, and Use*. Norman: University of Oklahoma Press, 1977.

Leftwich, Rodney L. *Arts and Crafts of the Cherokee*. Cherokee, N.C.: Cherokee Publications, 1986.

Lyford, Carrie A. *Iroquois Crafts*. Stevens Point, Wisc.: Schneider Books, 1982.

——. *Ojibway Crafts*. Stevens Point, Wisc.: Schneider Books, 1982.

MacDonald, George. *Haida Art*. Seattle: University of Washington Press, 1996.

MacNair, Peter L. *Down from the Shimmering Sky: Masks of the Northwest Coast*. Seattle: University of Washington Press, 1998.

Mather, Christine. *Native America: Arts, Traditions, and Celebrations*. New York: Clarkson Potter, 1990.

McQuiston, Don, and Debra McQuiston. *Visions of the North: Native Art of the Northwest Coast*. San Francisco, Calif.: Chronicle Books, 1995.

Nabokov, Peter, and Robert Easton. *Native American Architecture*. New York: Oxford University Press, 1989.

Stewart, Hilary. *Cedar: Tree of Life to the Northwest Coast Indians*. Seattle: University of Washington Press, 1984.

——. *Looking at Indian Art of the Northwest Coast*. Seattle: University of Washington Press, 1979.

——. *Looking at Totem Poles*. Seattle: University of Washington Press, 1993.

Wissler, Clark. "Costumes of the Plains Indians." *Anthropological Papers, American Museum of Natural History*. Vol. 17, pt. 2. New York: American Museum of Natural History, 1915.

——. "Indian Costumes in the United States." *American Museum of Natural History*. Leaflet no. 63. New York: American Museum of Natural History, 1931.

Mythology, Language, and Literature

Burland, Cottie, and Marion Wood. *North American Indian Mythology*. New York: Peter Bedrick, 1985.

Campbell, Lyle. *American Indian Languages: The Historical Linguistics of Native America*. Oxford: Oxford University Press, 1997.

Campbell, Lyle, and Marianne Mithun, eds. *The Languages of Native America: Historical and Comparative Assessment*. Austin: University of Texas Press, 1979.

Cushing, Frank Hamilton. *Zuni Folk Tales*. Tucson: University of Arizona Press, 1992.

Feldmann, Susan, ed. *The Storytelling Stone: Traditional Native American Myths and Tales*. New York: Dell, 1991.

Fitzhugh, William W., and Susan A. Kaplan. *Inua: Spirit World of the Bering Sea Eskimo*. Washington, D.C.: Smithsonian Institution Press, 1982.

Fundaburk, Emma Lila, and Mary D. Forman, eds. *Sun Circles and Human Hands: The Southeastern Indian's Art and Industries*. Fairhope, Ala.: American Bicentennial Museum, 1957.

Goddard, Ives, ed. *Handbook of North American Indians, Vol. 17: Languages*. Washington, D.C.: Smithsonian Institution, 1996.

Hausman, Gerald. *Turtle Dream: Collected Stories from the Hopi, Navajo, Pueblo, and Havasupai People*. Santa Fe, N.M.: Mariposa Publishing, 1989.

———. *Turtle Island Alphabet: A Lexicon of Native American Symbols and Culture*. New York: St. Martin's Press, 1992.

Lankford, George E. *Native American Legends, Southeastern Legends: Tales from the Natchez, Caddo, Biloxi, Chickasaw and Other Nations*. Little Rock, Ark.: August House, 1987.

Seidelman, Harold, and James Turner. *The Inuit Imagination: Arctic Myth and Sculpture*. New York: Thames & Hudson, 1994.

Wallas, Chief James, and Pamela Whitaker. *Kwakiutl Legends*. Vancouver, B.C.: Hancock House, 1981.

Wardwell, Allen. *Tangible Visions: Northwest Coast Indian Shamanism and Its Art*. New York: Monacelli Press, 1996.

MAJOR JOURNALS

American Anthropologist. Arlington, Virginia, 1898–. Quarterly.

American Antiquity. Washington, D.C., 1935–. Quarterly.

Antiquity. Cambridge, England, 1927–. Quarterly.

Current Anthropology. Chicago, 1959–. Quarterly.

Historical Archaeology. California, Pennsylvania, 1967–. Quarterly.

Journal of Anthropological Archaeology. New York, 1982–. Quarterly.

Journal of Archaeological Method and Theory. New York, 1994–. Quarterly.

Journal of Archaeological Research. 1992–. Biannually.

Journal of Field Archaeology. Boston, 1974–. Quarterly.

Midcontinental Journal of Archaeology. Iowa City, 1976–. Biannually.

Plains Anthropologist. Lincoln, Nebraska, 1955–. Quarterly.

Southeastern Archaeology. Lawrence, Kansas, 1982–. Biannually.

World Archaeology. London, 1969–. Quarterly.

WORLD WIDE WEB SITES

American Anthropological Association
www.aaanet.org

Anasazi Heritage Center
www.co.blm.gov/ahc/index.htm
ArchNet
http://archnet.asu.edu
Canadian Archaeological Association
www.canadianarchaeolgy.com
Hopewell Culture
www.nps.gov/hocu/
Midwestern Archaeological Conference
http://www.indiana.edu/~mwarch/
Mississippian Moundbuilders
www.mississippian-artifacts.com
Moundbuilders of the Mississippi
www.cr.nps.gov/aad/feature/builder.htm
National Park Service Southeast Archaeological Center
www.cr.nps.gov/seac/seac.htm
Plains Anthropological Society
www.ou.edu/cas/archsur/plainsanth/index.html
Society for American Archaeology
www.saa.org
Southeastern Archaeological Conference
www.southeasternarchaeology.org/

About the Author

Cameron Wesson is an associate professor of anthropology at the University of Illinois at Chicago. He received his B.S. in architecture and B.S. in anthropology from Auburn University and his M.A. and Ph.D. in anthropology from the University of Illinois at Urbana-Champaign. He has held previous positions at the University of Oklahoma and Auburn University. His primary research focus is the political economy of the Native Americans of the Eastern Woodlands. He is the director of a long-term archaeological research project investigating the nature of Woodland period and Mississippian period archaeological sites in central Alabama. He is the author of numerous articles on the archaeology of southeastern North American, and is coeditor with Mark A. Rees of *Between Contacts and Colonies: Archaeological Approaches to the Protohistoric Period* (2002, University of Alabama Press). He is also the author of *Households and Hegemony: Early Creek Prestige Goods, Symbolic Capital, and Social Power* 2005i, University of Nebraska Press).